SUBVERSIVE SPIRITUALITY

SUBVERSIVE SPIRITUALITY

Eugene H. Peterson

Jim Lyster • John Sharon • Peter Santucci
Editors

WILLIAM B. EERDMANS PUBLISHING COMPANY
GRAND RAPIDS, MICHIGAN / CAMBRIDGE, U.K.

REGENT COLLEGE PUBLISHING
VANCOUVER, BRITISH COLUMBIA

This edition published jointly 1997 by

Wm. B. Eerdmans Publishing Co.

255 Jefferson Ave. S.E., Grand Rapids, Michigan 49503 /

P.O. Box 163, Cambridge CB3 9PU U.K.

and by

Regent College Publishing

an imprint of Regent College Bookstore

5800 University Boulevard, Vancouver, B.C. V6T 2E4

Published in association with the literary agency of

Alive Communications, Inc.

1465 Kelly Johnson Blvd., Suite 320, Colorado Springs, CO 80920

Printed in the United States of America

02 01 00 99 98   7 6 5 4 3 2

Library of Congress Cataloging-in-Publication Data

Peterson, Eugene H., 1932-

Subversive spirituality / Eugene H. Peterson : Jim Lyster,

John Sharon, Peter Santucci, editors.

p.   cm.

Includes bibliographical references.

ISBN 0-8028-4297-6 (pbk. : alk. paper)

1. Spiritual life — Christianity. 2. Spiritual life — Biblical teaching.

3. Evangelicalism. I. Lyster, Jim. II. Sharon, John.

III. Santucci, Peter. IV. Title.

BV4501.2.P4277   1997

248 — dc21   97-21465

CIP

Regent College Publishing ISBN 1-57383-071-2

For
Cuba Marie Dyer

"Stay alert. This is hazardous work I'm assigning you. You're going to be like sheep running through a wolf pack, so don't call attention to yourselves. Be as cunning as a snake, inoffensive as a dove."

ST. MATTHEW 10:16 (THE MESSAGE)

Contents

CONTENTS

Introduction

The Christian life, in one of its main aspects, is a recovery of what was lost in the Fall. We happen upon, we notice, we reach out and touch things and ideas, people and events, and among these the Holy Scriptures themselves, that were there all along but that our ego-swollen souls or our sin-blurred eyes quite simply overlooked — sometimes for years and years and years.

And then we do notice: we sight life, we realize God and hear his word, we grab the sleeve of a friend and demand, "Look! Listen!" More often than not our friend has been looking and listening all along and treats our sudden enthusiasm with courteous conde-scension.

In reading over these occasional and picked-up pieces, written over the past twenty-five years, I have the distinct feeling that they may be greeted in just that way, with courteous condescension. I remember Austin Farrer's stricture against pretensions to originality, "There is nothing new to say on the subject, only the fashions of speech alter, and ancient argument is freshly phrased." This gathering of articles and essays, poems and conversations, is a kind of kitchen midden of my noticings of the obvious in the course of living out the Christian life in the vocational context of pastor, writer, and, more recently, professor. The randomness and repetitions and false starts are rough edges that I am leaving as is in the interests of honesty. Spirituality is not, by and large, smooth. I do hope, however, that they will be found to be "freshly phrased." Later, some of these articles took on a life of their own and developed into books.

INTRODUCTION

My friends, Jim Lyster, John Sharon, and Peter Santucci of Regent College, were diligent in collecting, arranging, and editing what is here, and I thank them.

SPIRITUALITY

Saint Mark: The Basic Text for Christian Spirituality

Introduction

A quite remarkable thing has been taking place in this city in the last 25 years; spiritual theology has been named and recognized, appreciated and sought after. Spiritual theology is an honored, central, and ancient concern of the Christian church. But in the last two hundred years with the imperialistic ascendance of rationalism, accompanied by various and sundry reactions of romanticism, spiritual theology virtually disappeared from the scene. Rationalism and romanticism fought for the heart of humankind and between them pretty much divided up the spoils. Spiritual theology, pushed to the sidelines, survived academically in obscure corners of various libraries around the world. Spiritual theology, mostly ignored but sometimes demeaned in both church and world, became the specialty of small and often eccentric coteries of enthusiasts.

Meanwhile here in Vancouver, something quite different has been taking place: spiritual theology has been recovered as a discipline and concern that is basic to the entire Christian enterprise as

Originally published in *Crux* 29, no. 4 (December, 1993). Editor's note: This article is based on Dr. Peterson's inaugural lecture as the James M. Houston Professor of Spiritual Theology at Regent College, given October 17, 1993.

it is thought through and studied in classrooms, prayed and practised in home and workplace, believed in the church and proclaimed in the world. Both the necessity and the attractiveness of spiritual theology has been worked out and demonstrated among us — an immense gift to both church and world. And a gift most timely, for it is quite clear that our culture, toxic with rationalism and romanticism, is in a bad way and getting worse. Those of us who pray for the salvation of the world cannot do without the rich flocks of wisdom and insight and prayer and maturity to which spiritual theology is shepherd.

The name most associated with this recovery and demonstration is James M. Houston. No one person pulls off an historical and cultural feat like this single-handed. He had, and has, colleagues, friends, and family who were and are part of it in large and small ways. But his name — his focused vision, his sacrificial faithfulness, the clarity of his thinking, the passion of his prayers — his name more than any other identifies this recovery of spiritual theology at this critical time as we approach the third millennium.

Because of what has been taking place in this city in the last 25 years, spiritual theology is no longer confined to the academic pursuits of medievalists. Because of what has been taking place in this city in the last 25 years, spiritual theology now carries the connotation of robust and mature spiritual health instead of being suspect as religious neurosis.

And because James Houston's name is so thoroughly associated with all this, it is fitting that this professorship be distinguished by the title, the James M. Houston Chair of Spiritual Theology.

Saint Mark: The Basic Text

The Gospel of St. Mark is the basic text for Christian spirituality. I use the definite article deliberately, *the* basic text. The entire canon of Scripture is our comprehensive text, the revelation that determines the reality that we deal with as human beings who are created, saved, and blessed by the God and Father of our Lord Jesus Christ through the Holy Spirit. But St. Mark as the first Gospel holds a certain primacy.

1. The Form of the Text

No one had ever written a Christian Gospel before Mark wrote his. He created a new genre. It turned out to be a form of writing that quickly became both foundational and formative for the life of church and Christian. We are accustomed to believing that the Holy Spirit inspired the content of the Scriptures (2 Tim. 3:16), but it is just as true that the form is inspired, this new literary form that we call Gospel. There was nothing quite like it in existence, although Mark had good teachers in the Hebrew storytellers who gave us the Books of Moses and Samuel.

The Bible as a whole comes to us in the form of narrative, and it is within this large, somewhat sprawling narrative that St. Mark writes his Gospel. "We live mainly by forms and patterns," Wallace Stegner, one of our great contemporary storytellers, tells us, ". . . if the forms are bad, we live badly."[1] Gospel is a true and good form, by which we live well. Storytelling creates a world of presuppositions, assumptions, and relations into which we enter. Stories invite us into a world other than ourselves, and, if they are good and true stories, a world larger than ourselves. Bible stories are good and true stories, and the world that they invite us into is the world of God's creation and salvation and blessing.

Within the large, capacious context of the biblical story we learn to think accurately, behave morally, preach passionately, sing joyfully, pray honestly, obey faithfully. But we dare not abandon the story as we do any or all of these things, for the minute we abandon the story, we reduce reality to the dimensions of our minds and feelings and experience. The moment we formulate our doctrines, draw up our moral codes, and throw ourselves into a life of ministry apart from a continuous re-immersion in the story itself, we walk right out of the presence and activity of God and set up our own shop.

The distinctiveness of the form "Gospel" is that it brings the centuries of Hebrew storytelling, God telling his story of creation and salvation through his people, to the story of Jesus, the mature completion of all those stories, in a way that is clearly revelation — that is, divine self-disclosure — and in a way that invites, insists on, our participation.

---

1. Wallace Stegner, *When the Bluebird Sings to the Lemonade Springs* (New York: Random House, 1992), p. 181.

This is in contrast to the ancient preference for myth-making, which more or less turns us into spectators of the supernatural. It is also in contrast to the modern preference for moral philosophy which puts us in charge of our own salvation. "Gospel story" is a verbal way of accounting for reality that, like the incarnation that is its subject, is simultaneously divine and human. It *reveals,* that is, it shows us something we could never come up with on our own by observation or experiment or guess; and at the same time it *engages,* it brings us into the action as recipients and participants but without dumping the responsibility on us for making it turn out right.

This has great implications for our spirituality, for the form itself protects us against two of the major ways in which we go off the rails: becoming frivolous spectators, clamoring for new and more exotic entertainment out of heaven; or, becoming anxious moralists, putting our shoulders to the wheel and taking on the burdens of the world. The very form of the text shapes responses in us that make it hard to become a mere spectator or a mere moralist. This is not a text that we master, it is one that we are mastered by.

It is significant, I think, that in the presence of a story, whether we are telling it or listening to it, we never have the feeling of being experts — there is too much we don't yet know, too many possibilities available, too much mystery and glory. Even the most sophisticated of stories tends to bring out the childlike in us — expectant, wondering, responsive, delighted — which, of course, is why the story is the child's favorite form of speech; why it is the Holy Spirit's dominant form of revelation; and why we adults, who like posing as experts and managers of life, so often prefer explanation and information.

2. The Content of the Text

We don't read very long in this text by St. Mark before we realize that it is about Jesus Christ, and before we have finished we realize that it is about God revealed in Jesus Christ. This seems obvious enough, but I want to dwell on the obvious for a moment.

I have named St. Mark's Gospel as the basic text for our spirituality. Spirituality is the attention we give to our souls, to the invisible interior of our lives that is the core of our identity, these image-of-God souls that comprise our uniqueness and glory. Spirituality is the

6

concern we have for the invisibility that inheres in every visibility, for the interior that provides content to every exterior. It necessarily deals much with innerness, with silence, with solitude. It takes all matters of soul with utmost seriousness.

This would appear to be a wonderful thing, and our initial exclamation is most likely, "Would that all the Lord's people were so engaged!" But twenty centuries of experience in spirituality qualifies our enthusiasm considerably. In actual practice it turns out to be not so wonderful. When you look at our history, it is no wonder that spirituality is so often treated with suspicion, and not infrequently with outright hostility. For in actual practice spirituality very often develops into neurosis, degenerates into selfishness, becomes pretentious, turns violent. How does this happen? The short answer is that it happens when we step outside the Gospel story and take ourselves as the basic and authoritative text for our spirituality; we begin exegeting ourselves as a sacred text. We don't usually throw the Gospel out; we merely put it on the shelf and think that we are honoring it by consulting it from time to time as an indispensable reference work.

Our spiritual guides tell us, "You are wonderful, glorious beings, precious souls. Your aspirations for holiness and goodness and truth are splendid. But you are not the content of spirituality; God revealed in Jesus is that. You need a text to read and study and learn from — here's your text, the gospel of Jesus Christ. Start with St. Mark's Gospel as your basic text."

We open the text and read the story of Jesus. It is an odd kind of story. It tells us very little of what interests us in a story. We learn virtually nothing about Jesus that we really want to know. There is no description of his appearance. Nothing about his origin, friends, education, family. How are we to evaluate or understand this person? And there is very little reference to what he thought, to how he felt, his emotions, his interior struggles.

At some point or other we realize that this is a story about God — and about us. Even though Jesus is the most referred-to person in the story, there is a surprising reticence in regard to Jesus. Jesus is the revelation of God, so we are always being faced in Jesus with what we are faced with in God: most of what is here we don't get, we don't see, don't understand. We don't figure Jesus out, we don't search Jesus out, we don't get Jesus on our terms. It follows that neither do we get God on our terms. As a story, it is a most unsatisfying story.

And then we realize that our attention has been drawn away from ourselves and is on Jesus, God revealed in Jesus. True spirituality, Christian spirituality, takes attention off of ourselves and focuses it on another, on Jesus.

There are others in the story, of course, many others — the sick and hungry, victims and outsiders, friends, and enemies. But Jesus is always the subject. No event and no person appears in this story apart from Jesus. Jesus provides both context and content for everyone's life. Spirituality — the attention we give to our souls — turns out in practice (when we let St. Mark shape our practice) to be the attention we give to God revealed in Jesus. The text trains us in such perception and practice. Line after line, page after page — Jesus, Jesus, Jesus. None of us provides the content for our own spirituality; it is given to us; Jesus gives it to us. The text allows for no exceptions.

3. The Emphasis of the Text

As we read this text we soon discover that the entire story funnels into the narration of the events of a single week of Jesus' life, the week of his passion, death, and resurrection.

And of these three items, death gets the most detailed treatment. If we are asked to say as briefly as possible what St. Mark's Gospel consists of, we must say, "the death of Jesus."

That doesn't sound very promising, especially for those of us who are looking for a text by which to live, a text by which to nurture our souls. But there it is. There are sixteen chapters in the story. For the first eight chapters Jesus is alive, strolling unhurriedly through the villages and backroads of Galilee, bringing others to life — delivering them from evil, healing their maimed and sick bodies, feeding hungry people, demonstrating his sovereignty over storm and sea, telling marvellous stories, gathering and training disciples, announcing that they are poised on the brink of a new era, God's Kingdom, which at that very moment is breaking in upon them.

And then, just as he has everyone's attention, just as the momentum for life and more life is at its crest, he starts talking about death. The last eight chapters of the Gospel are dominated by death talk.

The death announcement also signals a change of pace. As the story is told through the first eight chapters, there is a leisurely and meandering quality to the narration. Jesus doesn't seem to be going anywhere in particular — he more or less drifts from village to village, goes off by himself into the hills to pray, worships in the synagogues, gives the impression that he has time to take meals with anyone who invites him over, goes boating with his friends on the lake. We do not construe this relaxed pace as aimlessness or indolence, for energy and intensity are always evident. But through these Galilean years, Jesus appears to have all the time in the world, which, of course, he does have.

But with the death announcement that changes: now he heads straight for Jerusalem. Urgency and gravity and destination now characterize the narration. The direction changes, the pace changes, the mood changes. Three times Jesus is explicit: he is going to suffer and be killed and rise again (8:31; 9:31; 10:33).

And then it happens: death. Jesus' death is narrated carefully and precisely. No incident in his life is told with this much detail. There can hardly be any question about the intent of St. Mark: the plot and emphasis and meaning of Jesus is his death.

It is not as if this death emphasis was an idiosyncrasy of Mark, a morbid obsession of his that distorted the basic story, for this sequence and proportion is preserved by St. Mark's successors in Gospel narration, Matthew and Luke. They elaborate St. Mark's basic text in various ways, but preserve the proportions. John, who comes at the story from a quite different angle, dazzling us with images of light and life, actually increases the emphasis on death, giving half of his allotted space to the passion week. All four Gospel writers do essentially the same thing; they tell us the story of Jesus' death, and write their respective introductions to it. And Paul — exuberant, passionate, hyperbolic Paul — skips the narration completely and simply punches out the conclusion, "Christ died for us" (Rom. 5:8); "I decided to know nothing among you except Jesus Christ and him crucified" (1 Cor 2:2).

But there is far more here than the simple fact of death, although there is that most emphatically — this is a carefully *defined* death. It is defined as voluntary. Jesus did not have to go to Jerusalem; he went on his own volition. He gave his assent to death. This was not accidental death; this was not an unavoidable death.

9

It is defined as sacrificial. He accepted death that others might receive life, ". . . his life as a ransom for many" (Mark 10:45). He explicitly defined his life as sacrificial, that is, as a means to life for others, when he instituted the Eucharist, "He took a loaf of bread. . . . Take, this is my body. . . . Then he took a cup . . . this is my blood of the covenant, which is poured out for many" (Mark 14:23-24).

And it is defined in the company of resurrection. Each of the three explicit death announcements concludes with a statement of resurrection. The Gospel story as a whole concludes with a witness to resurrection. This doesn't make it any less a death, but it is a quite differently defined death than we are accustomed to dealing with.

Tragedy and procrastination are the words that characterize our culture's attitude to death.

The view of death as tragic is a legacy of the Greeks. The Greeks wrote with elegance of tragic deaths — lives that were caught up in the working out of large, impersonal forces, lives pursued with the best of intentions, but then enmeshed in circumstances that cancelled the intentions, circumstances indifferent to human heroism or hope.

The death of Jesus is not tragic.

The procrastinated death is a legacy of modern medicine. In a culture where life is reduced to heartbeat and brainwave, death can never be accepted as such. Since there is no more to life than can be accounted for by biology — no meaning, no spirituality, no eternity — increasingly desperate attempts are made to put it off, to delay it, to deny it.

The death of Jesus is not procrastinated.

It is essential that we counter our culture by letting St. Mark's storytelling shape our understanding of death and eventually come to understand our own death within the rich dimensions and relations of Jesus' story.

4. The Spiritual Theology of the Text

I noted earlier that one of the distinctive qualities of "Gospel story" is that it draws us into participation. The first half of St. Mark's Gospel does that — all sorts of people are drawn into the life of Jesus, experience his compassion, his healings, his deliverance, his call, his peace. We find ourselves implicitly included. In the second half of the Gospel this experience of personal participation becomes explicit.

Right at the center of St. Mark's text is a passage that I am going to designate as the "spirituality" of the text. By using the term spirituality at this juncture I intend to call attention to the place where our concern for our souls, our lives, and Jesus' concern for our souls, our lives, converge. By spirituality I mean the particular way in which St. Mark wrote his Gospel to help us who read him experience truly the message he writes. It goes without saying, I think, that Mark was not a journalist, writing daily bulletins on the first-century activities of Jesus. Nor was he a propagandist, attempting to enlist us in a cause that had designs on history. This is spiritual theology in action, a form of writing that draws us into participation with the text.

St. Mark 8:27–9:9 is the passage. It is set at the center of the Gospel story so that one half of the Gospel, the multiple Galilean evocations of life, falls symmetrically on one side, and on the other side, the single-minded travel to Jerusalem and death.

The passage consists of two stories. The first story, Jesus' call for renunciation as he and his disciples start out on the road to Jerusalem, provides the ascetic dimension in spirituality. The second story, Jesus' transfiguration on Mount Tabor, provides the aesthetic dimension in spirituality.

The stories are bracketed at either end by affirmations of Jesus' true identity as God among us: first, Peter saying, "You are the Christ, the Son of the living God"; second, the voice out of heaven saying, "This is my beloved son, listen to him." Human testimony at one end, divine attestation at the other.

Before we consider the two stories, I want to insist we keep them in context and that we maintain their connection. These stories must never be removed from their context. Their context is the life and death of the God-revealing Jesus. St. Mark's Gospel has Jesus as its subject. Out of context, these stories can only be misunderstood. They do not stand on their own. They do not give us a spiritual theology that we can walk off with and exploit on our own terms.

And these stories are organically connected. They must not be torn apart. They are the two-beat rhythm in a single spiritual theology, not two alternate ways of doing spiritual theology. The two stories bring together the ascetic and aesthetic movements, the No and the Yes that work together at the heart of spiritual theology.

The Ascetic. First, the ascetic movement. This is God's No in Jesus. Jesus' words are succinct and stark: "If any want to become my followers, let them deny themselves and take up their cross and follow me" (8:34). The ascetic life deals with life on the road.

The verbs that leap out of the sentence and pounce on us are "deny yourself" and "take up your cross." Renunciation and death. It feels like an assault, an attack. We recoil.

But then we notice that these two negatives are bracketed by the positive verb, "follow," first as an infinitive, then as an imperative. "If anyone wants to follow *(akolouthein)*" opens the sentence; "you follow me *(akoloutheito)*" concludes it. Jesus is going some place; he invites us to come along. There is no hostility in that. It sounds, in fact, quite glorious. So glorious, in fact, that the great verb "follow," sheds glory on the negative verbs that call for renunciation and death.

There is always a strong ascetic element in true spiritual theology. Following Jesus means *not* following your impulses and appetites and whims and dreams, all of which are sufficiently damaged by sin to make them unreliable guides for getting any place worth going. Following Jesus means *not* following the death-procrastinating, death-denying practices of a culture which, by obsessively pursuing life under the aegis of idols and ideologies, ends up with a life that is so constricted and diminished that it is hardly worthy of the name.

Grammatically, the negative, our capacity to say No, is one of the most impressive features of our language. The negative is our access to freedom. Only humans can say No. Animals can't say No. Animals do what instinct dictates. No is a freedom word. I don't have to do what either my glands or my culture tell me to do. The judicious, well-placed No frees us from many a blind alley, many a rough detour, frees us from debilitating distractions and seductive sacrilege. The art of saying No sets us free to follow Jesus.

If we adhere carefully to St. Mark's text, we will never associate the ascetic with the life-denying. Ascetic practice sweeps out the clutter of the god-pretentious self, making ample space for Father, Son, and Holy Spirit; it embraces and prepares for a kind of death that the culture knows nothing about, making room for the dance of resurrection. Whenever we are around someone who is doing this well, we notice the lightness of step, the nimbleness of spirit, the quickness to laughter. H. C. G. Moule wrote that these dominical negatives ". . . may have to carve deep lines in heart and life; but the chisel need never deface the brightness of the material."[2]

The Aesthetic. Alongside St. Mark's ascetic is his aesthetic. This is God's Yes in Jesus. Peter, James, and John see Jesus transfigured before them on the mountain into cloud-brightness in the company of Moses and Elijah, and hear God's blessing, "This is my beloved, listen to him" (Mark 9:7). The aesthetic deals with life on the mountain.

The word "beauty" does not occur in the story, but beauty is what the disciples experienced, and what we find ourselves experiencing — the beauty of Jesus transfigured, law and prophets, Moses and Elijah integrated into the beauty of Jesus, the beautiful blessing, "My beloved . . .": Everything fitting together, the luminous interior of Jesus spilling out on to the mountain, history, and religion beautifully personalized and brought into deep, resonating harmony, the declaration of love.

There is always a strong aesthetical element in true spiritual theology. Climbing the mountain with Jesus means coming upon beauty that takes our breath away. Staying in the company of Jesus means contemplating his glory, listening in on this vast, intergenerational conversation consisting of law and prophet and gospel that takes place around Jesus, hearing the divine confirmation of revelation in Jesus. When God's Spirit makes its appearance, we recognize the appearance as beautiful.

Now here's the thing about the transfigured Jesus. Jesus is the form of revelation, "and the light does not fall on this form from above and from outside, rather it breaks forth from the form's interior."[3] The only adequate response that can be made to light is to keep our eyes open, to attend to what is illumined — adoration.

The aesthetical impulse in spiritual theology has to do with training in perception, acquiring a taste for what is being revealed in Jesus. We are not good at this. Our senses have been dulled by sin. The world, for all its vaunted celebration of sensuality, is relentlessly anaesthetic, obliterating feeling by ugliness and noise, draining the beauty out of people and things so that they are functionally efficient, scornful of the

2. H. C. G. Moule, *Veni Creator* (London: Hodder & Stoughton, 1890), p. 104.
3. Hans Urs von Balthasar, *The Glory of the Lord* (San Francisco: Ignatius Press, 1984), vol. 1, p. 151.

aesthetic except as it can be contained in a museum or flower garden. Our senses require healing and rehabilitation so that they are adequate for receiving and responding to visitations and appearances of Spirit, God's Holy Spirit, for as Jean Sulivan says, "The fundamental insight of the Bible . . . is that the invisible can speak only by the perceptible."[4]

These bodies of ours with their five senses are not impediments to a life of faith; our sensuality is not a barrier to spirituality but our only access to it. Thomas Aquinas was convinced that *asensuality* was a vice, the rejection of one's senses too often leading to sacrilege.[5] When St. John wanted to assure some early Christians of the authenticity of his spiritual experience, he did it by calling on the witness of his senses of sight, hearing, and touch — "that which we have heard . . . seen with our eyes . . . touched with our hands concerning the word of life" (1 John 1:1). In his opening sentence, he calls on the witness of his senses seven times.

St. Mark sets this story of glorious affirmation in immediate juxtaposition to his story of stern negation. In company with Jesus, these bodies of ours so magnificently equipped for seeing, hearing, touching, smelling, and tasting, climb the mountain (itself a strenuous physical act), where, in astonished adoration, we are trained to see the light and hear the words that reveal God to us.

This seems simple enough, and it is. St. Mark does not go in for subtleties — he sets it before us plainly. But he also knows that, simple and obvious as it is, it is easy to get it wrong. Peter's initial response in both the ascetic road story and the aesthetic mountain story was wrong.

On the road, Peter tried to avoid the cross; on the mountain, he tried to possess the glory. Peter rejected the ascetic way by offering Jesus a better plan, a way of salvation in which no one has to be inconvenienced. Jesus, in the sternest rebuke recorded in the Gospels, called him Satan. Peter rejected the aesthetic way by offering to build memorials on the mountain, a way of worship in which he could take over from Jesus and provide something hands-on and practical. This time Jesus just ignored him.

Peter's propensity to get it wrong keeps us on our toes. Century

4. Jean Sulivan, *Morning Light* (New York: Paulist Press, 1988), p. 18.
5. Quoted by Beldon Lane, *Landscapes of the Sacred* (New York: Paulist Press, 1988), p. 81.

after century we Christians keep getting it wrong — and in numerous ways. We get the ascetic wrong; we get the aesthetic wrong. Our history books are full of ascetic aberrations, full of aesthetic aberrations. Every time we get sloppy in reading this text of St. Mark and leave the company of Jesus we get it wrong.

Conclusion

One more thing. These two stories, carefully placed at the center of the gospel story, are not the center of the story. St. Mark's story, remember, is a story about Jesus, not us. In fact, if we deleted this section from the story, the story would still be the same story. Nothing in this road and mountain narrative is essential to understanding the story of Jesus as he lived, was crucified, and rose from the dead. Without this account of the road and the mountain, we would still know everything St. Mark chose to tell us about Jesus as the revelation of God, a full accounting of Jesus' work of salvation.

What happens here is that we are invited into becoming full participants in the story of Jesus and shown how to become such participants. We are not simply *told* that Jesus is the Son of God; we not only *become* beneficiaries of his atonement; we are invited to die his death and live his life with the freedom and dignity of participants. And here is a marvelous thing: we enter the center of the story without becoming the center of the story.

Spirituality is always in danger of self-absorption, of becoming so intrigued with matters of soul that God is treated as a mere accessory to my experience. This requires much vigilance. Spiritual theology is, among other things, the exercise of this vigilance. Spiritual theology is the discipline and art of training us into a full and mature participation in Jesus' story while at the same time preventing us from taking over the story.

And for this St. Mark provides our basic text. The two stories at the center, the road and mountain stories, are clearly proleptic — they anticipate Jesus' crucifixion and resurrection. They immerse us and train us in the ascetic negations and aesthetic affirmations, but they don't leave us there; they cast us forward in faith and obedience to the life that is finally and only complete in the definitive No and glorious Yes of Jesus crucified and risen.

Back to Square One: God Said

(The Witness of Holy Scripture)

A number of years ago when I was in the first few months of learning how to be a grandparent, my son Eric, daughter-in-law Lynn, and little grandson Andrew were visiting us in our home for a few days. It had been twenty-five years since I had experienced a baby in daily and close-up detail and I was taking it all in. I had missed a lot the first time around; I was determined not to miss it this time. One day it was just Andrew, his mother, and me in the living room. Lynn was reading a book. Andrew had been practicing his American adaptation of the Australian crawl for a few weeks and was getting close to perfection. I was sitting on the floor watching with wonder this small body perform a series of highly skilled muscular operations, calling for the precise coordination of eyes and arms and legs. He had a tennis ball which he would pick up, throw, and then crawl after. The ball caromed nicely off walls and furniture, providing challenge and variety for showing off to his grandfather his finely honed skills of crawling. Nothing I have ever seen on a baseball field or hockey rink rivaled my interest and admiration that day as I watched Andrew's athletic prowess at crawling. This went on for ten or fifteen minutes, and just then, the ball that he was crawling after rolled under a dry sink and disappeared from view. The moment it disappeared, Andrew stopped, sat back on his well-diapered bottom and looked around

"Back to Square One: God Said" was originally published in *Crux* (Vancouver: Regent College) 31, no. 1 (March 1995): 2-10.

for something else to do, as if there had never been a tennis ball to chase. I looked to his mother, "Lynn, what's wrong with Andrew?" My extravagant admiration had quickly become anxiety. Why did he quit chasing the ball? Was there a missing gene in his DNA? Was he showing early signs of dyslexia and a short attention span? Lynn, not bothering to look up from her book, said coolly, and just a bit condescendingly I thought, "Andrew has not yet acquired object permanence."

"What does that mean?"

"It means that if he can't see it, it doesn't exist."

It took a few seconds for that to sink in, and then I said, "Oh. I've got a whole congregation like that."

*   *   *

I had never heard that phrase before, "object permanence." We talked about it, Lynn and I. She told me that during those early months of being a mother, virtually everything in Andrew's life required immediate gratification — feeding, comforting, diapering. There was no waiting. There was no reality for Andrew other than what he could see and taste and smell and feel and hear. And most of what he saw, tasted, smelled, felt, and heard was his mother. If she was going to be a good mother, she had to be there physically with her body, around the clock, day and night. She also observed that if she continued being a good mother in that way, past a certain point she would be a bad mother.

"How could you be a bad mother? You could never be a bad mother." Lynn was (and is) as good at mothering as Andrew was at crawling. She couldn't be a bad mother if she tried.

She led me to see that her good mothering would become bad mothering if Andrew never learned object permanence — if he never learned to deal with her absence in the same way he had learned to deal with her presence. Most of Lynn, to say nothing of most of the world, was not at that moment accessible to his senses. If she insisted on being indispensable to him, she would narrow his life to only what he could see of her.

*   *   *

I am always a little surprised when I come across yet another way in which biology provides a grounding for spirituality. But here it was again. And in the unlikely psychological abstraction, "object permanence." Through that conversation that day, and learning about a critical item in child development, I acquired a fresh perspective regarding the starting point of the uniquely human adventure which finds its fullest expression in the Christian life. I am calling this starting point, Square One, the place where we acquire object permanence. This is the place from which we launch the distinctly human journey.

The first few months of our lives are spent in getting things ready, getting our basic needs met so that we *can* journey. Many of you have had an analogous experience in, say, going for a backpacking trip into the mountains. You spend days getting things ready, laying out the proper clothing, measuring out quantities of food, making sure the tent is waterproofed, checking the first-aid kit for essentials. And then you are at the trailhead. Up to this point nearly everything has been under your control; after this point almost nothing is under your control — most of what you are dealing with now is invisible, uncertain, unpredictable — changes in the weather, the appearance and behavior of wild animals, your own physical endurance and the mood of your hiking companions. You have arrived at Square One.

Up to Square One, you live by sight; after Square One you live by faith. Basic biology now gives way to basic spirituality. No longer confined by sense, feelings, and immediacy, we are launched into exploration and participation in the immense world of memory, anticipation, waiting, trust, belief, sacrifice, love, loyalty, faithfulness — none of which can be reduced to what you can see and handle. None of these things that go into making up what is distinctively and characteristically human in us can be possessed — they all must be entered into. Most of what *is,* is not where we can touch it, put it in our mouths, be wrapped in its warm comfort. Square One is the place from which we begin learning how to live with Absence with the same ease with which we have come to live with Presence. The generic word that we use for this is Faith — in its classic and never yet improved upon definition, "the substance of things hoped for, the evidence of things not seen" (Heb. 11:1).

It is essential to keep in mind that our five senses do not become less important at this point; in fact they may even become more important because they are no longer limiting. Our spiritual life is no less physical, sensual, immediate than our biological life, but it is not confined to the physical. Our bodies, instead of being prisons in which we are locked up on ourselves, are open roads along which we set out on our travels towards what "eye hath not seen nor ear heard." Biology is not fate, as Freud would have us believe; it is rather a free pass to tasting and seeing that the Lord is good, as the Psalmist has it. We do not leave biology behind when we get to Square One; what we do is acquire object permanence. We no longer have to see something to know that it exists.

Andrew has acquired it very well. He is six years old now, and most of his world is composed of invisibilities and words. I come across him in his back yard, wielding a sword, shouting anathemas and knocking the heads off dandelions. I ask him what he is doing and he tells me that he is fighting giant trolls. As he tells me this, I think I catch a note of condescension in his voice similar to what I heard in his mother five years ago when she was instructing me in object permanence.

I

The characteristic element of Square One is this: God Said. There is, of course, much else, too. As we step into Square One the entire sweep of heaven and earth opens up before us. We are not capable of handling it all at once. It's best to take it in small bits and pieces. A story here, a prayer there, a song, a dream. Words are our primary tools for getting our bearings in the world — most of which we can't see, most of which we'll never touch — large, expanding, mysterious existence that is so much larger, more intricate, more real even, than we are.

We learn the word "ball," and by means of the word acquire the ability to experience the reality of the tennis ball even after it rolls under the dry sink and cannot see it. As we add words to our working vocabulary, we become conversant with more and more reality. The absolutely indispensable word that we learn at Square One is God. We learn the word "God" and acquire the ability to experience everything that is beyond us as connectedly real and personally congenial. We don't learn this immediately, suddenly, absolutely; there are misunderstandings, superstitions, twists and turns in the imagination, advances and regressions. But we learn it. Everybody learns it. "For that which can be known about God is plain to them, because God has shown it to them. Ever since the creation of the world his invisible nature, namely, his eternal power and deity, has been clearly perceived in the things that have been made" (Rom. 1:19-20). The unknown takes precedence over the known. That which we can't see accounts for what we can see. And this mysterious unknown, unseen, is purposeful and personal: God.

Purposeful. For there is coherence and design and plan previous to my experience of life.

Personal. For there is something or other that connects with me that is more me than I am: God is more than I am, not less. Not just more powerful or more wise, but more *person,* more of whatever it is that makes me capable of thinking, believing, loving, hoping, trusting — all these great invisibles that I become aware of at Square One.

God. There is no single term that is as common and indispensable to human beings. There is no language in which the word does not occur. There is hardly a moment in our lives when the word does not figure in some way or other in the way we account for ourselves and the world around us — whether through denial, or modification, or blasphemy, or adoration. God.

In scientific theory and philosophy "the criterion of simplicity is crucial."[1] Richard Swinburne is the Nolloth Professor of the Christian Religion at Oxford University. He is one of our premier contemporary defenders of the Christian faith. A central thrust of his work revolves around this criterion of simplicity. The world, no matter from which direction you approach it, from the scientific or the religious, is amazingly diverse, with millions of details to be accounted for. Anyone can come up with a Rube Goldberg theory that explains by the most complicated mental machinery some aspect of what is going on. Much philosophical work consists of just such intellectual monstrosities. But the most convincing and useful theory is the simplest — the theory that uses the simplest vocabulary and fewest variables that leads us to expect the diverse phenomena that

---

1. Richard Swinburne, "The Vocation of a Natural Theologian," in *Philosophers Who Believe,* ed. Kelly James Clark (Downers Grove, IL: InterVarsity, 1993), p. 184.

form the evidence which we face. Richard Swinburne wrote a trilogy of books that applied this criterion of simplicity to the word "God."[2] What he has done, in effect, is account for all the material that our scientific and philosophical studies come up with, and account for it with the simple profundity of "God." He has returned us to our first insights and basic experiences of object permanence.

Professor Richard Swinburne and my grandson Andrew tell me the same thing and in virtually the same language to return us to Square One.

II

But you will notice that I am using the verb "return" and not "bring." We were there once, but chances are we are there no longer.

Square One is the place at which we realize that there is a huge world that we have not yet seen, an incredible creation that we cannot account for, a complex reality that is not defined or controlled by our experience of it. There is more — far more. Our experience, while authentic enough, is not encompassing. There is far more that we don't know than what we do know. We are enveloped, to use one of the classic phrases in our tradition, in "the cloud of unknowing."

There is something wonderfully exhilarating about this, the sense of space and time, of mystery and beauty. We become explorers, adventurers, knights errant.

But there is also something seriously disappointing, the realization that we are not at the center of the universe. In an infantile state — and this is true regardless of our chronological age — we have the perception that we are the center of everything. Our needs take precedence over everything, absolutely everything. Our appetites, our welfare, our comfort. We are as gods and goddesses, worshiped and adored and served.

Then we arrive at Square One and are told that we must wait our turn, or that our behavior is quite despicable and we must go to our room, or that we must share our toys with our sisters. There is a lot more going on than you and me. We experience finitude.

---

2. The books in order are *The Coherence of Theism, The Existence of God,* and *Faith and Reason.*

And we don't like it. For anyone who has had a taste of glory as a sovereign queen, as an almighty king, it is quite a come-down to be treated as a brat with bad manners. For anyone who has acquired enough money to be able to demand and pay for any conceivable whim, it is a shock to be told to walk away from it and start keeping company with a homeless and jobless itinerant preacher (Mark 10:17-31). For anyone who through long disciplined study has mastered an important body of knowledge, it is an impertinent insult to be assigned nursing care to a victim of random street violence (Luke 10:25-37).

When we first arrive at Square One, we are breathless before the unguessed splendors of infinity, stretching out endlessly. That is wonderful. And then we begin to realize the corollary, if there is such a thing as infinity, I am not it. I am finite. If there is God then there is no room for me as god.

The virtually unanimous response to this realization is some form or other of either narcissism or prometheanism. Narcissism is the attempt to retreat from Square One back into the spiritual sovereignty of self. Forget infinity. Forget mystery. Cultivate the wonderful self. It might be a small world, but it is my world, totally mine.

Prometheanism is the attempt to detour around Square One into the spirituality of infinity, get a handle on it, get control of it, and make something of it. All that spirituality sitting around idle needs managing. Prometheanism is practical. Prometheanism is entrepreneurial. Prometheanism is energetic and ambitious. Prometheanism wants to put all that power and beauty to good use.

Most of us, most of the time, can be found to be practising some variation on narcissism or prometheanism. It goes without saying then that most spirituality is a combination of narcissism and prometheanism, with the proportions carefully customized to suit our personal temperaments and circumstances.

And that is why I use the word "return" — it's *back* to Square One, back to the place of wonder, the realization of infinity, the worship of God.

The primary way in which we counter our stubborn propensities to narcissism and prometheanism is by cultivating humility. Learning to be just ourselves, keeping close to the ground, practising the *human,* getting our fingers in the *humus,* the rich, loamy, garden dirt out of which we have been fashioned.

And then listen.

III

Because returning to Square One is not only the return to a realization of God, but also to listening to what God says. God *said*. Did you listen? Do you listen?

Listening is linked, not only lexically (*akouo* and *hupakouo*), but spiritually to obedience, to response. "The hearing of man represents correspondence to the revelation of the Word, and in biblical religion it is thus the essential form in which this divine revelation is appropriated."[3]

Language is the primary means we have of acquiring "object permanence." The discovery that there is a word "ball" that refers to that round green fuzzy object that rolled under the dry sink, is a key to dealing with the reality of "things unseen." Words attest to the reality and distinctiveness of people and things and events that are outside the realm of my sensory experience. As I develop facility in words, my world expands; before long I am inhabiting remote centuries, dealing with faraway continents, having conversations with men and women in the cemeteries.

So it is not surprising that God, who is "far beyond what we can ask or think" should deal with us by means of language. God speaks. For Christians, basic spirituality is not only a noun, *God,* but also a verb, *Said* (or *Says*).

My purpose right now is not to argue this — it has been skillfully and competently reasoned and argued by our best Christian minds, some of them my colleagues here at Regent. What I want is simply to call your attention to the obvious, the accepted, the basic: when we go back to Square One, we listen, for God speaks.

And we do need reminding. For just as the realization of the world of Spirit that centers in the person and power of God frequently results in a proliferation of spiritualities that attempt to become or use God, so the acquisition of language that enables response and participation in the world of Spirit then results in spiritual talk that bypasses God.

Most, but certainly not all, of the spiritual talk that goes on in and out of Christian churches is of this kind. It is not listening to

3. G. Kittel, ed., *Theological Dictionary of the New Testament* (Grand Rapids: Eerdmans, 1964), vol. 1, p. 216.

God; it is not answering God; it is not believing in the Word of God. It is chatter.

Sometimes very interesting chatter. Often it is fascinating chatter. But it is *our* commentary on *our* experience with the spiritual, not a proclamation of *God's* address to us from the world of Spirit. We give witness, we testify endlessly — but more often than not we are talking about ourselves, not God. It is not proclamation, which is the basic form which language about God takes, but gossip.

*　　*　　*

The Book of Job is our classic exposé of this kind of thing. Job is back to Square One: God Said. But the noun, God, and the verb, Said, are separated in the Book of Job by a lot of spiritual talk that has nothing to do with God. Job has no question but that he is dealing with God. He is faced with mystery — none of the familiar ways of accounting for life work any more. He is confronted with unknowing. He will be satisfied by nothing less than God speaking to him, a God who tells him what's what, a God who reveals. And God does speak, "out of the whirlwind," and Job is satisfied. God does not answer his questions, does not explain the mystery — but he speaks. And that is enough. It is always enough.

But most of the text of Job is taken up with the spiritual talk of Job's religious advisors, Eliphaz, Bildad, Zophar, and Elihu. Almost all of what they say is true. But at the same time, almost nothing of what they say is true. None of it is a participation in listening to and answering God. One of the most arresting of the speeches is that of Eliphaz. It is his first speech, and he supports what he has to say by documenting it with the authority of spiritual experience. Eliphaz tells Job that he must have sinned, otherwise he would not be suffering. It's a logical, cause-effect spiritual universe that we live in. There is no mystery. There are answers to everything. But Eliphaz is not all logic — he attempts to give authority for his speech by testifying to a supernatural experience.

A word came to me in secret,
　　a mere whisper of a word, but I heard it clearly.
　　It came in a dream that disturbed my sleep
　　after I had fallen into a deep, deep sleep;

Dread confronted me, and Terror,
I was scared to death, trembled from head to foot.
A ghost glided right in front of me,
the hair of my head stood straight up.
It stood there, but I couldn't tell what it was,
a blur . . . and then I heard a muffled voice.

4:12-16 (my trans.)

After an experience like that, you might think there would be some profound revelation to impart. But, no, it is more of the same — the conventional wisdom that Eliphaz could have picked up at some Babylonian shrine or Egyptian temple.

Can mere mortals be more righteous than God?
Can humans be more pure than their maker?
Why, God doesn't even trust his own servants,
doesn't even laud his angels,
So how much less these bodies composed of mud,
fragile as a moth?
These bodies of ours can be unmade in no time at all
and no one even notice — gone without a trace.
Someone pulls the plug and that's it,
we die and are never the wiser for it.

4:17-21 (my trans.)

Later on Eliphaz again attempts to give spiritual authority to his worn-out banalities by referring to "the vision I had" (15:17).

Job is not impressed. He is not impressed by the supernatural. He wants God. And he wants the God who speaks; he doesn't want to hear Eliphaz talk about his experience with a ghost. He has no interest in Eliphaz's stories about spooky whispers and blurs in the middle of the night; he wants to hear God speak. The Word of God.

When God speaks through his prophets he does so clearly. Isaiah is nothing if not clear: "I heard the voice of the Lord saying, 'Whom shall I send, . . . Go, and say to this people . . .'" (Isa. 6:8-9). Jeremiah is nothing if not clear: "Now the Word of the Lord came to me saying, 'Before I formed you in the womb I knew you. . . . I have set you this day over nations and over kingdoms, to pluck up and to break down, to destroy and to overthrow, to build and to plant'" (Jer.

1:4-10). Ezekiel is nothing if not clear: "And he said to me, 'Son of man, stand upon your feet, and I will speak with you.' And when he spoke to me, the Spirit entered into me and set me upon my feet; and I heard him speaking to me. And he said to me, 'Son of man, I send you to the people of Israel, to a nation of rebels . . .'" (Ezek. 2:1-3). "The prophets experienced the word in unequivocal terms; it was placed directly in their mouths as an oracle for public proclamation."[4]

And Eliphaz is nothing if not vague: ". . . a mere whisper of a word . . . a ghost glided in front of me . . . a blur . . . a muffled voice" (Job 4:12-16). "For Eliphaz the word steals in through the back door furtive, indistinct, and faint. Its origin and author are unknown. It is simply identified as a word, a passing sound, a noise in the night."[5]

This kind of stuff is the plague of spiritualities of all times and all places. The bizarre, the enigmatic, the pretentiously exotic. There is no suggestion here that Eliphaz is a fraud, that the experience itself is not real. But it is put before us in such a way that we realize that it is not significant. All these testimonies of brushes with the supernatural, descriptions of mystical states and heightened consciousness — not significant. All these techniques offered to us by which we can be in tune with the voices, feel the vibrations, hear the harmonies — not significant.

I am not suggesting that all this is sheer fraud and fantasy. The experiences might very well be real enough. There is nothing in Job to suggest that Eliphaz was a fraud. He may very well have had this supernatural experience that gave him goose bumps.

What I am saying is that it is not significant. Eliphaz was the Shirley McLaine of ancient Edom.

Christian spirituality is not impressed with the supernatural. Supernatural is neither here nor there for those of us who are standing at Square One, getting ourselves oriented, coming to terms with our human finitude, getting a glimpse of God's infinitude.

We are immersed in a world of Spirit, and so why wouldn't we have spiritual experience? But such experience does not confer authority upon *our* counsel or *our* character. The return to Square One

4. Norman C. Habel, *The Book of Job* (Philadelphia: Westminster Press, 1985), p. 126.
5. Habel, *The Book of Job,* p. 127.

is not only a return to God, but to God *Said*. For not only is there God, there is God's Word.

Christian spirituality does not begin with us talking about our experience; it begins with listening to God call us, heal us, forgive us.

This is hard to get into our heads. We talk habitually to ourselves and about ourselves. We don't listen. If we do listen to each other it is almost always with the purpose of getting something we can use in our turn. Much of our listening is a form of politeness, courteously waiting our turn to talk about ourselves. But in relation to God especially we must break the habit and let him speak to us. God not only is; God *Says*.

Christian spirituality, in addition to being an attentive spirituality, is a listening spirituality.

*   *   *

Words are our primary tools for getting our bearing in a world, most of which we can't see, most of which we'll never touch — this large, expanding, mysterious existence that is so much larger, more intricate, more real even, than we are.

When Andrew learned the word "ball," he had a means for dealing with an object he couldn't see. When I learn the word "God" I am able to deal with a person I cannot see. God uses words to train us in object permanence.

But now I want to amend the phrase, from *object* permanence to *subject* permanence. For God is not an object that I deal with, but a subject who speaks to and addresses me. It is in learning to listen to God speak that I become familiar with and participate in basic spirituality.

There is an interesting detail here that I want to note. I said earlier that when we get to Square One we do not leave biology and embrace spirituality. Our physical senses do not become less important; they become more important because we are not limited by them. When we discover that God reveals himself by word, we are back in the realm of the sensory again — a word is spoken by a mouth/lips/tongue/throat; it is heard by ears, or in the case of the written word, seen with eyes. But once the word is uttered and heard, or written and read, it enters into us in such a way that it transcends

27

the sensory. A word is (or can be) a revelation from one interior to another. What is inside me can get inside you — the word does it. Which is why language is the major bridge from basic biology to basic spirituality.

And why Christian spirituality insists on listening.

By God's grace, God's Word is also written. And that makes Holy Scripture the text for Christian spirituality. Holy Scripture is the listening post for listening to God's Word.

IV

Something remarkable takes place when we return to Square One, to the place of adoration and listening — a terrific infusion of energy within us; a release of adrenaline in our souls which becomes obedience. The reason is that the word that God speaks is the kind of word that makes things happen. When God speaks it is not in order to give us information on the economy so that we will know how to do our financial planning. When God speaks it is not as a fortune teller, looking into our personal future and satisfying curiosity regarding our romantic prospects or the best horse to bet on. No, when God speaks it is not in explanation of all the things that we have not been able to find answers to from our parents or in books or from reading tea leaves. God's Word is not, in essence, information or gossip or explanation. God's Word makes things happen — he makes something happen in us. The imperative is a primary verb form in Holy Scripture: "Let there be light . . . Go . . . Come . . . Repent . . . Believe . . . Be still . . . Be healed . . . Get up . . . Ask . . . Love . . . Pray. . . ."

And the intended consequence of the imperative is obedience. I love the Psalm phrase, "I will *run* in the way of thy commandments, when thou givest me understanding" (Ps. 119:32). Yes, *run*. Square One, with its attentiveness and listening, is that place of understanding — we know who we are and where we are . . . and who God is and where he is. At that place and in that condition, there is an inward gathering and concentration of energy that on signal from God's imperative expresses itself in, precisely, obedience — *running* in the way of God's commandments. For there is nothing grudging or hangdog or foot dragging in the biblical narrations of obedience.

St. Mark gives us a sharply etched detail of this aspect of God's Word when he tells the story of the healing of Bartimaeus at Jericho, the city where a millennium earlier Jesus' namesake, Joshua (in Greek, "Jesus"), signaled the acts of salvation and deliverance that launched the campaign that turned the promises of God into actual possession of the land. Jesus returns to Jericho to launch his final campaign — going up to Jerusalem against the forces of darkness and then, by means of crucifixion and resurrection, taking possession of the country of salvation. Jericho is a Square One kind of place.

Here's the detail: as Jesus starts out, Bartimaeus is sitting beside the roadside begging. He hears that it's Jesus and calls out for help, for mercy — persistently. Jesus hears him, stops, and calls for him. When Bartimaeus receives the summons there is not a moment of hesitation — he leaps to his feet and goes to Jesus (Mark 10:50). The verb "leaps" (*anapedesas*) — this is its only occurrence in the New Testament — catches our attention. Bartimaeus *jumps up*. Like a sprinter at the signal of a starting pistol, he explodes from his place and is off and running. Yes, "I will run in the way of thy commandments, when thou givest me understanding." Bartimaeus is at Square One, poised and ready, and so when Jesus speaks the word of invitation, *God's Word* no less, Bartimaeus at Square One is a rocket launched.

For Square One is not a place where we sit around discussing what to do next. It is not an oasis of repose from the strenuous business of pilgrimage. It is not a return to inaction when the action gets too much for us. It is the place to which we return so that our faith is God-initiated, our discipleship is Christ-defined, our obedience is Spirit-infused.

Eugen Rosenstock-Huessy, whom I honor as one of the wonderful, if maverick, teachers on the spirituality of language and life in our century, took as his life motto: *Respondeo etsi mutabor,* "I respond although I will be changed!"[6] For when we return to Square One where we hear God's Word, the obedience which follows will certainly change our lives. Repentance and commitment, belief and faithfulness — all the energy-filled actions that are initiated at Square One, do not run in the ruts of our willful habits and routines, but are

6. Quoted in *Judaism Despite Christianity,* ed. Eugen Rosenstock-Huessy (University, AL: University of Alabama Press, 1969), p. 4.

transformative: they take us with Jesus to Jerusalem and the cross and the resurrection.

We do not progress in the Christian life by becoming more competent, more knowledgeable, more virtuous, or more energetic. We do not advance in the Christian life by acquiring expertise. Each day, and many times each day, we return to Square One: God Said. We are constantly being "thrown back on the start and always opening up afresh."[7] We are always beginners. We begin again. We hear Jesus say, "Unless you turn and become like children, you will never enter the kingdom of heaven" (Matt. 18:3). And so we become as little children. We return to the condition in which we acquired subject permanence, God said. We go back to Square One. We adore and we listen.

*   *   *

I want to simplify your lives. When others are telling you to read more, I want to tell you to read less; when others are telling you to do more, I want to tell you to do less. The world does not need more of you; it needs more of God. Your friends do not need more of you; they need more of God. And you don't need more of you; you need more of God.

The Christian life consists in what God does for us, not what we do for God; the Christian life consists in what God says to us, not what we say about God. We also, of course, do things and say things; but if we do not return to Square One each time we act, each time we speak, beginning from God and God's Word, we will soon be found to be practicing a spirituality that has little or nothing to do with God. And so it is necessary, if we are going to truly live a Christian life, and not just use the word Christian to disguise our narcissistic and promethean attempts at a spirituality without worshiping God and without being addressed by God, it is necessary to return to Square One and adore God and listen to God. Given our sin-damaged memories that render us vulnerable to every latest edition of journalistic spirituality, daily re-orientation in the truth revealed in Jesus and attested in Scripture is required. And given our

7. Karl Barth, *Church Dogmatics,* I/1 (Edinburgh: T. and T. Clark, 1936), p. 15.

ancient predisposition for reducing every scrap of divine revelation that we come across into a piece of moral/spiritual technology that we can use to get on in the world, and eventually to get on without God, a daily return to a condition of not-knowing and non-achievement is required. We have proven, time and again, that we are not to be trusted in these matters. We need to return to Square One for a fresh start as often as every morning, noon, and night.

Spirit Quest

If all your friends were suddenly to begin talking about the state of their digestion — comparing symptoms, calling up for advice, swapping remedies — you would not consider it a hopeful sign. Nor does the widespread interest in spirituality today lead me to think that the North American soul is in a flourishing condition.

A person who has healthy digestion does not talk about it. Neither does a person who has a healthy soul. When our bodies and souls are working well, we are, for the most part, unaware of them. The frequency with which the word *spirituality* occurs these days is more likely to be evidence of pathology than health.

By taking this stance, I am not dismissing current interest in spirituality as sick. The interest itself is not sick, but sickness has provoked the interest. There is considerable confusion regarding the appropriate treatment, but virtual unanimity in the diagnosis: Our culture is sick with secularism.

But deeper and stronger than our illness is our cure. The Spirit of God that hovered over the primordial chaos (Gen. 1:2) hovers over our murderous and chaotic cities. The Spirit that descended on Jesus like a dove (Matt. 3:16) descends on the followers of Jesus. The Holy Spirit that filled men and women with God at nine o'clock in the morning in Jerusalem during Pentecost (Acts 2:1-4) fills men and women still in Chicago and Calcutta, Moscow and Montreal, around the clock, 365 days a year.

This article first appeared in the November 8, 1993, issue of *Christianity Today*.

What's more, there is a groundswell of recognition spreading through our culture that all life is at root spiritual; that everything we see is formed and sustained by what we cannot see. Those of us who grew up in the Great Spiritual Depression and who accustomed ourselves to an obscure life in the shadow of arrogant Rationalism and bullying Technology can hardly believe our eyes and ears. People all around us — neighbors and strangers, rich and poor, Communists and capitalists — want to know about *God*. They ask questions about meaning and purpose, right and wrong, heaven and hell.

For several years I was recruited by the state university, not far from where I lived, to teach a course in New Testament. The course had been inserted into the curriculum in the Department of Philosophy and Religion 40 years before by a Christian professor who headed the department. It was a surreptitious move on his part, hoping to provide university students access to the New Testament. He taught the course himself to a few students, never very many. And then he died. By that time, all the professors in the department were either atheist or Marxist, and since there was no one to teach the course, it was left untaught.

Through atheistic carelessness, it continued to be listed in the catalogue. Some students spotted it and demanded that it be offered. The professors had to go looking for someone outside their ranks to teach it and found a good friend of mine. When he moved away, they tried to drop it. But by then, it had become the most popular course in the department. Student movements being what they were in those days, they again had to go looking for a Christian to teach it, and they found me.

This kind of thing happens a lot these days — spiritual interest gathering force underground and erupting into unlikely and often secular settings. Overnight, it seems, the tables are turned: instead of plotting ways in which we can get people interested in God, they are calling *us* up, pulling on our sleeves, asking, "We would see Jesus." They, of course, do not always (not even often) say *Jesus*. But they have had it with the world and their lives the way they are, and they have the good sense to realize that improved goods and services are not going to help.

We may well be living during a wonderful moment in history, as those old frauds, the world, the flesh, and the Devil, are discredited by the very culture they have nearly destroyed. As the dust settles and the air clears, we see a widespread readiness to respond to the Father, Son, and Holy Spirit.

Spirituality is not always recognized in the terms I am using to define it — the presence and activity of God the Spirit — but the *awareness* is there; the *hunger* is there.

Bored with Freedom

In order to respond appropriately, it is necessary to take stock of this failed culture out of which a hunger for God is emerging.

Our culture has failed precisely because it is a *secular* culture. A secular culture is a culture reduced to *thing* and *function*. Typically, at the outset, people are delighted to find themselves living in such a culture. It is wonderful to have all these *things* coming our way, without having to worry about their nature or purpose. And it is wonderful to have this incredible freedom to *do* so much, without bothering about relationships or meaning. But after a few years of this, our delight diminishes as we find ourselves lonely among the things and bored with our freedom.

Our first response is to get more of what brought us delight in the first place: acquire more things, generate more activity. Get more. Do more. After a few years of this, we are genuinely puzzled that we are not any better.

We North Americans have been doing this for well over a century now, and we have succeeded in producing a culture that is reduced to thing and function. And we all seem to be surprised that this magnificent achievement of secularism — all these things! all these activities! — has produced an epidemic of loneliness and boredom. We are surprised to find ourselves lonely behind the wheel of a BMW or bored nearly to death as we advance from one prestigious job to another.

And then, one by one, a few people begin to realize that getting more and doing more only makes the sickness worse. They realize that if it gets much worse, the culture will be dead — a thoroughly secularized culture is a corpse.

People begin to see that secularism marginalizes and eventually obliterates the two essentials of human fullness: intimacy and transcendence. *Intimacy:* we want to experience human love and trust and joy. *Transcendence:* we want to experience divine love and trust and joy. We are not ourselves by ourselves. We do not become more human, more *ourselves,* when we are behind the wheel of a BMW, or, when capped and gowned we acquire another academic degree so we can get a better job and do more and better things. Instead, we long for a human touch, for someone who knows our name. We hunger for divine meaning, someone who will bless us.

And so spirituality, a fusion of intimacy and transcendence, overnight becomes a passion for millions of North Americans. It should be no surprise that a people so badly trained in intimacy and transcendence might not do too well in their quest. Most anything at hand that gives a feeling of closeness — whether genitals or cocaine — will do for intimacy. And most anything exotic that induces a sense of mystery — from mantras to river rafting — will do for transcendence.

It is commendable that we have a nation of men and women who, fed up with things as such and distraught with activity as such, should dignify their hearts with something more than a yearly valentine card. It is heartening that our continent is experiencing a recovery of desire to embrace intimacies and respond to transcendence. But it is regrettable that these most human and essential desires are so ignorantly and badly served.

But then, a culture as thoroughly secularized as ours can hardly be expected to come up with its own medicine. For the most part, North Americans come up with a secularized spirituality, which is no spirituality at all. They ransack exotic cultures and esoteric groups in a search for wholeness; but being new at this and without experience, they have no way of discriminating between the true and false. Fraudulence is rampant. Our leaders, ignorant of human nature, promote pseudo-intimacies that dehumanize. Our celebrities offer a pseudo-transcendence that trivializes.

Internalizing the World's Ways

Historically, evangelical Christians have served the church by bringing sharpness and ardor to matters of belief and behavior, insisting on personal involvement, injecting energy and passion, returning daily to the Scriptures for command and guidance, and providing communities of commitment. But presently there is not an equivalent precision in matters of spirituality. It turns out that we have been affected by our secularizing culture far more than we had realized. Evangelicals have been uncritically internalizing the world's ways and bringing them into churches without anyone noticing. In particular, we have internalized the world's fascination with technology and its enthusiasm for activities.

Instead of being brought before God ("O come, let us worship and bow down") and led to acquire a taste for the holy mysteries of transcendence in worship, we are talked to and promoted endlessly, to try this and attend that. We are recruited for church roles and positions in which we can shine, validating our usefulness by our function.

After a few years or decades of this, we find ourselves in churches (*evangelical* churches) where there is as little intimacy and transcendence as in the world. We feel impoverished — defrauded, even. We look around for evidence of what we desire most. It is there in our Scriptures. We catch glimpses of it in other people. We see signs of it in other parts of the church, in other centuries, sometimes in other countries, sometimes in other denominations. We want it for ourselves. What's wrong? We are *believing* the right things. We are *doing* the right things.

Things! — that's what is wrong. We become avid for spirituality: we long to be in community, experiencing love and trust and joy with others. We are fed up with being evaluated by how much we can contribute, how much we can do. We hunger for communion with God, something beyond the satisfaction of self, the development of *me*. We are fed up with being told *about* God.

We go to our leaders for help, and they don't seem to know what we are talking about. They sign us up for a program in stress management. They recruit us for a tour of the Holy Land. They enroll us in a course in family dynamics. They give us a Myers-Briggs personality-type indicator so they can fit us into the slot where we can function efficiently. When we don't seem interested, they talk faster and louder. When we drift somewhere else, they hire a public-relations consultant to devise a campaign designed to attract us and our friends. Sometimes the advertising campaign is successful in enlisting people who want something to do without the inconvenience of community and want to know how to be on good terms with God without having to give up the final say-so on their own lives. But they don't attract *us*. We are after what we came for in the first place: intimacy and transcendence, personal friends and a personal God, love and worship.

Focus, Precision, and Roots

It is my sense that spirituality is mostly of concern among the laity these days, the men and women who are running markets, raising children, driving trucks, cooking meals, selling cars, believing in God while changing a flat tire in the rain, and praying for an enemy while studying for an exam. Religious professionals, by and large, are working from a different agenda.

Contemporary spirituality desperately needs focus, precision, and roots: focus on Christ, precision in the Scriptures, and roots in a healthy tradition. In these times of drift and dilettantism, evangelical Christians must once again serve the church by providing just such focus and precision and rootage. That it is primarily lay Christians who are left to provide this service to the church is not at all crippling. The strength and impact of evangelicalism has often been in its laity — transcending denominational divisions, subverting established structures, working behind the scenes, beginning at the bottom.

I have five items of counsel in matters of spirituality for all who hunger and thirst after intimacy and transcendence. Each item provides evangelical focus, precision, and rootage to spirituality. As we get it straight ourselves, we will be equipped to provide leadership to others, an *evangelical* leadership that is so conspicuously lacking at present.

1. Discover what Scripture says about spirituality and immerse yourself in it. This is not a matter of hunting for a few texts, but of acquiring a biblical imagination — entering into the vast world of the Bible and getting a feel for the territory, an instinct for *reality*. The scriptural revelation is not only authoritative for what we believe about God and the way we behave with each other, but also for shaping and maturing our very souls, our *being,* in response to God. The Scriptures provide as much precision in matters of our being as they do in our thinking and acting. Spirituality that is not continuously and prayerfully soaked in the biblical revelation soon either hardens into self-righteousness or dissolves into psychology.

2. *Shun spirituality that does not require commitment.* Personal commitment to the God personally revealed in Jesus is at the heart of spirituality. Faddish spiritualities, within and without the church, ignore or deny commitment. Evangelical counsel places the Lord's commands — believe, follow, endure — at the core of all spirituality. A lifelong faith commitment to God as revealed in Jesus Christ is essential to any true spirituality.

"Ecstasy doesn't last," wrote novelist E. M. Forster, "but it cuts a channel for something lasting." Single-minded, persevering faithfulness confirms the authenticity of our spirituality. The ancestors we look to for encouragement in this business — Augustine of Hippo and Julian of Norwich, John Calvin and Amy Carmichael, John Bunyan and Teresa of Avila — didn't flit. They *stayed.*

Spirituality without commitment is analogous to sexuality without commitment — quick and casual, superficial and impersonal, selfish and loveless — eventually a parody of its initial promise. Deprived of commitment, sexuality degenerates into addiction, violence, or boredom. Deprived of commitment, spirituality, no matter how wise or promising, has a short shelf life.

3. *Embrace friends in the faith wherever you find them.* This may mean friends across town in another church, on another continent, or, through books from another century. Spirituality digs wells deep into our traditions, and at some point, we find we have tapped into a common aquifer.

I grew up in an atmosphere of strident anti-Catholicism. Being Roman Catholic was far worse than being unsaved, for Catholics were the enemy, obedient soldiers of the Antichrist, ready to wipe us out on signal from the Vatican. And then one day, to my great surprise, my Pentecostal-minister mother came home from a retreat she had led, talking with warmth and appreciation about several nuns she had met. Soon she was referring to them as "my" nuns. The "sisters" had become her sisters.

This is a common experience in our age of a recovered spirituality. We find ourselves praying with Quakers and Orthodox, Carmelite nuns and Mennonite pacifists. Baptists lie down with Presbyterians, and Anglicans play with the Methodists.

4. *But then return home and explore your own tradition.* Hunger

for a deeper spirituality, a Christian life in which God is authenticated in everyday circumstances and personal relationships, is almost always accompanied by a sense of deprivation; we suspect we were not provided our rightful heritage by our church or pastor or family, that we were not guided and nurtured in the ways of robust holiness. That sense of deprivation often turns into anger: "Why didn't you tell me about this? Why did you use my hunger for God to recruit me for your religious projects? Why did you flatten my longing for God into explanations that would keep me in my place?"

Angry over our impoverishment, we cannot help noticing churches or movements that look better. We see places and people who are risking themselves in love and God, and we know we would flourish if we could only live among them. They have already stimulated and nourished us so wonderfully. We get ready to jump ship.

Our wisest counselors usually tell us to stay put. Every place, every congregation, every denomination, has a rich spiritual tradition to be discovered and explored.

Evangelicalism is *also* a tradition — representing centuries of prayer and holy living, witness and wisdom, and treasures for our nurture. Recover what is yours by right by going *deep,* not away. The grass is not greener on the other side of the fence. Every religious community has its dead spots; your task is to dig wells in your desert.

Baron Friedrich von Hugel, a Roman Catholic layperson, was one of the most respected spiritual directors in England in the early years of this century. As men and women came under his influence and sought his direction, they frequently wanted to become Catholics. He never encouraged it. He insisted they stay where they were, as Presbyterians and Anglicans and Baptists. He consistently sent people back to their own churches. There is plenty of digging to be done in our own back yard.

There are, to be sure, exceptional cases. But spirituality does not normally thrive by transplant. Those of us suddenly awake to the rich heritage we missed all these years, who now want to become Orthodox or Catholic or charismatic, need to ask if Jesus is speaking to me in his command to the healed demoniac in Gerasa who, when he begged to return with Jesus to Galilee, was sent back to the "church" he grew up in: "Go home to your friends, and tell them how much the Lord has done for you, and how he has had mercy on you" (Mark 5:19).

5. Look for mature guides; honor wise leaders. There are many holy friends and pastors, teachers and priests, brothers and sisters among us. But they do not advertise themselves. Seek them out. Cultivate their company either in person or through books.

Because an appetite for God is easily manipulated into a consumer activity, we need these wise, sane friends as guides and companions. There are entrepreneurs among us who see the widespread hunger for spirituality as a marketplace and are out there selling junk food. The gullibility of the unwary who bought relics from itinerant monks in the Middle Ages — splinters of wood from the true cross, finger bones from the saints, a few pieces of thread from Jesus' seamless robe — is more than matched by North Americans in matters of spirituality.

We are trained from the cradle to be good consumers. It is understandable that we seek to satisfy our hunger for God along the lines in which we have been brought up. But it is not excusable, for we have clear counsel in the Gospels to steer us away from this consumer world: "Blessed are the poor. . . . Deny yourself, take up your cross, and follow me. . . . Love not the world nor the things that are in the world." And our Lord's counsel is confirmed and expanded in numerous ways by our wise evangelical ancestors in the faith.

Spirituality is not the latest fad but the oldest truth. Spirituality, the alert attention we give to a living God and the faithful response we make to him in community, is at the heart of our Scriptures and is on display throughout the centuries of Israel and the church. We have been at this a long time. We have nearly four millennia of experience to draw upon. When someone hands you a new book, reach for an old one. Isaiah has far more to teach us about spirituality than Carl Jung.

Writers and Angels:
Witnesses to Transcendence

One winter, as I was walking with my dog along the North Fork of the Flathead River in Montana, he suddenly plunged his head into fourteen inches of snow and came up with a field mouse in his teeth. Similar things, not always dramatic, happen all the time. I am always impressed with how much more the dog sees and hears and smells than I do. The dog's senses are fine-tuned, constantly picking up signals to which I am oblivious. Would he be as impressed with how much more I believe and pray and love than he does? Probably not, for I seem to be as limited in detecting the supersensual as I am in detecting the sensual.

But fortunately, I am not without resources. Persistent reports keep coming in on the activity of angels — beings that call attention to the rich and complex world of spirit much as animals do the rich and complex world of sense. At least, that is what most of my Christian ancestors, the accounts of Holy Scripture confirmed in their own experience, have believed. After a century of partial eclipse due to our fascination with the machine, interest in angels seems to be picking up again.[1]

"Writers and Angels" was originally published in *Theology Today* 5, no. 3 (October 1994): 396-404.

1. Sophy Burnham's *A Book of Angels* (New York: Ballantine Books, 1990) and *Angel Letters* (1991) are representative of the many angel books and letters that have been appearing in the last few years.

Angels and animals. They make a nice combination, extending our awareness in the twin dimensions of spirit and sense. Animal stories, pets, photography, and observation extend our participation more deeply into the sensual beauty and vitality that is all around us, so much of which we are unaware. Angel stories, letters, books, and glimpses extend our participation more deeply into the spiritual beauty and vitality that is all around us, so much of which we are unaware. It is significant that in St. John's *Revelation,* our most prominent biblical integration of the sensual and spiritual, animals and angels flank the human representatives of Israel and the church in giving praise to God (Rev. 4–5). We humans need help from both sides in order to participate in the largeness of God's creation and salvation.

Angels have never lacked for notice. Angel stories that run the gamut from serious to silly abound in folk religion. And learned angel speculation has occupied some of the best minds in Christendom, most notably Pseudo-Dionysius and Thomas Aquinas. But it is the novelists and poets who have shown the most immediate and natural affinity for angels. It is easy to see why, for writers and angels are alike concerned with bringing transcendence to our attention. Writers and angels are message-bringers, bringing the message that there is more here than meets the eye.

Writers and angels share another quality, a penchant for elusiveness, for staying out of the way. Our best writers hide themselves in their work. And angels are for the most part invisible and inaudible, neither noticed nor heard. For transcendence cannot be forced upon us. It doesn't yell, doesn't announce its presence with a bullhorn, doesn't advertise itself on roadside billboards. There is nothing bullying about transcendence.

What it requires is noticing. Witnesses to transcendence don't create transcendence. The transcendence is already here, or there. But in our hurry to get someplace else, we miss it. There is always more here than meets the eye. We miss a lot. We need friends who will grab our shirttails, turn us around, and show us what we just now missed in our hurry to get across the street on the way to the bank. We need friends who will tap us on the shoulder, interrupting our non-stop commentary on the talk of the town so that we can hear the truth. We need witnesses to transcendence. Writers. Angels. We stop, we look, we listen.

Because they have this natural affinity for one another, it is to be expected that writers would use angels as they go about their business of giving witness to transcendence. Milton in his *Paradise Lost* will always occupy the place of honor among writers who have used angels to persuade and convince us of what "eye cannot see nor ear hear." Or is it the angels that used Milton?

While no one is likely to do this better than Milton, many writers continue to do what he did so well. I have selected four works of contemporary fiction in which major writers of our century follow this long and venerable practice of employing angels to provide witness to transcendence. I have chosen these four to provide some indication of the variety and range of transcendence that we inhabit. Each writer goes about his work in very different ways; about the only thing they have in common, besides their use of angels, is that it is a specifically Christian *transcendence* to which they give witness.

It will be apparent that none of these novels is *about* angels as such. What I find interesting is the theologically serious and spiritually accurate roles that angels play as these writers bring into our awareness huge dimensions of reality that are too often unremarked or unnoticed in the everydayness of our lives. Since each of these novels is complex in its own way and operates skillfully at several levels of meaning at once, I will not deal with them as wholes. I only want to notice with pleasure this affinity between writers and angels for calling us to attention before the divine presence.

Witness to Divine Purpose

John Irving creates the character of Owen Meany[2] to serve as a subversive evangelist in a culture in which explicit evangelists can't be trusted. A most unlikely evangelist — a waif-like runt with a squeaky voice who accidentally kills his best friend's mother by hitting her with a foul ball in a baseball game — but an evangelist all the same. The opening lines of the novel announce the theme: "I am doomed to remember a boy with a wrecked voice — not because of his voice, or because he was the smallest person I ever knew, or

2. John Irving, *A Prayer for Owen Meany* (New York: William Morrow, 1989).

even because he was the instrument of my mother's death, but because he is the reason I believe in God; I am a Christian because of Owen Meany."[3]

Owen Meany is one of the outstanding characters in contemporary fiction not because of comic effects of his appearance and sound, the sheer oddness of his presence, but because of the sheer oddness of his conviction that he is an instrument of God. In a culture that understands itself primarily through the categories of psychology and economics, Owen Meany understands himself theologically, and in terms of a most unfashionable expression of theology, predestination. These parallel oddnesses of appearance and conviction reinforce one another, and both together, through the writer's art, become believable. We end up believing that someone who looked and spoke like this could actually exist in our neighborhood; we end up believing that someone like this, living out a conviction that there is nothing odd or apparently accidental or seemingly useless — even when it's me! — that does not serve the divine purpose, could actually exist in our culture.

The conviction pivots on an angel appearance. Owen Meany is sleeping overnight with his best friend, Johnny Wheelwright. Owen is sick with a fever during the night and wakes Johnny. Johnny's mother is sleeping in the next room, and Johnny sends Owen to her. Owen returns and tells Johnny that he has just seen an angel by the bed. Johnny assumes that he has feverishly mistaken the dressmaker's dummy that always stood by his mother's bed for an angel, but returns with Owen to the room to see for himself. The angel is no longer there. When Johnny suggests to Owen that he mistook the dummy for an angel, Owen says, "The angel was on the other side of the bed."[4]

The angel sighting was pivotal because Owen came to believe that he had walked in on the Angel of Death at its holy work and thereby upset the scheme of things. The angel's task was then reassigned to him. Later, when Owen hit the foul ball that killed Johnny's mother, it was no accident, but "fated." Johnny Wheelwright as narrator says, "It made him furious when I suggested that *anything* was an 'accident' — especially anything that had happened to him; on the

3. Irving, *A Prayer for Owen Meany,* p. 13.
4. Irving, *A Prayer for Owen Meany,* p. 99.

subject of predestination, Owen Meany would accuse Calvin of bad faith. There were *no* accidents; there was a reason for that baseball — just as there was a reason for Owen being small, and a *reason* for his voice."[5]

Life, in our everyday experience of it, often seems absurd. Circumstances turn up at random; nothing is connected. By means of narrative art, the novelist attempts to convince us that life is not random, that there is plot and resolution, that things make sense. But a narration is not an explanation; in some ways it is the opposite of explanation, it is imagination. Explanation has its honored place, but it is a poor substitute for imagination. The writer puts things on the page in such a way that our imaginations are enlisted in seeing the connections, the interlaced meanings in people and things and events. In attempting to account for the events on the night when Owen saw the angel, a neighbor says, "Ah, that explains everything!" The narrator then comments, "What a phrase that is: 'that explains everything' today."[6]

It is most interesting that, in a day when predestation, at least in its extreme forms, has been largely abandoned by theologians and pastors as they attempt to account for the coherent connectedness of life, it is picked up by a novelist and successfully put to the uses of the imagination. The test of the novel is not whether we end up believing in predestination, but whether we are convinced that Owen Meany believed it and that Owen Meany is, in fact, believable. For that opens up the possibility for the reader to accompany the narrator from "I didn't believe in angels then" to "I believe in angels now."[7]

The pivotal function of the angel in this novel is confirmed in a scene in the cemetery on the night Johnny's mother is buried. Johnny and his cousin Hester go to the cemetery looking for Owen. They find him at the grave with a flashlight, reading prayers from the Burial Service, "Into paradise the angels lead you. . . ."[8] The scene is picked up again on the last page of the novel and provides the title for the book. As Johnny, the novel's narrator, is summing up, he says, "There's a prayer I say most often for Owen. It's one of the little

5. Irving, *A Prayer for Owen Meany,* p. 99.
6. Irving, *A Prayer for Owen Meany,* p. 102.
7. Irving, *A Prayer for Owen Meany,* p. 134.
8. Irving, *A Prayer for Owen Meany,* p. 131.

prayers he said for my mother, the night Hester and I found him in the cemetery — where he'd brought the flashlight, because he knew how my mother had hated the darkness. 'Into paradise may the angels lead you,' he'd said over my mother's grave; and so I say that one for him — I know it was one of his favorites. I am always saying prayers for Owen Meany."[9]

Rebel Angels

Near the end of Robertson Davies' novel *What's Bred in the Bone*,[10] there is a conversation between the two angels, the Lesser Zadkiel and the Daimon Maimas, who, invisibly and in the background, have been present throughout the story overseeing the destiny of the principal character, Francis Cornish. As Cornish dies, the angels reminisce over their assigned angel work throughout his lifetime. In the midst of their reminiscence, the Daimon Maimas says, "Of course, we know that it is all metaphor, you and I. Indeed, we are metaphors ourselves."[11]

Calling an angel a metaphor says nothing one way or another about the reality of angels as such. Metaphor is a primary means by which language deals with what is unseen and yet real. If we say, as the psalmists often did, that God is a rock, and that "rock" in the sentence does not refer to an idol but is a metaphor for God, there is no implication that the rock is not real on its own account. Angels as metaphors provide a means for making story and sense out of elusive energies and forces for which abstract terms seem unsatisfactorily thin.

In an earlier novel, *The Rebel Angels*,[12] in which Francis Cornish also played a part, the writer worked from the other direction — he used humans as metaphors for angels. Two scholars, Simon Darcourt and Clem Hollier, professors at the College of St. John and the Holy Ghost ("Spook" to its residents), are made to represent the rebel angels, Samahazai and Azazel.

9. Irving, *A Prayer for Owen Meany*, p. 542.
10. Robertson Davies, *What's Bred in the Bone* (New York: Viking Press, 1985).
11. Davies, *What's Bred in the Bone*, p. 435.
12. Robertson Davies, *The Rebel Angels* (New York: Viking Press, 1981).

In an old Gnostic myth, the angels Samahazai and Azazel betrayed the secrets of heaven to King Solomon — told him everything there was to be told about everything that was. God, naturally, threw them out of heaven. "And did they mope and plot vengeance? Not they! They weren't soreheaded egotists like Lucifer. Instead they gave mankind another push up the ladder, they came to earth and taught tongues and healing and laws and hygiene — taught everything. . . ."[13]

One of the conspicuous results of this is the university. The energetic and colorful life of learning and research and teaching is given full play in the university setting of the story. But it is anything but a glorification of learning and knowledge in themselves, for evil is rendered most powerfully here. Most people who inhabit an institution of learning, whether as teachers or students, often naively suppose that the enemy is Ignorance, or Stupidity. Davies tells us that it is Evil.

The angels, remember, are *rebel* angels. The learning and knowledge are all good and true, but, divorced from God's presence and will, they breed evil. Angel-imparted knowledge, that is, knowledge that originates in the mind of God, ruined King Solomon and it can ruin us. Knowledge is a dimension of spirituality and has moral qualities. It is not neutral. The most brilliant and learned person in the novel (John Parlabane), who also talks the most about God, is the most evil. The two professors, each in quite a different way, teeter on the edge of evil but regain their balance before the story is finished.

They do it in relation to Sophia, another figure from Gnostic mythology. Maria Magdalena Theotoky, a student of the two professors, becomes a metaphor for Sophia, the feminine personification of Wisdom, a companion figure to God in the creation of the universe. Her name combines the two elements of Sophia: Maria Magdalena, the Mary from whom Jesus cast seven devils (and in legend a whore), and Mary the virgin mother of Jesus ("Theotoky" is the Greek for "the one who gives birth to God"). One of the professors reflects on the Gnostic myth thus: ". . . anybody who concerns himself with the many legends of the Sophia knows about the 'fallen Sophia' who put on mortal flesh and sank at last to being a whore in a brothel in Tyre, from which she was rescued by the Gnostic Simon Magus. I myself

13. Davies, *The Rebel Angels*, p. 257.

think of that as the Passion of Sophia, for did she not assume flesh and suffer a shameful fate for the redemption of mankind? It was this that led the Gnostics to hail her both as Wisdom and also as the *anima mundi*, the World Soul, who demands redemption and, in order to achieve it, arouses desire."[14]

Maria, as a metaphor for Sophia, is in quest of learning at the university each day; she also goes home each night to her Gypsy mother and uncle, who are full of the old lore of spells and incantations and magic. As she integrates her modern university learning, under the tutelage of her two professors (her rebel angels), with the medieval earthiness of religion and sexuality insisted upon by mother and uncle, she shows the way to goodness and wisdom.

As a writer, Davies show that any failure to deal with both of the Mary names, Mary Magdalene and Mary the Virgin Mother, turns into a life of evil. The two "rebel angel" professors, in quite different ways, learn to deal with both and arrive at a kind of restorative humility.

Two others, John Parlabane and Urquhart McVarish, do not. They also are rebel angels, but by refusing to deal seriously with Maria/Sophia, they lose their credibility even as metaphors. They mock and scorn her, and, as they do, they become thoroughly evil. It is not easy for a writer to provide a convincing rendition of an evil person who does not take over and grab the spotlight, exciting our admiration. One of the complaints frequently lodged against Milton is that he made Lucifer and the Fallen Angels more interesting than God and the Good Angels. By skillful use of the rebel angel myth, Davies manages to fashion these two evil men in such a way that we are interested enough to keep reading about them, all the while realizing that their evil is a complete bore. Not all transcendence is glorious. Malign transcendence is not even interesting.

The Beauty of Goodness

It is as difficult to provide an accurate witness to goodness as to evil. Again, transcendence must be conveyed. If there is no transcendence, we end up with mere niceness or piety or some variation on a grim

14. Davies, *The Rebel Angels*, p. 236.

and stoical decency. It is rare to find a "good" character in a novel or poem who is compelling and truly interesting. Most of them appear on the page as insipid do-gooders. Our everyday experience is so deficient in genuine goodness, that our imaginations lack the raw materials for recognizing it.

But occasionally a writer happens along who shows us the blazing and breathtaking beauty of goodness, shows us that it has nothing to do with being nice or keeping rules or avoiding moral mudpuddles. C. S. Lewis is preeminent among them.

In his space trilogy *Out of the Silent Planet, Perelandra,* and *That Hideous Strength,* Lewis re-tells the Christian story of the conflict between good and evil in the form of space fantasy set successively on Mars (Malacandra), Venus (Perelandra), and Earth (Thulcandra). Evil is necessarily given much attention; but what stands out wonderfully is the portrait of goodness, most particularly in *Perelandra,*[15] which is a retelling of the temptation story of Eden in which there is no Fall. On the planet Perelandra (Venus), Lewis shows us a mirror opposite of Thulcandra (Earth). Venus is a planet on which goodness is overwhelmingly present, with evil trying its best to get a foothold, in contrast to Earth where evil is overwhelmingly present with goodness asserting itself against great odds.

Angels are background figures in the realization of this goodness. In Lewis's mythmaking, the angels are called *eldila.* Lewis's description of them rivals anything that the medieval angelologists were able to imagine. "The eldila are very different from any planetary creatures. Their physical organism, if organism it can be called, is quite unlike either the human or the Martian. They do not eat, breed, breathe, or suffer natural death, and to that extent resemble thinking minerals more than they resemble anything that we should recognize as an animal. Though they appear on planets and may even seem to our senses to be sometimes resident in them, the precise spatial location of an eldil at any moment presents great problems. They themselves regard space (or 'Deep Heaven') as their true habitat, and the planets are to them not closed worlds but merely moving points — perhaps even interruptions — in what we know as the Solar System and they as the Field of Arbol."[16]

15. C. S. Lewis, *Perelandra* (New York: Collier Books, 1962).
16. Lewis, *Perelandra*, p. 9.

The function of angels (eldila) is to break down the distinction between natural and supernatural. We characteristically divide the universe into two halves, nature and supernature, and avoid thinking of them both in the same context. We put scientists and engineers in charge of the natural and pastors and poets in charge of the supernatural. We think we can keep things simpler and less confusing that way. But, in fact, we incapacitate ourselves for dealing with reality. We are always working with one hand tied behind our backs. Angels come to our rescue by untying the other hand, whether nature or supernature, for they are witnesses to essential oneness of the two halves. They are not animals to which we can assign predictable behavior and habitat, supported by scientific verification. But at the same time they have some kind of material vehicle or capacity through which they can make their presence known.[17] Nearly the same thing can be said of writers.

An Oxford philologist named Ransom is the primary character in *Perelandra*. On an earlier visit to Malacandra (Mars), he had passed a child who said she was speaking to an eldil, but Ransom could see no one. Later he asked a Malacandrian about it and was told, ". . . *eldila* are hard to see. They are not like us. Light goes through them. You must be looking in the right place and the right time; and that is not likely to come about unless the *eldil* wishes to be seen. Sometimes you can mistake them for a sunbeam or even a moving of the leaves; but when you look again you see that it was an *eldil* and that it is gone."[18]

More often than not, what is conveyed in the angel witness is goodness, and, as every writer knows, goodness is a most difficult subject to render honestly and realistically. Foundational to the experience of goodness is beauty. (The pitiful attempt of evil to compete with it ends up in the banalities of pornography, one of the sub-themes in *The Rebel Angel*.) Goodness is not an abstraction, not an idea, not a spiritual essence distilled out of the coarse materiality of human experience. Goodness is experienced as beauty, an emphatically *sensuous* beauty, a beauty apprehended and relished by the entire human sensorium. Arrival on Perelandra is an immer-

17. Lewis, *Perelandra*, p. 11.

18. C. S. Lewis, *Out of the Silent Planet* (New York: Collier Books, 1962), p. 76.

sion in colors, shapes, odors, textures, and tastes that are sheer delight. As Ransom, the central character in the novel, takes a drink, ". . . it was almost like meeting Pleasure for the first time."[19] As he gradually gets the feel of "goodness" through this immersion in sensual novelty and delight, the narrator comments, ". . . more than all these [sensual delights] was something else at which I have already hinted and which can hardly be put into words — the strange sense of excessive pleasure which seemed somehow to be communicated to him through all his senses at once. I use the word 'excessive' because Ransom himself could only describe it by saying that for his first few days on Perelandra he was haunted, not by a feeling of guilt, but by surprise that he had no such feeling. There was an exuberance or prodigality of sweetness about the mere act of living which our race finds it difficult not to associate with forbidden and extravagant actions."[20]

There must be nearly as many ways in which writers and angels collaborate in giving witness to transcendence as there are angels who can dance simultaneously on the head of a pin. In *The Tongues of Angels* by Reynolds Price,[21] the witness is given by developing the character of a fourteen-year-old boy, accumulating various hints and guesses about angels, and then letting the sustained observation and accumulating guesses overlay one another until we are not sure where the boy ends and the angel begins, or where the angel ends and the boy begins. What we become sure of, though, is that both "boy" and "angel" take place in the same location.

And because the boy is a strikingly unlucky boy, a veritable lightning rod for bad luck, what we get in this writer/angel collaboration is a witness to the transcendence of humanity in the unfinished and untidy setting of adolescence.

Adolescence is the form of our humanity that is least likely to exhibit anything like divine transcendence. Our stereotypical response to adolescence is to treat it as a welter of hormones and confusion and cliché. Price witnesses transcendence. If it can be witnessed in adolescence, it can be witnessed in anyone.

19. Lewis, *Perelandra,* p. 35.
20. Lewis, *Perelandra,* p. 37.
21. Reynolds Price, *The Tongues of Angels* (New York: Atheneum, 1990).

The story is narrated by a fifty-five year old artist as he remembers and sorts through the story of the summer of 1954 when he, as a twenty-year-old college student, was a counselor at a religious camp for boys in the mountains of North Carolina. Transcendence that incorporates elements of the predestination, evil, and goodness witnessed by Irving, Davies, and Lewis, is now observed in the person of an adolescent camper, Raphael ("Rafe"), who was named by his mother for the painter but in the course of the story is seen more and more under the aegis of the archangel.

The artistic imagination and perspective provide the data for the plot and character development. The artist/counselor/narrator says, "All my life . . . I'd been fascinated by the fairly worldwide idea of angels. The English word comes from the Greek, *angelos,* and *angelos* translates the Hebrew word for *messenger.* So an angel, in the sacred sense, is a messenger from and to a divine center. Since for years I'd been sure that my work [as an artist] came from such a supremely powerful and knowing center, I'd taken to keeping a sketchbook devoted to it. In special moments . . . I'd try to set down quickly and with a minimum of forethought a guess at the face of an angelic messenger. Not that I really thought they have faces. I was making my own contribution to a line of glorious-to-silly guesses that stretch from at least the Ark of the Covenant down to those American primitives who even now portray the flaming message and the messenger through whom it reaches their minds and guides their hands."[22]

One of his assignments at the summer camp is to conduct a drawing class for the campers. He himself wants to be an artist vocationally (and does become that) but it is during this summer that his desire solidifies into a conviction: ". . . I made a vow to spend my whole life, if fate agreed, in using the one real block of capital I knew I'd been given. And that, of course, was my old need to watch those parts of the world that caught me, then to copy them out for others less patient or with eyes less lucky."[23]

His passion in teaching his boys to draw was to teach them to observe, to really *see.* "If I taught anything . . . I hope it was this. *Keep your eye on the object,* or it will trick you and keep its own

22. Price, *The Tongues of Angels,* pp. 127-28.
23. Price, *The Tongues of Angels,* p. 244.

secrets. For secrets are what the whole visible world tries constantly to keep, for some mysterious reason."[24]

All the while that he is observing and teaching others to observe the rocks and trees and mountains of the Smoky Mountains, waiting for them to give up their secrets, he is also observing Rafe, watching attentively, waiting for the message. At one point he speaks to him, " 'Would you let me draw your picture?' He was the first human being I'd wanted to add to my messenger file."[25] For even though Rafe has lived through unspeakable and tragic suffering, he cannot be accounted for by what has happened to him. His suffering-battered life resists reduction by explanation. He cannot be condescended to. In the grace and nobility of his life, his camp counselor senses "a direct messenger from central control, for life or death."[26] He realizes, finally, that he cannot put Rafe in his angel sketchbook. Angels are, precisely, *messengers*. Rafe is delivering a message, a message that his counselor spends the next thirty-five years of his life meditating and assimilating, of which this novel with its evocative title, "the tongues of angels," is the accounting.

Not all writers, of course, give witness to transcendence. Some of them work quite diligently to show that there is not and never has been any such thing. But most writers find themselves working in a reality larger than they know, writing out of some mysterious depth beyond themselves. A surprising number of them are explicit in naming the mystery *God*. These four novelists — Irving, Davies, Lewis, Price — are more representative than not in providing contemporary Christian writer/angel witness to transcendence in predestination, evil, goodness, and our ever so badly damaged humanness.

---

24. Price, *The Tongues of Angels*, p. 103.
25. Price, *The Tongues of Angels*, p. 138.
26. Price, *The Tongues of Angels*, p. 229.

The Seminary as a Place of Spiritual Formation

The most frequently voiced disappointment by the men and women who enter seminary has to do with *spirituality*. They commonly enter seminary motivated by a commitment to God and a desire to serve their Lord in some form of ministry, and then find that they are being either distracted or deflected from that intention at every turn.

They find themselves immersed in Chalcedonian controversies, they find themselves staying up late at night memorizing Greek paradigms, they wake up in the morning, rubbing their eyes, puzzled over hairsplitting distinctions between *homoousios* and *homoiousios*.

This is not what they had bargained on. Their professors seem far more interested in their spelling than in their spirituality. They find themselves spending far more time on paradigms than in prayer.

*   *   *

I grew up surrounded by warnings regarding the dangers of seminaries. The sectarian tradition in which I was reared had no use for learning. Thinking about God got you into nothing but trouble. *Only believe*. And praise! The brain was more or less bypassed as the Holy Spirit filled the praising heart with blessings.

Originally published in *Theology, News and Notes*, October 1993.

The Seminary as a Place of Spiritual Formation

Seminaries were regarded as the graveyard of spirituality. Seminaries were where men and women lost their faith. The doomsday warnings that today's youth get regarding drugs and "safe sex" for me were all posted on *seminaries*. The brain, if used to carry out basic everyday functions (like counting out change and reading the comic strips), was considered fairly harmless. But if it presumed to think about God and his ways, to ask hard questions and read big books, it was almost certain to develop a malignancy which would spread rapidly to the soul. Intellectual cancer was the highest known cause of death to the soul. Many of the warnings had stories attached to them. I knew some of the people in those stories and had no reason to doubt the validity of the warnings. The only prudent thing to do was avoid seminaries at all possible costs. Bible schools were acceptable, for one had to learn some thing or other, but *seminaries* with their intellectual intensities and spiritual laissez-faire were too dangerous to risk a vocation.

But despite the warnings and the stories, I went to seminary. Not without considerable trepidation, but I went. And now, forty years later, having not only gone to one seminary but having taught at half a dozen others, I have found no evidence that any of the warnings were wrong — or even exaggerated. Seminary education *is* dangerous — and many have lost their faith in its classrooms and libraries. Many others, though not taken out in a coffin, have been left crippled or stunted in ways either subtle or conspicuous.

All of us, pastors and professors alike, who have attended seminaries, returned to them from time to time, and continue to send men and women under our spiritual care to them, know this. It is no secret. None of us has come through unscathed.

*   *   *

By and large, a seminary is not a congenial place in which to nurture spirituality — a life of prayer, a community of love, a risky faith. A seminary is a place of learning, learning about God to be sure, but still *learning*. Ever since the Enlightenment-split between the heart and the head in the seventeenth century, schools have not been easy allies in a life of worship, prayer, and the love of God. Talking *about* God is almost the antithesis of talking *to* God. Even though the same words are used in the talk, they are not the same thing at all.

But if the seminary is not a congenial place for spiritual formation, neither is any other place I have inhabited. I haven't found it any better in the congregation, home, retreat center, or ocean beach. I haven't yet attempted the monastery (they wouldn't let me bring my wife), but I am good friends with some who have, and they report similar conditions.

Not only that, but I keep running across holy men and women in seminaries in the guise of professors and students and staff. They are no *more* frequent, but certainly no *less,* than in other places I have lived and done my work. If the seminary itself is not holy ground, it does not prevent bushes from breaking into flame from time to time and evoking holy responses. "Midian Theological Seminary" would not be an inaccurate generic name for our schools of theology.

Spirituality, it seems, is not a function of place or curricula. I spent my formative work years in my father's butcher shop, carving pork loins and grinding hamburger. That is where I learned much of the spirituality that I have been working out ever since. It has been supplemented, of course — challenged, corrected, redirected, developed, sidetracked, abandoned, and then taken up again. But that, and my mother's prayers and presence, provided the raw material that the Holy Spirit has been working with ever since. It took me a long time to recognize that rather simple and obvious fact. But once I did, I quit expecting either *persons* or *institutions* to provide for me what was already sitting in my backyard.

And from the moment of that recognition, I was freed from a lot of grumbling and complaining in the wilderness.

It is the same for all of us. Seminary does not provide the *materials* for spiritual formation, but a particular *condition* in which the formation takes place for a relatively brief period of time.

The condition is characterized by *words* — words spoken, words written, words read. Books, containers for words, are everywhere. Classrooms, designed for the audition of words, are the primary architecture. Computers, a technology for the recording and retrieval of words, are ubiquitous. *Seminary is a world of words.*

Recognizing this is essential in dealing with matters of spiritual formation in the seminary. For the main question is not, as it so often is put, What can we do to make the seminary a better place for spiritual formation? but rather, How can we enter into and embrace the unique condition that constitutes the seminary in such a way that we grow up into the maturity of Christ Jesus?

*   *   *

The distinctiveness of the particular *word-world* comprised by the seminary has to do with the "Word made flesh," the *Logos* which Jesus Christ incarnated. *Logos* is God speaking the world into being, Jesus crucified and raised for our salvation, the Holy Spirit shaping a holy life in us. *Logos* is the word spoken personally by a personal God in such a way that persons can respond to and participate in it. The personal response is formed through a life of obedience and prayer.

Because *Logos* is absolutely foundational and pivotal to what the world is and how it functions, the nature and meaning of history, and everything we are and do, it is extremely important to get it right. Seminary is a school designed to teach us to get it right — to read the Hebrew and Greek Scriptures accurately and appropriately (exegesis and hermeneutics), to develop a theological habit of thinking and inquiry (God, not my culture or my ego, as subject), and to acquire a feel for the ways the human community continually misapprehends the *Logos* of God — whether willfully or ignorantly — occasionally hears and understands, and sometimes believes and obeys (church history), and gives due consideration to the complexities of the personal, social, and political situations in which this *Logos* is spoken (ethics). And more!

But always it is the *Logos,* the Word of God, that determines the subject matter. This is what the seminary is charged to do: honor and understand, teach and consider this *Logos.* It is no easy task, and requires an entire faculty of specialists in various areas to carry it out.

*   *   *

And now comes the hard part. For as much as the seminary is formed to honor and preserve and explicate the *Logos,* the words that are used are not the *Logos* itself, but *logoi* about the *Logos,* human words about the divine Word. And because there are so many of them, so many *logoi,* they some times threaten to upstage the *Logos* itself. And not only threaten, they often *do* upstage it. And because these words

57

about the Word are not life-giving — not creating, not saving, not sanctifying — in the same fundamental and original way that the Word is, those of us who both speak and hear them get overwhelmed, burdened by the very words (and those who speak and write them) that we thought were going to be our salvation.

Calls go out that the seminary must become more intentional about spirituality and spiritual formation. Requests are made, sometimes as demands, sometimes as suggestions, that spirituality be integrated into the curricula with a seriousness equivalent to Hebrew exegesis and historical theology. However the requests are made, whether stridently or gently, they never seem to amount to much. A course added here and there, a committee formed to report back in a few months, a student questionnaire distributed. But all these and other attempts at solution or reform fail to take into account the nature of a seminary, the *conditions,* and the ways of spirituality.

The feelings of betrayal and frustration are understandable, but there is no remedy. Or at least no outside, imposed remedy.

Rather, the remedy is inherent in the nature of seminary itself, namely as a place of Word and words, of *Logos* and *logoi.* Any attempt to make things better by denigrating the intellect or de-emphasizing concern with Word and words is unacceptable. But how do we encounter the frequent and dismaying experience of alienation between God's Word and our words?

*   *   *

It is an old problem to which first-rate Christian minds have attended in nearly every century of the church's existence. An approach to dealing with it that I like very much is that of Evagrius Ponticus, sometimes referred to as "Evagrius the Solitary." Evagrius had the best theological education of his day, studying with the best theologians of the fourth century, Basil of Caesarea and Gregory Nazianzus, theologians who were also saints. But the last sixteen years of his life were spent in Egypt nurturing a life of spirituality and prayer with the desert fathers. He died in 399 at about 53 years of age.

It was during the Egyptian "desert" years that he wrote about matters of the intellect and prayer with the clarity and wisdom that make him such a good guide for us still. Evagrius used the word *logismos* for the thought or kind of thinking that gets in the way of, or interferes with, the *Logos*. A *logismos* is a thought that gets separated from the *Logos* and more or less takes on a life of its own, going its own way, doing its own thing. Evagrius uses words like *befogged* and *besotted* to describe what happens to our minds when they get filled and busy with *logismos* instead of prayerfully attending to the *Logos*.

Evagrius described in careful detail — using his well-trained intellect with great precision — the various ways in which the *logismos*, the thought that is inattentive or unresponsive or indifferent to God's Word, no matter what its content (and actual contents could be very good indeed), becomes a diversion from God or even an actual defiance of God. The goal, the highest good of the human creature, is that the *knowledge of* God and *prayer to* God converge. Knowledge of God that does not lead to or become prayer to God is, in Evagrius's analysis, demonic — a spirituality divorced from obedience to God. (See *The Philokalia*, Vol. I; London: Faber and Faber, 1979.)

It is a simple distinction, which, with a little practice, we can learn to make for ourselves. The seminary is as good a place as any to begin making these distinctions. In fact, it is probably the very best place to begin doing it, for there is hardly an hour in a seminary day when there is not an occasion in which to exercise these fundamental discernments.

The French have a wonderful phrase, *déformation professionale,* to refer to maladies that we are particularly liable to in the course of pursuing our line of work. Physicians are in constant danger of becoming calloused to suffering, lawyers in danger of cynicism about justice, and those of us who think and talk and read and write God are in danger of having the very words we use about God separate us from God, the most damning deformation of all.

St. Paul wrote about taking "every thought captive to obey Christ" (2 Cor. 10:5). There is not even a hint of anti-intellectualism in that phrase. He is not banning thought. (Have we ever witnessed a more exuberant exercise of the intellect than in Paul?) But he knows that thought, even when it is about God (maybe even *especially* when it is about God), soon becomes self-serving, prideful, and (using Evagrius's bold designation), demonic — if it is not brought vigorously, regularly, and devoutly before the living God in prayerful obedience.

There is a sense in which the seminary cannot do this for itself. But all of us who count seminaries as an important part of the church's ministry can contribute to the spiritual formation that takes place in them by practicing these discernments and posting these warnings at appropriate times and places. It might not seem like much, but an accurate road sign posted at the right place prevents considerable disaster. And an occasional "Capture the *logismos*" scrawled on a classroom wall wouldn't be a bad idea either.

BIBLICAL STUDIES

The Holy Stump

As an adolescent, one of the visions that filled my head with flash and color and glory was the French Revolution. I actually knew very little about it. Some vague impressions, incidents and names, were mixed haphazardly in my mind to produce a drama of pure romance, excitement, and triumph. I think I would probably have used the word Holy to sum it up: something spiritually blazing and extravagant and glorious.

I had this picture of idealistic, devoted men and women with the ringing affirmations of Liberty, Equality, Fraternity on their lips, marching through a corrupt, sinful world and purging it with their righteous ideas and actions. Names like Marat, Robespierre, and Danton had a ringing and righteous sound in my ears. Evil dungeons in the Bastille were deep shadows against which the fires of liberation burned purely. Heroism and villainy were in apocalyptic conflict. The guillotine was an instrument of the Last Judgment, separating the sheep from the goats. Thus my imagination, untroubled by facts, spun a wonderful fantasy of the glorious French Revolution.

When I arrived at college and looked through the catalogue of courses, I was delighted to find listed a course on the French Revolution. I had to wait a year to take it since first year students

---

"The Holy Stump" was originally published in *Crux* 32, no. 3 (September 1996).

were not admitted, but that only heightened my appetite. And so, returning for my second year, my first move was to enroll in the course.

The class was one of the significant disappointments of my college years. I brought the kind of great expectations to it that adolescents often do to adult enterprises, but nothing of what I expected took place.

The professor was a slight, elderly woman with thin, wispy grey hair. She dressed in dark, shapeless silks, and spoke in a soft, timorous monotone. She was a wonderfully nice person and was academically well-qualified in her field of European history. But as a teacher of the French Revolution, she was a disaster. She knew everything about the French, but nothing about revolution.

I, meanwhile, knew practically nothing about the subject and those few facts I had in my possession were nearly all of them wrong. What I possessed, in fact, was a vast ignorance about the whole business. But I was right about one thing: it was a revolution. Revolutions turn things inside out and upside down. Revolutions are titanic struggles between antagonistic wills. Revolutions excite the desire for a better life of freedom, promise a better life of freedom. Sometimes they make good on their promises and set people free. More often they don't. But after a revolution nothing is quite the same again.

Sitting in her classroom, though, day after day no one would ever know that. Ill-fated Marat, murderous Charlotte Corday, the black Bastille, the bloody guillotine, venal and opportunistic Danton, giddy Marie-Antoinette, ox-like Louis XVI — all the players and props in that colorful and violent age were presented in the same platitudinous, tired, and pious voice. Everybody sounded the same in her lectures. They were all presented as neatly labeled specimens, like butterflies on a mounting board on which a decade or so of dust had settled.

For a long time after that the French Revolution seemed to me a very great bore. Say the words, "French Revolution," and I yawned.

*   *   *

A few years later I had become a pastor and was astonished to find men and women in my congregation yawning. Matt Ericson went to

64

sleep every Sunday; he always made it through the first hymn but ten minutes later he was sound asleep. Red Belton, an angry teenager, sat on the back pew out of sight of his parents and read comic books. Karl Strotheim, a bass in the choir, passed notes supplemented by whispers to Luther Olsen on stock market tips. One woman gave me hope — she brought a stenographic notebook with her every Sunday and wrote down in shorthand everything I said. At least one person was paying attention. Then I learned that she was getting ready to leave her husband and was using the hour of worship to practice her shorthand so she could get a self-supporting job.

These were, most of them, good people, nice people. They were familiar with the Christian faith, knew the Christian stories, showed up on time for worship each Sunday. But they yawned. How could they do that? How could anyone go to sleep ten minutes after singing "Blessing and Honor and Glory and Power . . ."? How could anyone sustain interest in Batman when St. Paul's *Romans* was being read? How could anyone be content to practice shorthand when the resurrected Christ was present in Word and Sacrament? I had, it seemed, a whole congregation of saints and sinners who knew everything about the Christian life except that it was *life*. They knew the word "Christian" pretty well, and identified themselves as Christians. But *life?*

I knew I had my work cut out for me. When I was ordained and called to be their pastor, I had supposed that my task was to teach and preach the truth of the scriptures so that they would know God and how he works their salvation; I had supposed that my task was to help them make moral decisions so that they could live happily ever after with a clear conscience. I had supposed that my task was to pray with and for them, gathering them into the presence of a holy God who made heaven and earth and sent Jesus to die for their sins. Now I was realizing that more than accurate learning was at stake, more than moral behavior was at stake, more than getting them on their knees on a Sunday morning was at stake. *Life* was at stake. People can think correctly and behave rightly and worship politely and still live badly — live anemically, live bored and insipid and trivial lives.

*   *   *

65

That's when I got seriously interested in the word "holy," what Gerard Manley Hopkins described as the "dearest freshness deep down things."[1] I started looking for signs of the holy, evidence of the holy — holy lives, holy places, Holy Spirit.

I soon found that there were no adequate definitions of it; the dictionary didn't yield much, etymologies didn't get me very far, word-studies left me claustrophobic. And as I continued searching the Holy Scriptures and the faces and lives of holy men and women I discovered that there was no standard behavior dictated by the word. There are no instruction manuals written on the holy.

But whereas my lexicons and concordances didn't get me very far, I did find myself often surprised by the holy: the life of God brimming over out of unlikely containers — plain and unassuming stories in Scripture unexpectedly backlit by the "Dayspring," the beauty of God shining out of plain looking faces and catching me off-guard; the goodness of God welling up out of circumstances that I had concluded were parched and barren.

*   *   *

One of the basic stories in our western culture is the quest for the Holy Grail — the chalice from which, at his last meal with his disciples, Jesus drank with them the wine that became by his promise and command, his life in them. It is the Holy Cup from which we drink the Holy Life, the life that Jesus set before us when he said, "I came that they may have life, and have it abundantly" (John 10:10). Abundantly, *perisson*. The adverb, not surprisingly, became one of St. Paul's favorites (in various forms at least 18 occurrences). There are numerous variations on the hunt for the holy — holy grail, holy places, holy men and women, and, perhaps most wonderfully, Holy Scripture. Many of the quest stories are by now thoroughly secularized, but the quest for something other than and more than muscle and money keeps reappearing in unlikely guises. Holy Quest is ingrained in us — biological researchers will probably turn up a quest chromosome in our genetic make-up, someday. We are after something — more life than we get simply by eating three meals a day

1. Gerard Manley Hopkins, "God's Grandeur," *Poems and Prose of Gerard Manley Hopkins,* ed. W. H. Gardner (Baltimore: Penguin Books, 1953), p. 27.

and getting a little exercise. We're after the God-originated and God-shaped life: a holy life.

For Christians, the authoritative source for the holy is Holy Scripture, and at the center of Holy Scripture there is Isaiah at worship in the temple, feeling the rafters shake and hearing the angels sing,

> Holy, Holy, Holy is the Lord of Hosts,
> The whole earth is full of his glory. (Isa. 6:3)

*   *   *

In order to see and hear Isaiah's Holy/Holy/Holy in all its glory, we need an adequate context. Isaiah, chapter 6, is an intense, concentrated representation of the holy — we need a stage large enough to take it all in, a huge stage, as it turns out. I want to construct a stage that has Moses on one side, and St. John on the other, with Isaiah in the middle. Without this large horizon stretched from Moses to John, Isaiah cannot be fully appreciated.

Moses was surprised by the holy in Midian. Midian was an austere country and Moses was an exile there. Midian was not an attractive place and Moses was not doing attractive work. A hard country, hard work, a hard life.

Moses had been reared in luxury in one of the world's highest cultures and most accomplished civilizations. Moses was used to political power, intellectual conversation, and architectural splendor. And now Moses was in Midian — no books, no temples, no servants, no influence.

And then, without preamble, he found himself immersed in the holy: God's holy angel flaming out from a burning bush. Moses addressed by name, "Moses, Moses." Moses answering, "Here am I." Moses called to worship, "Put off your shoes . . . you are standing on holy ground." Moses addressed by God and given a job to do (Exod. 3:1-12).

Holy angel, holy ground, holy God, a holy word that forms a holy people and shapes a holy history. And in Midian of all places.

John was surprised by the holy on the prison island, Patmos, a place as barren and unfriendly as Midian. And John, like Moses in Midian, was there in exile. In that place of rejection and austerity he was given a holy vision. Instead of Moses' burning bush, John was given

67

Jesus ablaze with the holy and speaking words that the Holy Spirit used to make a holy people faithful and enduring in unholy times.

The word "holy" (*hagios*) as either noun or adjective occurs 26 times in St. John's Revelation. Whatever else we get out of this concluding book in our Scriptures, we know for sure that we are in on something huge and robust, burgeoning blessing and salvation and the glory of God: Holy, Holy, Holy.

Now we have an adequate context for Isaiah's vision: Moses in Midian and John on Patmos bracketing Isaiah in church — in the sanctuary. We need all of Scripture, all of history, all of experience to provide a horizon large enough to take in the holy. The holy cannot be cramped into a little box. The holy cannot be perceived through a peep hole.

One summer Jan and I were hiking in the Rocky Mountains of Montana. It was a misty, wet, cold day; not an especially good day for hiking in the mountains. But it had been rainy and wet and cold for weeks and we wanted air, even if it was wet, cold air. We had been slogging along the trail through thick stands of Engleman spruce and Douglas fir for a couple of hours and came out on a slope that had been burned off in a huge forest fire, over fifty years ago when I was ten years old, and in all those years had not grown back. The sudden openness gave us an immense vista — glacier-cut peaks soaring upwards to one side of us, and on the other side a valley floor carpeted by golden grain and rivered in meanders of blue. Then we spotted a tiny but bright splash of bird on a dead snag about 75 feet away. We looked at it through our binoculars, but couldn't identify it. Then, as we looked, it flew — a hummingbird! But one that we had never identified before, a rufous hummingbird. The tiny explosion of bright, coppery orange on that rain-soaked trail was more dramatic than a sunrise. The minuscule bird, framed by mountain and valley, provided a center to the majestic setting. But the delicate, exquisite bird needed a frame that large for us adequately to appreciate its color and flight. Anything less would have crowded the imagination.

Isaiah 6 is a rufous hummingbird in that great exposed wilderness framed by Moses in Midian and John on Patmos.

*　　*　　*

Isaiah is a large presence in the lives of those of us who live by faith, who submit ourselves to being shaped by the Word of God, and keep on the lookout for the holy. We know very little about Isaiah. It is always a marvel, isn't it, that we can be so influenced by someone we hardly know? But once a life is saturated in the Holy, in God Alive, it doesn't take much. What we mostly know about him was that he was a great preacher and that he was attracted to and formed by God's holiness, the Holy. "The Holy One of Israel" is Isaiah's special title for God.[2]

His very name was a sermon: Isaiah, "Yahweh is salvation." Wouldn't you love to have a name like that?

"What's your name?"

"Yahweh is salvation."

Every time you get introduced the gospel would be preached. Every time through your school years that the teacher calls on you in class, the gospel is proclaimed. Every time someone greets you on the street, the word of God is announced. An atheist can't even call up without preaching a mini-sermon. What were our parents thinking of anyway when they named us? Eugene . . . Beverly . . . Walter . . . Elmer . . . Kim . . . Where's the gospel in names like these? Why didn't they name us with sermon texts?

Isaiah continued the text-name tradition in the naming of his own children. He had three sons, each of their names doubling as a sermon text. When he went off to preach a sermon, instead of taking his Bible, he grabbed the hand of one of his boys, these boys whose names were sermon texts: Shear-jashub, Immanuel, and Maher-shalal-hash-baz.

There was enough variety in Isaiah's text-names to suit most of the occasions that called for preaching. When he went off on a preaching assignment instead of lugging an unwieldly Torah scroll, he simply grabbed the hand of one of his sons and brought him along.

One of Isaiah's more important assignments that we know about in some detail was preaching to King Ahaz. Ahaz was a particularly bullheaded, unbelieving king who insisted on dealing with the powerful and highly visible Assyrians rather than God. Isaiah never did get

---

2. J. A. Motyer, *The Prophecy of Isaiah* (Downers Grove, IL: InterVarsity Press, 1993), p. 77.

through to him. (But, interestingly, the sermons to which Ahaz turned a deaf ear have gotten through to millions of others down through the centuries). All three sons made their appearance before Ahaz as sermon texts.

Shear-jashub — Don't be agitated; hope. Everything is going to turn out all right. You aren't in charge here, God is, and he will make sure that there will be always be a faithful few to experience his grace and carry out his commands. Live trustfully.

Immanuel — Don't be intimidated by circumstances; trust. God is right here with us. When everything is falling apart around you, God is not falling apart. God, not your standard of living, is the reality that determines your life. Live courageously.[3]

Maher-shalal-hash-baz — Don't be smug, supposing that you can control the world by your own genius; repent. The world as you have constructed it is going to go smash. Live humbly.

The second name, Immanuel, took on a life of its own (8:8 and 10) and reverberated down through the centuries until it found its final and complete exposition in Jesus (Mt. 1:23). Isaiah's one-word sermon text continues to release insights and give witness to God's holy presence in improbable and, to all appearances, unholy circumstances.

*   *   *

But the Isaiah story doesn't begin with his preaching but with his praying — and with the Holy. The story's context is given in Isaiah 6 with the sentence: "In the year that king Uzziah died."

That simple sentence puts Isaiah's experience of the holy into a setting that is similar to that of Moses and John, which is to say, a bad time, an unlikely time, a time mighty uncongenial to what we think of as the abundant life — Jerusalem under the rule of Uzziah.

---

3. Not everyone agrees that Immanuel was one of Isaiah's sons. Elmer Dyck in a careful exegesis argues that Immanuel and Maher-shalal-hash-baz are the same child, but still leaves us with two sons with "text" names. Calvin, representing many, interprets the name as referring directly and only to Jesus. See Elmer Dyck, ed., *The Act of Bible Reading* (Downers Grove, IL: InterVarsity Press, 1996), pp. 45-64.

Uzziah was king for 52 years in Jerusalem (2 Chron. 26). He was a good king by all accounts — he subdued the Philistines, built up a strong defense system, developed the country, learned the fear of the Lord from his pastor, Zechariah. "And his fame spread far, for he was marvelously helped, till he was strong" (2 Chron. 26:15).

Then he did a terrible thing; he desecrated the holy temple. He arrogantly walked into the temple and took it over for his own purposes. He decided to take charge of his own spirituality, manage his own religion, put God to his own uses. He went to the holy altar of incense, pushed the priest out of the way, and proceeded to run things according to his own tastes and desires. The priests warned him; he lost his temper, told them to get lost and proceeded to offer holy incense on the holy altar of incense in the holy temple. He was king, after all, and he would deal with God the way and when he wanted to deal with him.

But what in his mind was royal prerogative, was in fact inexcusable sacrilege. It would be like you or me entering our home church with a can of black spray paint and spraying graffiti on pulpit and communion table, baptismal font and cross, "Under new management: from now on, I'm in charge here!"

Uzziah, with many honorable years of serving God's people behind him, but now proud and angry and willful, takes over the holy temple for his own purposes. Royal vandalism. Violent desecration.

Immediately, the desecration backfired and Uzziah turned leprous. His face broke out in leprosy. The dread disease that in the Hebrew mind had come to symbolize sin gave public visibility to the inward profanity.

Uzziah spent the rest of his life in isolation, banned by his leprous condition not only from the holy temple but from all contact with the community of holy people. He was still king, but no longer in touch with either temple or people. Judah's king a leper. The government of Judah focused in a man who defiled God's holy temple. The entire society and culture of Judah living under the shadow of unholiness, of desecration; the social, political, cultural, and religious atmosphere defiled by the king's leprosy. Judah under Uzziah was as barren as Midian, as austere as Patmos, for it was ruled by a leper king.

But despite Uzziah, Isaiah was in the temple praying, the same temple in which Uzziah had become a leper king. Isaiah was there

71

worshiping because he knew that the temple was not defined by Uzziah; the times were not defined by Uzziah; the culture didn't take its impress from Uzziah. Not for Isaiah, anyway, for in the year that king Uzziah died, Isaiah was at prayer in the temple.

The times in which we live are not definitive for our lives. Technology does not define our existence. Postmodern does not determine how we live. Psychologism does not account for who we are. Secularism is a slovenly, makeshift attempt to make sense of us and the world around us.

In unholy times, in an unholy place, Isaiah was plunged into the holy. He was given a holy vision, the Lord ruling in holiness, the songs of holy angels filling the air with holy sounds, Holy, Holy, Holy is the Lord of Hosts, The whole earth is full of his glory!

Not only was the desecrated temple bursting its seams with holiness, the desecrated earth was full of glory. *This* is the reality in which we live: Holy, Holy, Holy; Glory, Glory, Glory. No matter what Uzziah does to the church; no matter what the Assyrians do to the world, there is holiness in the church and glory in the land. Holiness in the Midian wilderness, holiness in the Patmos jailhouse, holiness in the leprously defiled Temple. And, don't ever forget it, holiness in all the defiled churches in Canada, holiness in every morally and physically polluted city and province in Canada. Holiness because God is still present in salvation and creation. We have to break the ignorant and faithless habit of letting the journalists of the day tell us what is going on. At least give Isaiah equal time: Holy, Holy, Holy.

* * *

At this point, though, I need to post a warning: go any further and you risk losing your life. Holy ground is dangerous ground.

A month or so ago a grizzly attacked a hiker not far from where we spend our summers in Montana and mauled him badly. He had heard of the wonder and beauty of the mountains of Montana and drove across the country from North Carolina to experience them for himself. Interviewed from his hospital bed, he said, "I'm never coming back to this place!" He didn't know that wonder and beauty can also be dangerous.

A week after that grizzly mauling, Jan and I with our son and daughter-in-law, plus another friend with her two-year-old son went hiking on that same trail. At the trailhead a notice was posted: "Danger: Grizzly activity on this trail. Hike at your own risk." None of the others knew of the previous week's mauling and I didn't say anything. But I must admit that the notice gave me an extra spurt of adrenaline: the danger to life heightened the sense of life. The beauty and the wonder in which we were immersed, the love and affection that we shared, were not our secure possessions. A couple of hours later we reached the glacier-fed lake that was our destination. We stood at the lakeshore admiring the five waterfalls cascading off the mountain face, listened to and watched a couple of varied thrushes sing and eat bugs. Holy ground. And then I noticed a movement a hundred or so yards up the lakeshore. I took aim with my binoculars: a grizzly and her cub, playfully splashing in the water. I passed the binoculars around; we all had a good look. And then Amy, our daughter-in-law, who is five months pregnant and therefore especially aware of the fragility and preciousness of life, said, "I want to get out of here." And we got out. Holy ground, but dangerous ground.

Holiness is the most attractive quality, the most intense experience we ever get of sheer *life* — authentic, firsthand living, not life looked at and enjoyed from a distance. We find ourselves in on the operations of God himself, not talking about them or reading about them. But at the very moment we find ourselves in on more than ourselves, we realize we also might very well lose ourselves. We cannot domesticate the holy. Moses didn't take a photograph of the burning bush to take home and show his wife and children. Isaiah's singing angels were not accompanied by a Handel oratorio, which he then purchased on a CD for later listening at his leisure. John didn't reduce his vision of Jesus into charts which he used to entertain religious consumers with titillating views on the future

Holiness is a furnace that transforms the men and women who get too close to it. Holy, Holy, Holy is not Christian needlepoint — it is the banner of a revolution, *the* revolution.

*   *   *

Here is how it took place in Isaiah; take careful note for it is also how it takes place in us.

First, there is an overwhelming sense of inadequacy, of sin, of unworthiness: "Woe is me, I am lost. My very speech is defiled and dirty. I don't belong here. I don't fit here. Nothing I know or can do is appropriate here. Get me out of here" (6:5) It is very easy to suppose that we are doing just fine with our lives, thank you, if we can only manage to insulate ourselves against the Holy, and live in comparison with our surroundings. But judging ourselves by the standards set by our dogs and cats and neighbors, is a sorry business. It takes the Holy to make me aware of my unholiness. This excess of life makes me aware of my deficit of life. We have been lost ever since we left Eden, wandering the world, looking for home, and getting mighty dirty in the process.

Second, there is mercy and forgiveness. There is purification. Our lips are touched with purifying fire (6:6). It is our basic, fundamental, most pressing need. Apart from the Holy we think we can improve our lives simply by progressing — getting a little more of this and then of that. But like a badly aimed arrow, the farther we go the greater the miss. This misdirection is not an occasional lapse; we give evidence against ourselves every time we speak. Sin and impurity that are expressed as soon as and whenever we open our mouths, even in our most decorous and polite talk. But God's very first interest in us is fixing that: the angel, flaming witness to God's holiness, burns the impurities, the sin, out of our speech. God's primary interest in us is not condemnation but forgiveness. "Indeed, God did not send the Son into the world to condemn the world, but in order that the world might be saved through him" (John 3:17) Acceptance not rejection. Holiness no longer outside us, but inside us. If we don't stay around the holy long enough to first realize and then experience that live coal on our lips, we will spend our lives in a tragic ignorance of God and his ways.

Third, God's word is spoken, "Whom shall I send?" (6:8). God speaks vocationally; there is work to be done. Holiness always involves this word of God: God spoke to Moses at the burning bush; God spoke to John in the Patmos vision; God spoke to Isaiah in the Jerusalem temple. The effusion, the overflow of life that is holiness is not something to be hoarded, but delivered, spread around, spoken and acted. Holiness can never be reduced to an emotional, devotional experience that we cultivate in order to "feel spiritual." It has command-content to it. Holiness is not an experience of sublimity that abstracts us from the world of work; it is an invitation to enter into what God is doing and intending to get done in the world. And for everyone, for this is not a text targeted to an elite ministerial aristocracy.

Fourth, God's word is answered, "Here am I, send me" (6:8). We accept God's invitation, prepare to obey whatever he commands. We pull on our gloves and get ready to go to work. But it is not imposed work; God's call is spoken as a question, inviting response, and we have the freedom to say yes or no. However impelling this word is to some of us, it is never a matter of coercion. We are invited in.

Isaiah's encounter with and participation in the holiness that originates in God and spills over into our lives, provides a convenient and reliable story against which we can test the authenticity of our own stories. The four elements, but in various orders and proportions, are normative: first, the abolition of self-sufficiency ("Woe is me, I am lost"), then the experience of merciful forgiveness (the live coal: "your guilt has departed and your sin is blotted out"), third, God's invitation to servant work ("Whom shall I send . . ."), and finally, the human response of becoming present to God in faith and obedience ("Here am I; send me!"). I can think of no exceptions in Scripture or church in which these elements are not either explicit or implicit.

But — make careful note of this for this is often ignored — the four elements cannot be removed from the context and expected to amount to much. You cannot hand over these four elements to one of the fashionable spiritual technicians of the day and expect him or her to manage them for you. The context is the living God: Holy, Holy, Holy in the temple, and Glory, Glory, Glory in all the earth. Nothing in God or our relations with God can be secularized to our expectations, or customized to our conditions, or managed for our convenience. We acquire readiness and perceptiveness for this by worshiping God and practicing the posture and rudiments of worship wherever we find ourselves, in church or world, in Midian or Patmos or Jerusalem, sitting in a pew or driving a car, reading a book or watching a cloud, writing a letter or picking a wildflower. Wherever we are, whatever we are doing there is *more,* and the more is God, revealing himself in Jesus by the Spirit, the *Holy* Spirit. Holiness is transformative, although rarely sudden. And the *more* is not often obvious, but more than likely obscure. The Holy Revolution begins in the times and places and lives that ambition and pride ignores or despises.

But here's the thing: the least hint of holiness has the power to set off this chain reaction of holy living in any one of us. Even though dangerous, for we most certainly will lose our lives as we have conceived them (". . . our God is a consuming fire," Heb. 12:29) the Holy pulls, but often only at the far edges of our awareness, at every fiber of our God-created being. God, the living God, is what we men and women hunger and thirst for most deeply, and the Holy, seeping (or bursting!) through the containers in which we habitually confine and then label life, whets our appetite.

*   *   *

This context and these four elements are normative; what we all need to be alert to and welcoming of. But there is one more thing in Isaiah's experience that is not necessarily normative, but that happens so frequently that it must be mentioned.

As Isaiah is pulled into the holy life and finds himself involved in holy work, he is at the same time told that nothing much is going to come of it. He is to be a preacher but a conspicuously unsuccessful preacher. He is going to preach with incredible power and eloquence and people are going to go to sleep in the middle of his sermons. It will turn out that he will have access to King Ahaz, be an insider to the operations of statecraft, and will have his wise and godly counsel ignored. The end result of a lifetime of God-ordained and God-blessed preaching is that the country will be destroyed — "utterly desolate" (6:11). The Assyrians are going to march in and ravage the place. It is going to look like a forest that has been clear-cut by rapacious loggers — ugly, defaced, barren — all the trees cut down and hauled away with nothing left but stumps, an entire country of stumps. "This is what is going to happen, Isaiah, after a lifetime in my service. This is the end result of your immersion in holiness, your honest confession and cleansed speech, your vocation in holy orders. Stumps. A nation of stumps."

The germ of the story is told in Isaiah, chapters 7–9, and needs to be studied far more than it is by Christians who are intoxicated by success stories and dazzled by evangelical, so-called, patter and sleight-of-hand. George Adam Smith, that incomparable preacher and scholar on the Isaiah text, insists on the reality as Isaiah writes it. Commenting on the appearance of the second of Isaiah's text-named sons, Immanuel, he writes: "The Child, who is Israel's hope, is born; he receives the Divine name, and that is all of salvation or glory suggested. He grows up not to a throne or the majesty which the seventy-second Psalm pictures — the offerings of Sheba's and Seba's kings, the corn of his land shaking like the fruit of Lebanon, while they of the city flourish like the grass of the earth — but to the food of privation, to the sight of his country razed by his enemies into one vast common fit only for pasture, to loneliness and suffering. Amid the general desolation his figure vanishes from our sight, and only his name remains to haunt, with its infinite melancholy of what might have been, the thorn-choked vineyards and grass-grown courts of Judah."[4]

And then we come upon this pungent final sentence, "The holy seed is its stump" (6:13).

Oh, really? The word holy again, but now applied to a totally inappropriate noun. Not the holy angel anthems, filling the temple with glorious song, transforming Isaiah's world and Isaiah in the world. Not the holiness that blazes out of a desert bush or explodes over a prisoner in rocky exile. Not the holiness that is evident in Jesus as his words and acts reveal the comprehensive and energetic and gracious life of the Trinity to us.

None of that now, but in place of it all a squat stump. A stump in a field of stumps. But there is more to the stump than anyone supposes: "the holy seed is its stump." The stump, unlikely as it seems and against all appearances, is the holy seed from which salvation will grow. Five chapters later in Isaiah we come on this stump again, but now with some elaboration:

> "A shoot shall come out from the stump of Jesse,
>   and a branch shall grow out of his roots.
> The spirit of the LORD shall rest on him
>   the spirit of wisdom and understanding,
>   the spirit of counsel and might,
>   the spirit of knowledge and the fear of the LORD."
>
> (11:1-2)

4. George Adam Smith, *The Book of Isaiah* (London: Hodder and Stoughton, 1889), vol. 1, p. 117.

All of us know how that eventually turned out: in a word, Jesus. And so we joyfully and gratefully sing the praises of our holy Lord. We can never sing those praises loudly or joyfully enough, but while doing it we must not lose touch with that stump. For very often that stump and nothing but that stump will characterize and dominate our lives. Not for all of us, to be sure, but for many. It did for Isaiah. Never, never forget that holy stump.

The world, the flesh, and the devil are all working full time to fill our minds and emotions with pictures and longings for more life, for abundant life that have nothing to do with God and therefore are ignorant of the Holy. They not only control the public media and mass advertising as they propagate and glamorize their lies, they have also infiltrated large parts of the church, interpreting the Christian life for us in such ways that we are trained to avoid or be contemptuous of anything that doesn't promise us gratification. I want to counter these glamorous lies with Isaiah and his Holy Stump. Does it sound to you like an oxymoron? Holy . . . Stump. But everything in Scripture and the gospel tells us that this is the truth, the reality of Jesus and our lives with and in Jesus. Holy. Life that issues out of death. Beauty that begins in ugliness. A holy revolution.

Ten or so miles north of the small Montana town in which I grew up, there was a smaller town that in earlier days was called Stump Town. The setting was beautiful, nestled as it was under the rock-muscled shoulders of the great Rocky Mountains. But it had the bad luck to get selected as a major railroad switchyard by Jim Hill, who was building the Great Northern Railroad across the continent. Jim Hill was as rapacious and brutal as any of Isaiah's Assyrians — he ravaged the country, bribed the government, exploited the weak and bullied the strong in pushing through his railroad. Railroad beds require huge quantities of railroad ties, and so every tree in this little town was cut for making ties and the stumps left exposed, for this village was not good for anything, after all, but to serve the grand railroad-building empire. When I was growing up it was still an ugly place, a shanty-town of hoboes and railroad bums and stumps. I and my friends all referred to it with condescension, and sometimes contempt: Stump Town.

Twenty years ago my brother became a pastor there; and then four years ago my son moved there. Between my brother and my son, I began to hear stories told and see scenarios unfold that were full of life and beauty and God, stories of the Holy Revolution. Stump Town no longer sounds to me like a term of derogation; today it sounds more like a promise of salvation and, yes, revolution, for the "holy seed is its stump."

Holy Living — which involves being agents of the Holy Revolution — requires us to be obedient in the place we find ourselves, faithful in work and worship. The circumstances are more often than not wilderness circumstances. But what we can be quite sure of is that the Holy, God's unmanageable but irrepressible life, is ever present and hidden within and around us. Unpredictably but most surely it breaks forth into our awareness from time to time: the bush blazes, the heavens open, the temple rocks, the stump blossoms. Holy, Holy, Holy. But don't expect to see it reported on the evening news.

Amen.

Jeremiah as an
Ascetical Theologian

Ascetical theology informs Jeremiah 17:5-10. Ascetical theology is not as prominent among us today as the theologies designated biblical, systematic, and historical. There were centuries, though, when it distinguished itself among its cousins. It still has essential service to perform. Ascetical theology: How does the human condition shape our understanding of and response to God? Jeremiah knew, as all experienced pastors know, that it is not enough to clearly and accurately proclaim the kerygma to an assembled congregation. There is more to this business of preaching and teaching than getting the revelation of scripture and Christ out on the table so that it is accessible to one and all. We do our exegesis well, we get our people into the pews, we present our exposition with urgency. And what happens? Frequently, nothing. Or not much.

What's going on? Isn't the "Word of God living and active, sharper than any two-edged sword, piercing to the division of soul and spirit, of joints and marrow, and discerning the thoughts and intentions of the heart" (Heb. 4:12)? Have we not been promised that this Word that we preach "shall not return to me empty" (Isa. 55:11)? Was not Jesus quite clear that at least some of this Word-of-God-seed that we broadcast faithfully from our pulpits Sunday after Sunday

---

Originally published in *Lectionary Homiletics* 3, no. 3 (1992).

will come to harvest, "some a hundredfold, some sixty, some thirty" (Matt. 13:8)?

Soon or late, we realize that it is not enough to get the nouns and verbs right, to explain the articles of the Creed adequately, to present God revealed in Jesus truly and well. We also have to deal with ears and eyes, hearts and minds, kidneys and feet — all these organs of human receptivity and response, most of which seem to be malfunctioning in some way or other most of the time. We find ourselves in the thick of what our ancestors were apt to designate *ascetical* theology, the wisdom/knowledge in preparing, cultivating, correcting our human condition for an adequate response to the revelation of God.

Jeremiah was a good ascetical theologian. He gave as much attention to the details of human reception as to the good news of divine revelation. In chapter 17 verses 5-10 he deals with the ways of life that determine — well, maybe not determine, but strongly affect — what we see and hear of the divine revelation. The presumption here is that the kinds of lives we lead, who we *are,* not just what we *do,* are huge factors influencing our access to truth, any truth but especially the Truth that is God. If we interpret passages like this in terms of moralism, checking off items on a behavioral scorecard, we will miss the point. This is not moralism but *theology,* ascetical theology.

This is the great truth that Thomas Aquinas named *adaequatio* (adequateness): "Knowledge comes about insofar as the object known is within the knower." Plotinus's way of putting it was, "Knowing demands the organ fitted to the object." The understanding of the knower must be *adequate* to the thing to be known. The "thing to be known" above all is God. Our lives — these human intricacies of flesh and bone, mind and emotion, digestion and dream and dance — are our "organ" for knowing God. No wonder that there is such lavish attention given throughout Scripture to the properties and conditions of our humanity — our bodily parts, our emotional states, our physical circumstances, our mental processes, our geographical settings. Every human detail is part of this instrumentality of response to God.

This aspect of theology was given a great deal more attention by our pastor predecessors than by us. We have been trained to suppose that if we only communicate clearly our job is done. And when it comes to the human side of things, the "pastoral care," we tend to think that our task is to comfort and heal, and when that is taken care of the way is clear for experiencing the gospel. But there is far more to it than that.

Jeremiah uses organic images for ways of life that either prevent or invite access to God, and in this he is in the biblical mainstream. For ascetical theology is not a matter of imposed techniques, or managed "disciplines." It takes seriously and in detail life as it is, its glorious creation and its baffling fall, life itself — "like a shrub in the desert" or "like a tree planted by water." A shrub in the desert and a tree by the river are both alive, but not quite in the same way: The desert shrub meagerly survives, the watered tree abundantly reproduces. The shrub in the desert is a cursed way of life, for it is only responsive to what is human ("trusts in man"), in itself a very minuscule portion of reality. The tree by the river is a blessed way of life, for it is responsive to what is divine ("whose trust is the Lord"), and therefore open to the extravaganza of creation and redemption. Ascetical theology gives its attention to *conditions,* conditions which are congenial to developing God-awareness as over against growing God-calluses, looking out for rivers and steering away from deserts. The way we are — the way we spend our money, eat our meals, read a book, treat a stranger — affects our capacity to see the beauty of holiness, hear the word of absolution, feel the touch of love, enter into a life of prayer. Jeremiah's image of the tree by the river was refashioned a few years later in Psalm 1 to serve as preparation for developing intimacy with God, a kind of pre-prayer to praying the prayers which are the Psalms. Jesus continued the recycling in the Beatitudes. The Lukan redaction (6:17-26) shows clear links with Jeremiah.

Jeremiah also shows himself a practiced ascetical theologian in his suspicion of all religious good intentions: "The heart is deceitful above all things, and desperately corrupt, who can understand it?" Sigmund Freud did not originate the "hermeneutic of suspicion." Preaching the gospel in such ways that will win the assent of our listeners requires constant testing lest it merely curry favor among idol-shoppers. Neither of us, preacher or congregation, is to be trusted in matters having to do with the soul and God. Since the day we left Eden, we have had this hankering after idols; given free reign, we are far more likely to run after some Baal or Asherah than bow in humble adoration before the Holy One. In all matters of spirit, then, there needs to be an unrelenting scrutiny of means and motive. "Discernment" is the usual word for this in ascetical theology, and needs diligent exercise by preachers who care for souls.

Learning to Worship from
St. John's Revelation

Certain times pull particular books of the Bible into prominence. Augustine, looking for ways in which the City of God took shape in the rubble of a wrecked and decadent Roman Empire, used Genesis for his text.

In the exuberant eroticism of the twelfth century, Bernard fastened on to the Song of Songs as a means of praying and living into mature love. Luther, searching for a simple clarity of gospel in the garage-sale clutter of baroque religion, hit on Romans and made it the book of the Reformation.

As the twentieth century is well on its way into its final decade, the last book of the Bible, Revelation, has my vote as the definitive biblical book for our times. Revelation has had moments in the sun before, but the present age needs it as none other has. Whether it will dominate, and in a healthy way, remains to be seen, but that it is capable of providing a comprehensive text for the church's life as we live through this stretch of history is a deeply held conviction in me.

The conviction has been forged in the crucible of my life as a pastor. As a pastor I am responsible for preaching and teaching the gospel of Jesus Christ. In that preaching and teaching I have a text

---

Originally published in *Christianity Today,* October 28, 1991.

— the Christian scriptures of Old and New Testaments — and I have been vowed to faithfulness to that text. I am not permitted to make up whatever I think might promote the general good will. The church has given me an assignment: to accurately and patiently and stubbornly work from this text and no other.

The Gossip of Jane

When I first started out in this work, it seemed to be a simple enough task to learn Hebrew and Greek, study what scholars and theologians could teach me about why, how, and where these Scriptures were written, discover how pastors before me had done this, and then go at it, preaching with urgency and clarity the Christ who is "the same yesterday and today and forever."

But it turned out to be not quite that simple. The difficulty was not in deciphering the Hebrew poetry of Isaiah, or the Greek syntax of Paul (although these old masters sent me to my library and knees often enough). The difficulty came from patiently trying to penetrate the gossip of Jane, working around the television-drugged imagination of Bill. I found, in other words, that the people to whom I was preaching and teaching this gospel had things on their minds other than what I was so eager to tell them. They seemed to be generally intelligent people, and they were certainly polite, but they simply weren't getting it.

This was puzzling. I was speaking to a congregation of people who were better educated than most of the Christians who have ever lived. But they weren't understanding a word I was saying. I don't mean that they didn't understand the dictionary meaning of my words, but they were not understanding that it was, precisely, "gospel" — the proclamation of a new order, an inaugurated kingdom, in which every ordinary word and act was redolent with *glory*. They listened and commented and before I knew it had reduced it all to kaffee-klatsch gossip.

I was rubbing shoulders with men and women who had a higher standard of living than most of the Christians who have ever lived — nice homes and furnishings, excellent hospitals and shopping malls — but every inconvenience, every news report of war or volcano, every sickness and death became an occasion to call the competence of God into question. I don't mean that they disbelieved in God when trouble came their way, but that at the very moment it appeared, God became secondary to their trouble. They wanted to know what they had done wrong that God had allowed or visited this trouble on the Earth. They wanted to know what God was doing wrong to permit this interruption of their well-being.

My first reaction was to blame them. Blame them for being gossips and complainers who were disqualifying themselves from realizing this exuberant glory, from entering into this dazzling sovereignty. But then the conviction began to form that they needed help far more than blame. They were gossips and complainers because they grew up and lived in a gossipy and complaining culture. They took it in with their mother's milk, so before they could chew the strong meat of Isaiah and Paul, I had to wean them from the culture.

That is when I found an ally in John's Revelation, for Revelation is a re-presentation of the good news of Jesus Christ to congregations afflicted with these precise cultural conditions. They were experiencing a trivialization of the gospel by gossip, and a deflection of the gospel by trouble. But John silenced the gossips and put the trouble in its place. He did it in the simplest and most economical of ways. He called the people to worship.

When the Glorious Becomes Trivial

The trivialization in John's world was taking place through the gossip of those whose aberrant teachings would soon be known as gnosticism. The essential nature of gossip is that it talks about people instead of to them. Gossip leaves out all that is unique and glorious in a person and reduces him or her to an anecdote or a cliché or a stereotype. The gossip is never in awe. The gossip is never in love.

The Gnostics gossiped about God. They claimed to know a lot about God (Gnostic means "one who knows"), but it was all *about* God. Gnostics did not pray. They did not worship. Gnostics talked a lot to each other and wrote endlessly about what they thought. God was reduced to an anecdote, or fantasized into a speculation.

The last decade of the first century, when John was trying to preach and teach the gospel to his congregations, was overrun by these precursors to the Gnostics of the next century. We see in other places of the New Testament direct and indirect evidence of their presence, and the danger they boded for the gospel. As a pastor, John knew he had to help his people disentangle themselves from such gossip or the gospel would be trivialized beyond recognition. The references in Revelation to Balaam, Jezebel, and the Nicolaitans are references to leaders or sects with Gnostic tendencies. In the guise of leading people into deeper understandings of God, they were, in fact, accommodating him to the terms of the culture, and thereby reducing him to their ideas and fads.

The parallel with our culture is striking: So many aspects of the church's life are being reduced to items of gossip and consumer pricing. Christians have succeeded in marketing crosses to the varying tastes of consumers. We have replaced saints with celebrities. And it is increasingly difficult to take any of it seriously.

Tribulation Rears Its Head

As bad as such trivialization was for the years when John was a pastor, tribulation — occasioned by Roman persecution — also caused deflection from the gospel. It was not lawful to be a Christian. There were imprisonments and martyrdoms. There was economic discrimination, social ostracism. The crucifixion of Jesus was repeated in his followers.

It is one thing to believe in and follow Jesus when everything is going well, and blessings tumble out of the skies. But when troubles pile up and everything that society values contradicts and even condemns your way of life, it is difficult not to give in to the daily parade of evidence that trouble is the dominant reality. Roman cruelty was far more in evidence than gospel grace. Emperor worship, a feast to the senses that also guaranteed a certain worldly security, was far more impressive than the Christian belief in an invisible God and crucified Savior that put its followers in danger of their lives.

But while, at least in the West, it is no longer a criminal offense to be a Christian, the conditions of tribulation have, if anything, increased. Polish poet Czeslaw Milosz in a recent speech used the word *cruel* to describe our century. Cruel indeed. We have had two world wars that irreversibly changed the politics of the planet, and we live under the threat of a third, which, if nuclear, could finish things off. The advent and then collapse of communism have thrown nation after nation into chaos in which anarchy wrestles freedom for supremacy. Third World countries are barging into the arena, grabbing for their piece of the pie. Disasters (political, moral, ecological) pile up faster than we can write up the reports on them. Commitment to a just, peace-bringing, salvation-making God is at risk. Every news report deflects another Christian or two from their aim at the Cross. Proclamations that "the kingdom of God is at hand" are drowned out by a daily roar of information on world conditions that challenge the claims of God's sovereignty.

If we care at all about the integrity of the gospel, what do we do? Wring our hands? Hand wringing is not a strategy. John wasted no time on lament. What he did was worship, and call his people to worship. Just worship. He offered no plan for renewal of the church. He did not call for a convocation of his seven churches to discuss what could be done. He worshiped God and called his people to worship God.

Why Worship?

The parallel conditions in John's decade and ours, the trivialization and tribulation, and his astonishingly focused and simple response, calling the people to worship, commends Revelation as a text for recovering the integrity of the gospel in a bad time.

Essentially, that is what Revelation is — an act of worship that calls others into the act of worship. On the first page we see John at worship, "I was in the Spirit on the Lord's Day" (1:10). On the last page, we see John, momentarily distracted by the angel, commanded back to the center: "Worship God," he is told (22:9). Between that first and last page we have scene after scene of robust worship — the sights and sounds pulling together everything in heaven and earth, in creation and Cross, in history and salvation — all involving us in worship.

But we are so easily distracted: distracted as easily by trivialization as by tribulation. John's vision, if only we submit ourselves to it, is powerful enough to catch our attention and pull us back again to the main action, to the "God center." It is imaginative enough to enlist our bodies, minds, and emotions in participation, to worship.

It is telling that our Bible concludes with Revelation, which is to say, with a call to worship. By the time we have come to this final entry in the library of 66 books, our minds are bursting with knowledge and our hearts burning with desire. With all that knowledge and all that desire there is a great danger that we will just run off and put it to good use — tell everybody what we know, enlist everyone in our cause: communicate, motivate.

And that is just what we, the churches and church leaders of America, have done: run off to communicate and motivate. Between them, communication and motivation dominate the current Christian agenda. The communication conveys much accurate information and the motivation enlists many in good causes. So why aren't things any better? Why isn't the Truth well known? Why isn't Righteousness flourishing? Why is the American church such an embarrassment? Why are its pastors so demoralized? Maybe it is because we didn't stay around for the reading of this last book, didn't let ourselves be called to worship. We failed to become immersed in the act of worship so thoroughly that it would be unthinkable to run off and do anything on our own, no matter how biblical, no matter how urgent.

The truth of the gospel is that God in Christ rules and saves. The reality of the human condition is that we are determined to rule and save and that we make a thorough mess of it every time we do. We want to rule ourselves and save ourselves. We want to rule others and save others.

Even at our best, we can't do it — no matter how much we know, no matter how well intentioned we are. Even when we have mastered Genesis through Jude, we can't do it. We can't because only God in Christ can rule and save. We have, it is quite true, a part in the ruling and saving, but it is strictly an obeying and believing part. And the only way in which we can stay alert to the reality of God in Christ ruling and saving is in the act of worship. The only way we can be trusted to say anything about God that is close to true, to do anything for God that is halfway right, is by the repeated and faithful practice of singing and praying, listening and believing with the elders and animals around the throne, where the scroll is unsealed and the gospel read out clear and strong.

If we absent ourselves from worship or treat it as marginal to our agenda of communication and motivation, we become dominated by the visible. But most of the reality with which we deal is invisible. Most of what makes up human existence is inaccessible to our five senses:

emotions, thoughts, dreams, love, hope, character, purpose, belief. Even what makes up most of basic physical existence is out of the range of our unassisted senses: molecules and atoms, neutrons and protons, the air we breathe, the ancestors we derive from, the angels who protect us. We live immersed in these immense invisibles. And more than anything else, we are dealing with God "whom no one has seen at any time."

Worship is the primary and most accessible means we are given for orienting ourselves in the invisibilities, in God. And Revelation is, along with the Psalms, the most comprehensive rendering of worship that we have. It is, precisely, a vision — a seeing of the invisible. A Christian community that is not rooted in and shaped by the invisible — the throne and the Lamb — very soon falls under the control of communicators and motivators.

I do not mean to exclude other readings of Revelation by my insistence that it reveals and calls us into faithful acts of corporate worship. There is much else in John's vast, theological poem. There is prophecy and comfort, beauty and assurance, warning and blessing, puzzle and mystery. But I do insist that every word in the book takes place in an act of worship, and is designed to pull us into the act of worship. Nothing is worse than religion that goes off on its own, wanders from the living God, detours the crucified Savior — which is to say, neglects worship. But that is what is epidemic among us today — religion as communication, religion as motivation.

Too many worship services in churches today are mere fronts for the pastor's ego or the congregation's needs, or both. That is what John saw going on in his churches. He responded by energetically and magnificently setting them in the place of worship, before the living God, under the command of the risen Christ, renewed by the Holy Spirit. Everything they were concerned with, along with everyone they knew or could imagine, were shown by the preached vision to be comprehended in the action of worship. They still are.

John's Revelation can help us here. For once we are immersed in this exuberance of sound and color, we will certainly lose our taste for gossip, and once we comprehend the comprehensiveness of grace and the empty pretensions of evil, we are not likely to cave in to the bullying of the "principalities and powers." Once we have taken our place in a pew with John leading us into an act of worship, we will never again say "just worship" or willingly absent ourselves from the action.

Apocalypse:
The Medium Is the Message

Christian preachers, pastors, and teachers — those in the church who proclaim, converse, lecture, and listen — are in a better position today to discover and interpret the documents of the gospel message with accuracy and authenticity than their predecessors of several centuries.

The reason is that ears are back. Hearing is once again the primary means of communication. For long centuries, learning was dominated by the printed word; and the characteristic experience with the word was of something seen, not heard. But electronic media dominate the communications scene today. These electronic media are primarily oral/aural, which is essentially what communications were in the years in which the biblical material was in formation. That means that contemporary humanity is closer in terms of communications experience to the first century than to the nineteenth. And that is good news for the Christian communicator who is now able to share a milieu with biblical humanity which is important in discovering and interpreting the biblical message.

The source for much of this communications insight, Marshall McLuhan, has been provocative in interpreting the media of communication, both literary and electronic. Christian teachers and

---

Originally published in *Theology Today,* July 1969.

preachers, whose source documents mostly originated in oral form, will find his work proliferating with suggestive material. Anyone, in fact, who is engaged in biblical hermeneutics, whether as exegete or expositor, will find him to be a stimulating aid.

McLuhan has not himself applied his concepts to any biblical material. His most celebrated work, *Understanding Media,* deals with the mass media of the electronic age. Earlier he worked with more classical literary material in *The Gutenberg Galaxy.* His first book, *The Mechanical Bride,* was a cultural/literary analysis of the "folklore of the industrial age," with case-study material from advertising.

The Apocalypse of St. John is one of the more obvious instances where the stimulus and insight of McLuhan can provide hermeneutical help.

I

For years the originally oral nature of most biblical material has been recognized. But the knowledge of an "oral tradition" has been used mainly to understand the processes of composition and transmission. McLuhan shows the enormous effect that the communication medium has on interpretation. His central insight, that "the medium is the message," demonstrates that the *form* in which a message is transmitted has more effect, and thus is more important upon the person and his culture, than the *content* of the message.

The two basic media of communication are oral/aural and literary. The former is the medium in pre-literate and non-literate societies. Its use creates a holistic culture, an intensely participatory society with all the senses heightened and matured by constant use. Individualism is rare, or even unknown. Events are experienced as wholes, by peoples who understand themselves as communities.

The literary medium, on the other hand, separates the event from my experience of it. Furthermore, it fragments the event itself by phonetically separating it into individual words. Events come to be experienced in linear fashion. Life is fragmented into pieces. A person no longer lives with his whole sensorium in operation. The senses are suppressed, and atrophy as the medium of the written word dominates the learning life. This analysis of the shaping effect of media might be a major clue in understanding the Apocalypse. At the very least, it accounts for the prevailing difficulties that literate exegetes have had in making sense of the book.

II

The Apocalypse is non-literary in its inception. Only after St. John "saw" the "word of God" and the "testimony of Jesus Christ" (Rev. 1:2) did he write it (Rev. 1:3). Even then its basically oral character was preserved: "Blessed is he who *reads aloud* the words of the prophecy, and blessed are those who *hear.* . . ." It is an oral construct of visual, auditory, and tactile material. It is theological poetry, and like most ancient poetry (and some modern) it is primarily something said or sung. If it is written at all, it is written subsequently. The creation and the construction take place in the milieu of the senses.

Ironically, R. H. Charles, to whom this probably never occurred, gives the most convincing evidence of it. Professor Charles, whose commentary has become a classic, meticulously runs down every quotation and allusion in the book. Interestingly, there is not a single exact quotation from any source. It would have been impossible for anyone to copy so many things with such uniform inaccuracy. The evidence is that the relation to the source material was all oral/aural. It was material that had been heard. Charles's exegetical conclusion was that the Apocalypse was an elaborate scissors-and-paste job; McLuhan provides the insight which uses the same evidence to reveal it as a fusion of voices and images. Moreover, the grammar is bad; almost as if it had not been composed on paper at all but transcribed from a spoken vernacular — a small but significant indicator of the book's originally oral character.

The Apocalypse, it would seem, has no strictly literary dependencies — but a great many oral ones. It is a work of the imagination composed out of the sensory memory of the spoken and sung word.

And yet, nearly all the exegetical and hermeneutical work done on the Apocalypse has assumed the literary premise. The book has been treated, as only literate man can treat it, as a series of words put in neat linear fashion on paper. The very act of reading privately (public reading would have a different effect) has destroyed the sensory whole of the original work and fragmented it into pieces. The results are notorious. Charts, schemes, diagrams abound. The bits and pieces are arranged and rearranged. Everyone becomes confused with the deluge of detail. Numbers, colors, visions, sounds are all treated separately and significantly. But in their separateness they also become insignificant. One remembers Dr. Cuticle in Melville's *White-Jacket,* the surgeon who, in his concern to demonstrate his own skill, does not observe that the patient has died on the table. "They murder to dissect."

No biblical book has suffered such an extreme fate at the hands of its scholarly exegetes. The reason is now easy to see — no biblical book has been so far removed in its origin from the literary medium. The vision was written; but it was read aloud and very quickly put back into the oral medium. And the reason, of course, was that it was addressed to persons who, in the main, could not read. Sound was primary. The experience of *hearing* the Apocalypse, whatever else it might have been, was not a *literary* experience. The medium was the ear. If neither the cause nor effect of the message was determined by literacy, it can hardly bode well for the interpreter to assume exclusively literary tools in his hermeneutical work.

No one fails to be impressed by the massive erudition of the major commentators on the Apocalypse. R. H. Charles and C. C. Torrey are brilliant. All the same, one does not get the feeling that they are illuminating the *message* of the book by their work. They do a superb job on its syntax, its mythological associations, its theology. But they are deaf to its medium: they never hear the trumpets. They are Gutenberg men all the way. It is no damning accusation to say so. We all are caught in the same cultural deafness. But they do demonstrate the difficulty of interpreting the Apocalypse with the literary tools and cultural experience of western man.

Artists, the "antennae of the race" (Ezra Pound), whose sensory life is less numbed by literary experience, have been more successful with the Apocalypse. Marc Chagall's paintings, William Blake's drawings, Christina Rossetti's devotional commentary — all see the vision and hear the message. D. H. Lawrence, who understood the fragmenting power of industrial life, perceived the wholeness of total man in the book and wrote on it with compelling conviction (though with dubious orthodoxy). It seems that the artist whose senses have not been dulled by literacy has a chance to come to the material through its own medium.

Perhaps the theologian and exegete who has come closest to

making *total* sense of the Apocalypse has been Austin Farrer. He has done it by treating it as poetry, and instead of parsing verbs and correcting syntax he has dealt with the artistic imagination of St. John. Farrer's imaginative reconstruction of the making of the book is supported by McLuhan's media insights.

To use McLuhan's terminology, the effect of literate commentators on the book has been *explosive,* separating the parts in a "widening gyre;" the effect of McLuhan's insight will be *implosive,* joining all the sensory material into a single event. But it takes a special effort of the imagination to hear and see along with St. John. We feel more at home in tracking down clues. "Ours is a culture based on excess, on overproduction; the result is a steady loss of sharpness in our sensory experience," according to Susan Sontag.[1] Small wonder that we do so badly as interpreters of the Apocalypse.

What happens in the Apocalypse is that the frightening, disintegrative effects of evil (persecution, death, suffering, etc.) are reversed by the imaginative reconstruction of a universe in which the senses are used to bring about participation and a sense of totality.

III

Auditory and visual materials are most apparent in the Apocalypse. Tactile, olfactory, gustatory senses are peripherally represented. Hearing is basic. Underneath the message to be heard is the experience of hearing: "He who has ears let him hear!" Hear *what?* Never mind *what,* let him *hear.* Resonance is set up. Communication is established. God's voice and our ears are united.

Hearing is joined with seeing. The two senses operate in tandem. The testimony in the first chapter, "I turned to see the voice . . . ," sets the tone. Ears and eyes are put to interacting and complementary use. Sounds of voices, thunders and songs, fill the air. Silence is significant. Sights of colorful, composite beasts, a magnificent statuary Christ, visually composite women, and precious gems are rich fare for the eyes. A documentation of the sensory material of ear and eye would repeat nearly every line of the book.

1. Susan Sontag, *Against Interpretation* (New York: Farrar, Straus & Giroux, 1966), p. 13.

Not so obvious, perhaps, is the appeal to tactility. The symbolic use of numbers has been a recognized feature of the Apocalypse from the outset: its series of sevens, combinations of fours and threes, cryptic sixes, myriads, multitudes. But the significance of the numbers, interpretatively, has been dealt with exclusively as having symbolic reference. Four means "x," three means "y," etc. But the medium is the message. Number, according to McLuhan, is an extension of tactility; from counting on your fingers (digits), numbers become a way of extending the sense of touch. "Baudelaire had the true intuition of number as a tactile hand or nervous system for interrelating separate units, when he said that 'number is within the individual. Intoxication is a number.' That explains why 'the pleasure of being in a crowd is a mysterious expression of delight in the multiplication of number.' Number, that is to say, is not only auditory and resonant, like the spoken word, but originates in the sense of touch, of which it is an extension."[2]

This does not mean, of course, that there are no symbolic meanings to the numbers; that is obvious. It does provide a sensory dimension which gives a unity and a background. It explains the powerful effect the numbers have had on readers even when they didn't understand the symbolic reference. It accounts for the power that the numbers have held over the imagination of interpreters.

The importance of the mass numbers in Revelation, chapter seven, is an instance: the squared number, 144,000, and the indefinite "multitude which no man can number." The incursion of violent evil is inaugurated by the four horsemen in chapter six. It is met by the *feel* of righteous, victorious *magnitude* in chapter seven. The mass numbers provide a sensory response of victory. The effect of the numbers in the vision of chapter seven on a sensorily alive person is to extend his *feeling* of God's protection and victory in the face of pressing evil. The Hebrew anthropomorphisms of God's fingers, back, arm, face are intensified in this use of numbers as an extension of the sense of touch, communicating the sense of God's actual presence and help.

The tactile sense is also made use of in the imagery of the "city." Lewis Mumford in his book, *The City in History*, notes that the city was first of all an extension of the skin and functioned as the skin

2. Marshall McLuhan, *Understanding Media: The Extensions of Man* (New York: McGraw-Hill, 1964), p. 109.

functions as protection.[3] The grouping of houses in a city and the building of a city wall create a group consciousness and inter-relatedness. The city in the Apocalypse is pictured in two ways, as Babylon and as Jerusalem. Babylon is the self-consciousness and inter-relatedness of evil. When evil reaches its peak and becomes concentrated, it forms a city. The city becomes the dwelling place of evil and, of course, it is destroyed. It is not wicked people who are destroyed but the wicked city.

The new Jerusalem is a city with perfect proportions and infinite space. It is most striking that the new heaven is not pictured as a restored garden of Eden, but as a new city. The pagan vision of the future is Eden or Arcadia — a primitivistic return to uncomplicated individualism. (Gauguin gave artistic representation to this vision in our century.) But the biblical vision is a perfection of the city. This artifice of society for living consciously together is culminated, not eliminated. The city becomes the dwelling place for the new righteousness, which means that those who live in cities have a ready model at hand to understand the future of the extension of the consciousness of God. (Harvey Cox has perceptive things to say about this in *The Secular City*.[4]) The measuring of both temple and city (chapters 11 and 20) emphasizes this extension of tactility. "As electrically contracted," says McLuhan, "the globe is no more than a village." Likewise, in the theological, sensory poetry of the Apocalypse, the cosmos is no more than the city.

The sense of smell is associated sensorily with prayer in the Apocalypse. The bowls of incense, representing the prayers of the church, can be both seen and smelled (chapter 8). "The sense of smell is not only the most subtle and delicate of the human senses; it is, also, the most iconic in that it involves the entire human sensorium more fully than any other sense. It is not surprising, therefore, that highly literate societies take steps to reduce or eliminate odors from the environment. B.O., the unique signature and declaration of human individuality, is a bad word in literate societies. It is far too involving for our habits of detachment and specialist attention."[5]

3. Lewis Mumford, *The City in History* (New York: Harcourt Brace Jovanovich, 1968).

4. Harvey Cox, *The Secular City* (New York: Macmillan, 1965).

5. McLuhan, *Understanding Media*, p. 147.

The sense of smell, "most subtle and delicate . . . most involving . . . ," is obviously the appropriate sensory equivalent for prayer. The difficulties of literate man in developing and maintaining a satisfactory life of prayer may be directly related to the increase in body deodorants!

The sense of taste has incidental representation in the tepidity of the Laodicean church which must be spewed out of the mouth because of its tastelessness, and the little scroll (chapter 10) which was sweet in the mouth but bitter in the belly.

IV

None of this is intended to minimize the place of the rational, understanding mind in reading the Apocalypse. There are a couple of very famous appeals to reason within the book itself: ". . . let him who has understanding reckon the number of the beast . . ." (Rev. 13:18); ". . . this calls for a mind with wisdom . . ." (Rev. 17:9). But the place of the imagination and the effect of sensory media have surely been ignored overlong in interpreting the book.

Yet the persistence of the Apocalypse in the life of the church indicates that this imaginative-sensory dimension has not been missed by everyone. Generations of Christian scholars, if they have not rejected it (as Luther) or ignored it (as Calvin), have found it a place to exercise literary ingenuity; but it has been *the* most important book for many illiterate and common people. Its impact through the centuries has been basically sensory rather than mental. People have not gotten new ideas out of the Apocalypse — they have found new feelings.

Features analogous to the interpretive task in biblical material have appeared in the current discussions of the "theology of hope." Some of the difficulty among the discussants can be traced to a literary experience which stubbornly treats "hope" as simply another subject in the theological spectrum, even though Moltmann warns sharply against it. "Eschatology cannot really be only a part of Christian doctrine. Rather, the eschatological outlook is characteristic of all Christian proclamation, of every Christian existence and the whole church."[6]

6. Jürgen Moltmann, *The Theology of Hope* (New York: Harper and Row, 1967), p. 16.

A key sentence in understanding the "theology of hope" is: "The eschatological is not one element *of* Christianity, but it is the *medium* of Christian faith as such, the key in which everything in it is set, the glow that suffuses everything here in the dawn of an expected new day."[7] Hope, then, is not another subject to be discussed, nor another topic to be debated. It is something different in kind, the *medium* of theological discussion, the theological environment in which the church discovers and carries out its mission. Just as orality (or literacy) provides the shaping medium in communications, so hope (or presumption/despair) provides the shaping medium in the church's mission. And the medium is the message: hope proclaims the mission experience and the church's future ("faith has the priority, but hope the primacy").

But if the theology of hope has provided difficulty for some, it has been grasped almost intuitively by others — a younger, later generation which understands something about the importance of the *medium*.

So Moltmann joins McLuhan. Interest in eschatology revives at the same time that conceptual tools are provided for demonstrating its "medium" character. The future, at least for the Apocalypse, looks good, hermeneutically. The new generations of the electronic age, whose learning is shaped by the electronic media, will get the message of the instantaneous, participatory, imaginative medium of the book. St. Paul, the favorite of literate minds, will take second place to St. John.

The usefulness of McLuhan's insights is at this point still academic. They enable the reader of the Apocalypse to gain a perspective from which he can see the inadequacy of his literary treatment, to discover some of the reason for all the exegetical trouble commentators have gotten into, and to account for the persistent popularity of the Apocalypse among common folk and poets. The insights do not help us to hear, see, or feel as a preliterate person would. Our senses are numbed and we are not likely to make a quick recovery. What Susan Sontag advises in respect to literature in general has relevance to readers of this biblical book: "What is important now is to recover our senses. We must learn to see more, hear more, feel more."[8]

7. Moltmann, *The Theology of Hope,* p. 16, my italics.
8. Sontag, *Against Interpretation,* p. 14.

It may be two more generations before the Christian church will hear, see, and feel the message of the Apocalypse without "Gutenberg distortion." But the future looks good. The contemporary world provides the most favorable milieu for a hermeneutic of the Apocalypse since at least the fourteenth century, and maybe even the second. Television-trained lay Christians may discover that it is the one biblical book in which they hold an interpretive advantage over their more bookish pastors and theologians. It may again become the brilliant climax to the scriptural canon that it once was, instead of the bizarre embarrassment it has been for so many centuries.

Resurrection Quartet

There was one resurrection; there are four narratives of it. Matthew, Mark, Luke, and John tell the story, each in his own way. Each narrative is distinct and has its own character. When the four accounts are absorbed into the imagination, they develop rich melodies, harmonies, counterpoint. The four voices become a resurrection quartet.

Yet many people never hear the music. The reason, I think, is that the apologetic style for years has been to "harmonize" the four resurrection stories. But it never turns out to be harmonization. Instead of listening to their distinctive bass, tenor, alto, and soprano voices, we have tried to make the evangelists sing the same tune. Differences and variations in the resurrection narratives are denied, affirmed, doubted, and "interpreted."

There is a better way. Since we have the four accounts that supplement one another, we can be encouraged to celebrate each one as it is, and to magnify the features that make it distinct from the others. Instead of melting them down into an ingot of doctrine, we can burnish the features that individualize them.

When we do that, our imagination expands, and the resurrection acquires the sharp features and hard surfaces of real life. Through the artistry of the four evangelists, the particularity and detail of local history, the kind we ourselves live in, becomes vivid.

Originally published in *Christianity Today,* March 31, 1972.

I

The eye-catching sentence in Matthew's narrative is, "There was a great earthquake; for an angel of the Lord descended from heaven and came and rolled back the stone and sat upon it" (28:2). That is a detail no one else includes. What it tells us is that the resurrection is earthshaking. Matthew reports the resurrection event as something like the explosion of a bomb that throws out waves of energy. The earthquake becomes an image used to dramatize the historical impact of Christ raised from the dead.

The detail alerts us to consequences. When we hear that an earthquake has occurred, we want to know how it affected the community. We are curious about the lives lost and the lives saved, about the acts of selfishness and heroism. Matthew's earthquake detail gets us interested in what *happens*. As the waves of resurrection energy spread, what will be the results? How will men and women respond?

As the earthquake-impact of the resurrection moves into human history, Matthew notes six responses: "the guards trembled and became like dead men" (28:4); the women departed quickly from the tomb with fear and great joy, and ran to tell his disciples" (v. 8); the women "came up and took hold of his feet and worshiped him" (v. 9); the elders bribed the soldiers and told them to "tell people, 'His disciples came by night and stole him away while we were asleep'" (v. 13); the soldiers "took the money and did as they were directed" (v. 15); the eleven "when they saw him, they worshiped him; but some doubted" (v. 17).

These responses range across a spectrum that includes terror, lying, bribery, reverent fear, doubt, great joy, and worship. Not one of them is trivial. The resurrection did not produce the same thing in everyone present, but no one was unaffected by it. It made a profound impact on everyone in the vicinity.

Matthew gives about equal space to each response. Yet he holds up one above the others: worship. The women in verse 9 and the eleven in verse 17 respond by worshiping. The lying and bribery responses of the elders and soldiers are sandwiched between these and provide a contrast that sets them off even more clearly. Worship, says Matthew, is the most appropriate response that can be made to the resurrection.

Matthew's words support his perspective. Imperatives are re-
sponse-demanding words, and Matthew uses a lot of them. When a
man has a command addressed to him, he has to *do* something, either
positively or negatively. Matthew's choice of words shows how the
waves of resurrection energy moved through the interstices of human
response: "do not be afraid" (28:5); "come, see the place where he
lay" (v. 6); "go quickly and tell his disciples" (v. 7); "do not be afraid"
(v. 10); "go and tell my brethren" (v. 10); "tell people" (v. 13); "go
therefore and make disciples" (v. 19).

No event in history rivals the resurrection in its impact on the
human will. The way a person responds to it is the most characteristic
and significant response we will ever make. With great skill Matthew
makes us see that as he constructs his story around the earthquake-
impact of Jesus' resurrection.

II

Mark's Gospel is a rapid-fire narration of what Jesus said and did as
he gave "his life as a ransom for many" (10:45). Mark scraps all the
preliminaries (for instance, he does not describe Jesus' birth) and in
a breathless, hurried journey involves us in the action. "Straightway"
and "immediately" are characteristic words in English translations.
Caught up in the action, we are eager to find what happens next.

Mark carries this style into chapter sixteen — his account of
the resurrection. Three women come to the tomb and find it empty.
An angel tells them that Jesus is risen and gives them instructions
on what they are to do. Mark then gives us one of his most dramatic
scenes: "They went out and fled from the tomb; for trembling and
astonishment had come upon them; and they said nothing to anyone,
for they were afraid" (16:8).

That isn't quite what *I* would expect as a response to the resurrection. I want to know what comes next. How will the story end?

The experience of the women who come to the tomb, grieving
deeply, and expecting to carry out the burial amenities, is the material
Mark uses to tell the resurrection story. Their simple devotion is
interrupted by two surprises: the stone is rolled away from the tomb,
and the tomb is empty. In that surprised condition they receive an
angelic message. The message has four simple statements of fact:

Jesus is risen; he is not there; the tomb is empty; he is going on ahead to Galilee. Then it has two commands: do not be amazed; go, tell his disciples and Peter. Finally, there is a promise: you will see him. A foundation of fact supports a double command that is motivated by a single promise. Subjectively, surprise prevails; objectively, the divine message predominates. The combination produces the pivotal experience: "They went out and fled from the tomb; for trembling and astonishment had come upon them; and they said nothing to anyone, for they were afraid."

Psychologically, that is a situation that simply must be resolved. There is an overwhelming personal necessity to complete the story. Mark draws us into the center of the action and lets us feel for ourselves the emotion that accompanies the sudden realization that Jesus was actually risen from the dead. It is impossible to look at it analytically or objectively. The story needs to be completed. Our participation is evoked.

Yet the oldest Greek manuscripts stop just at that point, at verse 8. Whether Mark deliberately stopped there or, whether the ending of the original manuscript scroll became frayed through constant usage and simply wore off, nobody at this point knows. What everyone does know, though, is that no one, ancient or modern, is satisfied with the ending (or lack of ending). The vacuum has to be filled. An ending must be supplied. The manuscript history of Mark's Gospel shows repeated attempts to "finish" the story.

This everywhere observable attempt to supply an ending to Mark's resurrection narrative shows how well he told his story and how pivotal verse 8 is. The resurrection is not complete until it is concluded in personal history. When we realize that Christ is risen, we may experience fear, joy, doubt. But these reactions in relation to the facts, commands, and promise of the divine word must be incorporated in a personal conclusion. The resurrection requires a conclusion that only personal participation can supply.

III

In addition to the story of the women at the empty tomb on Easter morning (the story common to the other accounts), Luke tells two rather long stories about the risen Christ's appearance: first to two men at Emmaus on Easter afternoon and evening, and then to all the disciples in Jerusalem that night.

These two stories are vehicles for gathering together material that will expand our understanding of the resurrection. Luke's account prevents us from reducing the resurrection to an isolated event, however earth-shaking, or to a personal experience, however intense. He weaves its meaning into the fabric of what has gone before and what will follow. He sees all history to that point leading up to this event, and all future history flowing from it.

Luke's method is to lace the stories with references to the ancient Scriptures and the recent past. Two men at Emmaus are "talking with each other all about these things that had happened" (24:14); when Jesus meets them, they rehearse the life and ministry of Jesus of Nazareth (vv. 19-24); Jesus offers an exposition relating Scripture (the past) and resurrection (v. 27); the two men recognize the relation between the past and the resurrection (v. 32); meeting with the eleven, Jesus refers them to "everything written about me in the law of Moses and the prophets and the psalms" (v. 44); the resurrection is rooted in past prophecy: "thus it is written . . ." (v. 46); the concluding verses (vv. 47-53) project the resurrection event into the future where there will be repentance, forgiveness of sins, witness, the coming promise of power, great joy, and continuous praise.

Luke tells the resurrection story in a way that connects humanity's past experience to the resurrection. Human history is a single story that has the resurrection as its theme and climax.

Luke's account of the resurrection is the longest of the four. He includes more material and expands it more thoroughly than the other Gospel writers. He wants us to *understand* the resurrection. He develops his material in a manner designed to expand our imagination so it can take in the immense scope of the resurrection. The resurrection, in other words, is comprehensive. It takes the scattered pieces of humanity's historical-religious-cultural life and puts them all together.

IV

The resurrection of Jesus is not easy to believe in. There are a lot of tricksters in the world and a lot of fakes. How do we know that the resurrection was not a hoax? There have, after all, been plenty of religious hoaxes in the world. Resurrection is a common theme in ancient religion. What evidence do we have that the resurrection of Jesus wasn't just one among many?

John's account of the resurrection is written to provide convincing evidence for dealing with these very legitimate questions. John's story is designed to persuade: "These are written that you may believe that Jesus is the Christ" (20:31). "Believe," in John's lexicon, is a union of intellectual comprehension and life commitment. His purpose is to place before us information that will clear away honest doubts and impel us to commitment. In telling of the resurrection John takes special pains to emphasize the credibility of the resurrection by bringing out details that show its historical reality.

In verses 1-10 Peter and John, told by Mary that the tomb is empty, run to see for themselves. What they *see* causes them to believe. The arrangement of linen cloths and napkin provided the kind of visible evidence that was convincing to those first observers: "Then the other disciple, who reached the tomb first, also went in, and he saw and believed" (20:8).

In verses 11-18, Mary, weeping outside the tomb, has a conversation with Jesus. At first she doesn't recognize the One to whom she is talking, but identifies the risen Christ when he speaks her name, she turns and sees his tangible form. Note what she says to the others: "I have *seen* the Lord."

In verses 19-23, the disciples are huddled in fear on the evening of the resurrection. Jesus appears to them. He reassures them of his resurrection reality by showing them the crucifixion marks in his hands and side. "Then the disciples were glad when they *saw* the Lord."

In verses 24-29 the disciples are again together, this time with Thomas who had not believed the report the others gave. Jesus makes another appearance, offering himself in tangible form: "Put your finger here, and see my hands; and put out your hand, and place it in my side . . ." (v. 27).

The senses of seeing, hearing, and touching are represented in the four stories John gives us. In each story people moved from a state where they lacked belief to one where they believed on the basis of first-hand evidence. The stories provide a framework in which people can move through doubt and skepticism. Thanks to John,

106

there is plenty of room in the Christian community for people to ask questions and express doubts.

John doesn't shout at us that we *have* to believe, no matter what. He knows that the best belief includes an intelligent, searching mind. He doesn't want us to believe blindly; he wants us to believe on the basis of good evidence. His Gospel is full of "signs" (we might almost call them "evidences") — events in Jesus' life that provide self-authenticating data that he is God's Son, the Savior of the world.

POETRY

Holy Luck

I. The Lucky Poor

"Blessed are the poor in spirit"

A beech tree in winter, white
Intricacies unconcealed
Against sky blue and billowed
Clouds, carries in his emptiness
Ripeness: sap ready to rise
On signal, buds alert to burst
To leaf. And then after a season
Of summer a lean ring to remember
The lush fulfilled promises.
Empty again in wise poverty
That lets the reaching branches stretch
A millimeter more towards heaven,
The bole expand ever so slightly
And push roots into the firm
Foundation, lucky to be leafless:
Deciduous reminder to let it go.

Originally published in *Theology Today*, April 1987. Editor's note: The word "lucky" has a bad odor among some people, Peterson says, but the old Wycliffe Bible referred to those faithful persons who had "holy luck," which should be reflective of our response to God's blessings. This was before the gamblers got hold of the word.

II. The Lucky Sad

"Blessed are those who mourn"

Flash floods of tears, torrents of them,
Erode cruel canyons, exposing
Long forgotten strata of life
Laid down in the peaceful decades:
A badlands beauty. The same sun
That decorates each day with colors
From arroyos and mesas, also shows
Every old scar and cut of lament.
Weeping washes the wounds clean
And leaves them to heal, which always
Takes an age or two. No pain
Is ugly in past tense. Under
The Mercy every hurt is a fossil
Link in the great chain of becoming.
Pick and shovel prayers often
Turn them up in valleys of death.

III. The Lucky Meek

"Blessed are the meek"

Moses, by turns raging and afraid,
Was meek under the thunderhead whiteness,
The glorious opacity of cloudy pillar.
Each cloud is meek, buffeted by winds
It changes shape but never loses
Being: not quite liquid, hardly
Solid, *in medias res*. Like me.
Yielding to the gusting spirit
All become what ministering angels
Command: sign, promise, portent.
Vigorous in image and color, oh, colors
Of earth pigments mixed with sun
Make hues that raise praises at dusk,
At dawn, collect storms, release
Rain, filter sun in arranged
And weather measured shadows. Sunpatches.

IV. The Lucky Hungry

*"Blessed are those who hunger
and thirst after righteousness"*

Unfeathered unbelief would fall
Through the layered fullness of thermal
Updrafts like a rock; this red-tailed
Hawk drifts and slides, unhurried
Though hungry, lazily scornful
Of easy meals off carrion junk,
Expertly waiting elusive provisioned
Prey: a visible emptiness
Above an invisible plenitude.
The sun paints the Japanese
Fantail copper, etching
Feathers against the big sky
To my eye's delight, and blesses
The better-sighted bird with a shaft
Of light that targets a rattler
In a Genesis-destined death.

V. The Lucky Merciful

"Blessed are the merciful"

A billion years of pummeling surf,
Shipwrecking seachanges and Jonah storms
Made ungiving, unforgiving granite
Into this analgesic beach:
Washed by sea-swell rhythms of mercy,
Merciful relief from city
Concrete. Uncondemned, discalceate,
I'm ankle deep in Assateague sands,
Awake to rich designs of compassion
Patterned in the pillowing dunes.
Sandpipers and gulls in skittering,
Precise formation devoutly attend
My salt and holy solitude,
Then feed and fly along the moving,
Imprecise ebb- and rip-tide
Border dividing care from death.

VI. The Lucky Pure

"Blessed are the pure in heart"

Austere country, this, scrubbed
By spring's ravaging avalanche.
Talus slope and Appekunny
Mudstone make a meadow where
High-country beargrass gathers light
From lichen, rock, and icy tarn,
Changing sun's lethal rays
To food for grizzlies, drink for bees —
Heart-pure creatures living blessed
Under the shining of God's face.
Yet, like us the far-fallen,
Neither can they look on the face
And live. Every blossom's a breast
Holding eventual sight for all blind and
Groping newborn: we touch our way
Through these splendors to the glory.

VII. The Lucky Peacemakers

"Blessed are the peacemakers"

Huge cloud fists assault
The blue exposed bare midriff of sky:
The firmament doubles up in pain.
Lightnings rip and thunders shout;
Mother nature's children quarrel.
And then, as suddenly as it began,
It's over. Noah's heirs, perceptions
Cleansed, look out on a disarmed world
At ease and ozone fragrant. Still waters.
What barometric shift
Rearranged these ferocities
Into a peace-pulsating rainbow
Sign? My enemy turns his other
Cheek; I drop my guard. A mirror
Lake reflects the filtered colors;
Breeze-stirred pine trees quietly sing.

VIII. The Lucky Persecuted

"Blessed are those who are persecuted"

Unfriendly waters do a friendly
Thing: curses, cataract-hurled
Stones, make the rough places
Smooth; a rushing whitewater stream
Of blasphemies hate-launched,
Then caught by the sun, sprays rainbow
Arcs across the Youghiogeny.
Savaged by the river's impersonal
Attack the land is deepened to bedrock.
Wise passivities are learned
In quiet, craggy, occasional pools
That chasten the wild waters to stillness,
And hold them under hemlock green
For birds and deer to bathe and drink
In peace — persecution's gift:
The hard-won, blessed letting be.

PASTORAL READINGS

Poetry from Patmos: St. John as Pastor, Poet, and Theologian

The most famous last words spoken or written are the last book of the Bible, the Revelation. No others come close in the competition. But "most famous" does not mean "most admired" or "best understood." Many, confused by the bloody dragons and doomsday noise, are only bewildered. Others, associating them with frequently encountered vulgarities and inanities, hold them in contempt.

Still, there have always been some, never perhaps a majority, who stopped to look and read out of curiosity, but who stayed to understand and admire because they discovered here rich, convincingly presented truth. I am among these people. The words, for us, are famous not because they are sensationally bizarre or teasingly enigmatic. They are famous because they are so satisfyingly *true,* backed up by centuries of mature experience and tested usage. The famous last words of the Revelation are famous because they memorably summarize and conclude centuries of biblical insight, counsel, and experience in the persons to whom God chose to reveal himself, and who in their turn chose to live by faith in God.[1]

The power of the Revelation to attract attention, and then, for

1. Northrop Frye, *The Great Code* (New York: Harcourt Brace, Jovanovich, 1982), p. 199.

Originally published in *Journal for Preachers,* Pentecost, 1987.

those who attend, to make the reality of God and the life of faith coherent, develops out of a striking convergence of the ministries of theologian, poet, and pastor in the person of its author, St. John.[2] The three ministries are braided into a distinguished plait in his introductory words: "I, John, your brother, who share with you in Jesus the tribulation and the kingdom and the patient endurance, was on the island called Patmos on account of the word of God and the testimony of Jesus. I was in the spirit on the Lord's day, and I heard behind me a loud voice like a trumpet saying, 'Write what you see in a book and send it to the seven churches. . . .' Then I turned to see the voice . . ." (1:9-12).

St. John was on Patmos, a prison island, "because of the word of God and the testimony of Jesus." The word (*logos*) of God (*Theos*) put him where he was; it also made him *who* he was. He did not identify himself by his circumstances as a prisoner but by his vocation as a theologian. He did not analyze Roman politics in order to account for his predicament, but exercised his intelligence on the word and testimony of God and Jesus: the task of the theologian.

The word and witness that shaped his life were then written down by command and under inspiration. "In the Spirit," he was commanded, "Write what you see." The result is a book that re-creates in us, his readers, that which he himself experienced: the work of the poet.

He did this in a conscious, double companionship with the Christians and the Christ whom he knew — "your brother, who shares with you in Jesus the tribulation and the kingdom and the patient endurance." Everything there was to share — the hard difficulties, the glorious blessings, the day-by-day discipleship — he shared: the life of a pastor.

A theologian takes God seriously as subject and not as object, and makes it a life's work to think and talk of God in order to develop knowledge and understanding of God in his being and work. A poet takes words seriously as images that connect the visible and invisible,

---

2. "St. John" can refer to the Apostle, the Elder in Ephesus, or to an otherwise unknown leader in the late first-century church. Scholars argue for the various identifications. It matters little, so far as I can tell, to an accurate interpretation of the book. I do take the position, though, that the St. John who wrote the Revelation also wrote the Gospel and Letters.

and becomes custodian of their skillful and accurate usage. A pastor takes actual persons seriously as children of God and faithfully listens to and speaks with them in the conviction that their life of faith in God is the centrality to which all else is peripheral. The three ministries do not always converge in a single person; when they do the results are impressive. Because St. John so thoroughly integrated the work of theologian, poet, and pastor, we have this brilliantly conceived and endlessly useful document, the Revelation.

St. John, the Theologian

A fourth-century scribe, set the task of copying the Revelation, wrote the title, "A Revelation of John," and then, in a moment of inspired doodling, scribbled in the margin, *tou theologou,* "the theologian." The next copyist, struck with their appropriateness, moved the two words from the margin onto the center of the page. It has been St. John the Theologian ever since. (AV translation, "John the Divine.")

St. John is a theologian whose entire mind is saturated with thoughts of God, his whole being staggered by a vision of God. The world-making, salvation-shaping Word of God is heard and pondered and expressed. He is God-intoxicated, God-possessed, God-articulate. He insists that God is more than a blur of longing, and other than a monosyllabic curse (or blessing), but capable of *logos,* that is, of intelligent discourse. John is full of exclamations in relation to God, quite overwhelmed with the experience of God, but through it all there is *logos:* God revealed is God known. He is not so completely known that he can be predictable. He is not known so thoroughly that there is no more to be known, so that we can go on now to the next subject. Still, he is known and not unknown, rational and not irrational, orderly and not disorderly, hierarchical and not anarchic.

It is of great importance for Christian believers to have, from time to time, a reasonable, sane, mature person stand up in their midst and say "God is . . ." and go on to complete the sentence intelligently. There are tendencies within us and forces outside us that relentlessly reduce God to a checklist of explanations, or a handbook of moral precepts, or an economic arrangement, or a political expediency, or a pleasure boat. God is reduced to what can be measured, used, weighed, gathered, controlled, or felt. Insofar as we accept these reductionist explanations, our lives become bored, depressed, or mean. We live stunted like acorns in a terrarium. But oak trees need soil, sun, rain, and wind. Human life requires God. The theologian offers his or her mind in the service of saying "God" in such a way that God is not reduced or packaged or banalized, but known and contemplated and adored, with the consequence that our lives are not cramped into what we can explain but exalted by what we worship. The difficulties in such thinking and saying are formidable. The theologian is never able to deliver a finished product. "Systematic theology" is an oxymoron. There are always loose ends. But even the crumbs from discourse around such a table are more satisfying than full-course offerings on lesser subjects.

St. John is a theologian of a particularly attractive type: all his thinking about God took place under fire: "I was on the isle, called Patmos," a prison isle. He was a man thinking on his feet, running, or on his knees, praying, the postures characteristic of our best theologians. There have been times in history when theologians were supposed to inhabit ivory towers and devote themselves to writing impenetrable and ponderous books. But the important theologians have done their thinking and writing about God in the middle of the world, in the thick of the action: Paul urgently dictating letters from his prison cell; Athanasius *contra mundum,* five times hounded into exile by three different emperors; Augustine, pastor to people experiencing the chaotic breakup of Roman order and *civitas;* Thomas, using his mind to battle errors and heresies that, unchallenged, would have turned Europe into a spiritual and mental jungle; Calvin, tireless in developing a community of God's people out of Geneva's revolutionary rabble; Barth arbitrating labor disputes and preaching to prisoners; Bonhoeffer leading a fugitive existence in Nazi Germany; and St. John, exiled on the hard rock of Patmos prison while his friends in Christ were besieged by the terrible engines of a pagan assault: *theologos.*

The task of these theologians is to demonstrate a gospel order in the chaos of evil and arrange the elements of experience and reason so that they are perceived proportionately and coherently: sin, defeat, discouragement, prayer, suffering, persecution, praise, and politics are placed in relation to the realities of God and Christ, holiness and healing, heaven and hell, victory and judgment, beginning and ending. Their achievement is that the community of persons who live by faith in Christ continue to live with a reasonable hope and in intelligent love.

The Christian community needs theologians to keep us *thinking* about God and not just making random guesses. At the deepest levels of our lives we require a God whom we can worship with our whole mind and heart and strength. The taste for eternity can never be bred out of us by a secularizing genetics. Our existence is derived from God and destined for God. St. John stands in the front ranks of the great company of theologians who convince by their disciplined and vigorous thinking that *Theos* and *logos* belong together, that we live in a creation and not a madhouse.

St. John, the Poet

The result of St. John's theological work is a poem, "the one great poem which the first Christian age produced."[3] If the Revelation is not read as a poem, it is simply incomprehensible. The inability (or refusal) to deal with St. John, the poet, is responsible for most of the misreading, misinterpretation, and misuse of the book.

A poet uses words primarily not to explain something, and not to describe something, but to *make* something. Poet *(poetes)* means "maker." Poetry is not the language of objective explanation but the language of imagination. It makes an image of reality in such a way as to invite our participation in it. We do not have more information after we read a poem, we have more experience. It is not "an examination of what happens but an immersion in what happens."[4] If the Revelation is written by a theologian who is also a poet, we must not read it as if it were an almanac in order to find out when things are going to occur, or a chronicle of what has occurred.

It is particularly appropriate that a poet has the last word in the Bible. By the time that we get to this last book we already have a complete revelation of God before us. Everything that has to do with our salvation, with accompanying instructions on how to live a life of

3. Austin Farrer, *A Rebirth of Images* (Westminster: Dacre Press, 1949), p. 6.
4. Denise Levertov, *The Poet in the World* (New York: New Directions, 1973), p. 239.

faith, is here in full. There is no danger that we are inadequately informed. But there is danger that through familiarity and fatigue we will not pay attention to the splendors that surround us in Moses, Isaiah, Ezekiel, Zechariah, Mark, and Paul. St. John takes the familiar words and by arranging them in unexpected rhythms, wakes us up so that we see "the revelation of Jesus Christ" entire, as if for the first time.

Some, when God is the subject, become extremely cautious, qualifying every statement and defining every term. They attempt to say no more than can be verified in logic. They do not want to be found guilty of talking nonsense. Others, when God is the subject, knowing how easily we drift into pious fantasies, become excessively practical. They turn every truth about God into a moral precept. But poets are extravagant and bold, scorning both the caution of the religious philosopher and the earnestness of the ethical moralist. St. John is a poet, not using words to tell us about God, but to intensify our relationship with God. He is not trying to get us to think more accurately or to train us into better behavior, but to get us to believe more recklessly, behave more playfully — the faith-recklessness and hope-playfulness of children entering into the kingdom of God. He will jar us out of our lethargy, get us to live on the alert, open our eyes to the burning bush and fiery chariots, open our ears to the hard-steel promises and commands of Christ, banish boredom from the gospel, lift up our heads, enlarge our hearts.

Denise Levertov wrote, "Since almost all experience goes by too fast, too superficially for our apperception, what we most need is not to *re*-taste it (just as superficially) but really to taste *for the first time* the gratuitous, the autonomous identity of its essence. My 1865 Webster's defines *translation* as 'being conveyed from one place to another; removed to heaven without dying.' We must have an art that translates, conveys us to heaven of that deepest reality which otherwise 'we may die without ever having known'; that *transmits* us there, not in the sense of bringing the information to the receiver but of putting the receiver in the place of the event — alive."[5] This is St. John's work: he takes the old, everyday things of creation and salvation, of Father, Son, and Spirit, of world and flesh and devil that we take for granted, and forces us to look at them and experience again (or maybe for the first time) their reality.

5. Levertov, *The Poet in the World*, p. 94.

Not long before his death in 1973, W. H. Auden stated what it is we demand of a poem: ". . . two things: firstly, it must be a well-made verbal object that does honor to the language in which it is written; secondly, it must say something significant about a reality common to us all, but perceived from a unique perspective."[6] St. John's theological poem meets both demands. It is well made: its complex structure is carefully crafted and commands the wonder and admiration of all who study it. And it takes "the reality common to us all," the gospel of Jesus Christ, and presents it in the "unique perspective" of the end, the fulfilled completion of all the details and parts of salvation.

St. John sings his songs, represents his visions, arranges the sounds and meanings of his words rhythmically and artistically. He juxtaposes images unexpectedly, and we see and hear what was there all the time if we had only *really* listened, *really* looked. He wakes up our minds, rouses our feelings, involves our senses.

St. John, the Pastor

St. John's passion for thinking and talking about God, and his genius for subjecting us to the power of language so that the images are re-born in us, connecting us with a reality other and more than us, that is to say, his theology and his poetry — these are practiced in a particular context, the community of persons who live by faith in God. *What* he talks of and the *way* he talks of it take place among persons who dare to live by the great invisibles of grace, who accept forgiveness, who believe promises, who pray. These people daily and dangerously decide to live by faith and not by works, in hope and not in despair, by love and not hate. And they are daily tempted to quit. St. John is their pastor, or, as he says, "your brother, who shares. . . ."

Persons who live by faith have a particularly acute sense of living "in the middle." We believe that God is at the beginning of all things, and we believe that God is at the conclusion of all life, in St. John's striking epigram "the Alpha and the Omega" (1:8). It is routine

6. W. H. Auden, "The Poems of Joseph Brodsky," *The New York Review of Books* 20, no. 5 (April 5, 1973): 10.

127

among us to assume that the beginning was good ("and God saw everything that he had made, and behold it was very good"). It is agreed among us that the conclusion will be good ("And I saw a new heaven and a new earth"). That would seem to guarantee that everything between the good beginning and the good ending will also be good. But it doesn't turn out that way. Or at least it doesn't in the ways we expect. That always comes as a surprise. We expect uninterrupted goodness, and it is interrupted: I am rejected by a parent, coerced by a government, divorced by a spouse, discriminated against by a society, injured by another's carelessness. All of this in a life which at its creation was very good and at its conclusion will be completed according to God's design. Between the believed but unremembered beginning and the hoped-for but unimaginable ending there are disappointments, contradictions, not-to-be-explained absurdities, bewildering paradoxes — each of them a reversal of expectation.

The pastor is the person who specializes in accompanying persons of faith "in the middle," facing the ugly details, the meaningless routines, the mocking wickedness, and all the time doggedly insisting that this unaccountable unlovely middle is connected to a splendid beginning and a glorious ending. Luther's acid test of the Christian pastor was: "Does he know of death and the Devil? Or is it all sweetness and light?"[7]

When we read a novel we have an analogous experience. We begin the first chapter knowing that there is a last chapter. One of the satisfying things about just picking up a book is the sure knowledge that it will end. In the course of reading we are often puzzled, sometimes in suspense, usually wrong in our expectations, frequently mistaken in our assessment of a character. But when we don't understand or agree or feel satisfied, we don't ordinarily quit. We *assume* meaning and connection and design even when we don't experience it. The last chapter, we are confident, will demonstrate the meaning that was continuous through the novel. We believe that the story will satisfyingly *end,* not arbitrarily stop.

It is St. John's pastoral vocation to reinforce this sense of connection in the chaotic first century. In the buzzing, booming confu-

---

7. Quoted by Norman O. Brown, *Life against Death* (Middletown, CT: Wesleyan University Press, 1959), p. 209.

sion of good and evil, blessing and cursing, rest and conflict, St. John discerns pattern and design. He hears rhythms. He discovers arrangement and proportion. He communicates an overpowering "sense of an ending."[8] We are headed towards not merely a terminus but a goal, an end that is purposed and fulfilled. He spells out this sense of an ending in such a way that the people in the middle acquire an inner conviction of *meaning* something good in God.

St. John is not concerned with heaven and hell as things in themselves. He has no interest in judgment and blessing apart from the persons to whom he is pastor. He does not speculate or theorize. Every word, every number, every vision, every song is put to immediate use among those persons in the seven little congregations to which he is pastor. He is with them in their experiences of worship and apostasy, martyrdom and witness, love and vengeance, and develops the connections that maintain coherence between the beginning and the ending. These people, served by such a pastor, steadily acquire confidence that they are included in God's ways and are able, therefore, to persevere meaningfully even when they cannot see the meaning.

It is generally agreed that the Revelation has to do with eschatology, that is, with "last things." What is frequently missed is that all the eschatology is put to immediate pastoral use. Eschatology is the most pastoral of all the theological perspectives, showing how the ending impinges on the present in such ways that the truth of the gospel is verified in life "in the middle." It shows us that believers are not set "at the high noon of life, but at the dawn of a new day at the point where night and day, things passing and things to come, grapple with each other."[9]

The Revelation is thick with meaning — there are layers and layers of truth here to be mined. There is a multiplicity of significance in nearly every image St. John uses. There is some of the many-sidedness of wild nature in this "great and vividly imagined poem, in which

---

8. The phrase is taken from the title of a study by Frank Kermode which discusses the modern instances of apocalyptic literature and the evidence that they give for our human requirement to live towards a proposed conclusion and not simply at random. *The Sense of an Ending* (New York: Oxford University Press, 1967).

9. Moltmann, *The Theology of Hope* (London: SCM Press, 1967).

the whole world of that age's faith is bodied forth."[10] Since no one person and no single generation can expect to take possession of more than a part of its complex truth, it is important at the outset that St. John's readers cultivate courtesy among each other, lest differences in discovery develop into antagonisms of dogma. A good place to begin is to be courteous to St. John himself by honoring the fundamental concerns that we discern in his life and that come to expression in the Revelation: that his subject is God (not cryptographic esoterica), and that his context is pastoral (not alarmist entertainment). When we accept St. John in the shape of these ministries of theologian, poet, and pastor, we can be wrong about specific details and still be correct in our total response to his work. Christians who honor these conditions will emphasize different aspects of the truth and uncover surprises not anticipated by previous readers, but still maintain a community of interpretation and response with all those who, in faith, read in order to run.

10. Austin Farrer, *A Rebirth of Images*, p. 6.

Masters of Imagination

Thirteen four-year-old children sat on the carpet of the sanctuary at the chancel steps on a Thursday morning in late February. I sat with them, holding cupped in my hands a last season's birdnest. We talked about the birds on their way back to build nests like this one and of the spring that was about to burst in on us. The children were rapt in their attention.

I love doing this, meeting with these children, telling them stories, singing songs with them, telling them that God loves them, praying with them. I do it frequently. They attend our church's nursery school and come into the sanctuary with their teachers every couple of weeks to meet with me. They are so *alive,* their capacity for wonder endless, their imaginations lithe and limber.

Winter was receding and spring was arriving, although not quite arrived. But there were signs. It was the signs that I was talking about. The birdnest to begin with. It was visibly weedy and grey and dirty, but as we looked at it we saw the invisible — warblers on their way north from wintering grounds in South America, pastel and spotted eggs in the nest. We counted the birds in the sky over Florida, over North Carolina, over Virginia. We looked through the walls of the church to the warming ground. We looked beneath the surface and saw the earthworms turning somersaults. We began to see shoots of color break through the ground, crocus and tulip and grape hyacinth.

Originally published in *Eternity,* January 1989.

The buds on the trees and shrubs were swelling and about to burst into flower and we were remembering and anticipating and counting the colors.

I never get used to these Maryland springs and every time am taken by surprise all over again. I grew up in northern Montana where the trees are the same color all year long and spring is mostly mud. The riotous color in blossom and bloom in Maryland's dogwood and forsythia, redbud and shadbush, catches me unprepared. But this year I was getting prepared and getting the children prepared for all the glorious gifts that were going to be showering in on us in a week or so. We were looking at the bare birdnest and seeing the colors, hearing the songs, smelling the blossoms.

There are moments in this kind of work when you know you are doing it right. This was one of those moments. The children's faces were absolutely concentrated. We had slipped through a time warp and were experiencing the full sensuality of the Maryland spring.

They were no longer looking at the birdnest, they were *seeing* migrating birds and hatching chicks, garlanded trees and dewy blossoms. Then, abruptly, at the center of this moment of high holiness, Bruce said, "Why don't you have any hair on your head?"

Why didn't Bruce see what the rest of us were seeing — the exuberance, the fecundity? Why hadn't he made the transition to "seeing the invisible" that we were engrossed in? All he saw was the visible patch of baldness on my head, a rather uninteresting fact, while the rest of us were seeing multi-dimensioned *truths*. Only four years old and already Bruce's imagination was crippled.

Visible and Invisible

Imagination is the capacity to make connections between the visible and the invisible, between heaven and earth, between present and past, between present and future. For Christians, whose largest investment is in the invisible, the imagination is indispensable, for it is only by means of the imagination that we can see reality whole, in context. "What imagination does with reality is the reality we live by," writes David Ignatow in *Open Between Us* (University of Michigan Press, 1980).

When I look at a tree, most of what I "see" I do not see at all. I see a root system beneath the surface, sending tendrils through the soil, sucking up nutrients out of the loam. I see the light pouring energy into the leaves. I see the fruit that will appear in a few months. I stare and stare and see the bare branches austere in next winter's snow and wind. I see all that, I really do — I am not making it up. But I could not photograph it. I see it by means of imagination. If my imagination is stunted or inactive, I will only see what I can use, or something that is in my way.

Czeslaw Milosz, the Nobel prize-winning poet, with a passion for Christ supported and deepened by his imagination, said in an interview in *The New York Times Review of Books* (Feb. 27, 1986) that the minds of Americans have been dangerously diluted by the rationalism of explanation. He is convinced that our imagination-deficient educational process has left us with a naive picture of the world. In this naive view, the universe has space and time — and nothing else. No values. No God. "Functionally speaking, men and women are not that different from a virus or bacteria, a speck in the universe."

Milosz sees the imagination, and especially the religious imagination which is the developed capacity to be in reverence before whatever confronts us, to be the shaping force of the world we really live in. "Imagination," he said, "can fashion the world into a homeland as well as into a prison or a place of battle. Nobody lives in the 'objective' world, only in a world filtered through the imagination."

Imagination and Explanation

The imagination is among the chief glories of the human. When it is healthy and energetic, it ushers us into adoration and wonder, into the mysteries of God. When it is neurotic and sluggish, it turns people, millions of them, into parasites, copycats, and couch potatoes. The American imagination today is distressingly sluggish. Most of what is served up to us as the fruits of imagination is, in fact, the debasing of it into soap opera and pornography.

Right now, one of the essential Christian ministries in and to our ruined world is the recovery and exercise of the imagination. Ages of faith have always been ages rich in imagination. It is easy to see why: the materiality of the gospel (the seen, heard, and touched

133

Jesus) is no less impressive than its spirituality (faith, hope, and love). Imagination is the mental tool we have for connecting material and spiritual, visible and invisible, earth and heaven.

We have a pair of mental operations, imagination and explanation, designed to work in tandem. When the gospel is given robust and healthy expression, the two work in graceful synchronicity. Explanation pins things down so that we can handle and use them — obey and teach, help and guide. Imagination opens things up so that we can grow into maturity — worship and adore, exclaim and honor, follow and trust. Explanation restricts and defines and holds down; imagination expands and lets loose. Explanation keeps our feet on the ground; imagination lifts our heads into the clouds. Explanation puts us in harness; imagination catapults us into mystery. Explanation reduces life to what can be used; imagination enlarges life into what can be adored.

But our technological and information-obsessed age has cut imagination from the team. In the life of the gospel, where everything originates and depends upon what we cannot see and is worked out in what we can see, imagination and explanation cannot get along without each other. Is it time to get aggressive? Is it time for the Christian community to recognize and honor and commission masters of the imagination — our poets and singers and storytellers — as partners in evangelical witness? How else is Bruce going to hear the gospel when he grows up? How will he hear Isaiah's poetry, Jesus' parables, John's visions? It will be sad if, when he is 40 years old and enters a congregation of worshiping Christians and ministering angels, all he sees is a preacher's bald head.

Sheep in Wolfe's Clothing

The most skilled theological allegorist of the century has, unhappily, been typed as a writer of murder mysteries. The stereotype is so fixed that no one recognizes that Rex Stout for the past fifty years has been elaborating a complex, analogical parable of the Christian ministry in his Nero Wolfe detective stories.

Our tastes, dulled and flattened, see nothing in Rex Stout's novels but detective stories. Stout has written a body of work every bit as theologically perspicuous as Swift with the result that he hits the bestseller lists as a clever and resourceful detective novelist. To his financial benefit, of course, but still, for a serious writer to be misunderstood so completely must be humiliating no matter what the bank balance.

Type of Ministry

Once theological intent is suggested, the barest sleuthing quickly shows Nero Wolfe as a type of the church's ministry in the world. The most evident thing about him, his body, provides an analogue to the church. His vast bulk is evidence of his "weight," recalling the etymology of the biblical "glory." More than anything else he is *there,*

"Sheep in Wolfe's Clothing" was originally published in *Christian Ministry,* January 1973, pp. 26-28. Reprinted with permission.

visibly. He must be reckoned with. He is corpulent or nothing. And the church is the *body* of Christ.

Along with an insistence on bodily presence there is a corresponding observation that there is nothing attractive about that body. His body is subject to calumny and jokes. His genius is in his mind and his style. He does not fawn before customers, nor seek "contacts" (a word, incidentally, that he would never use. He once was found ripping apart a dictionary, page by page, and burning it because it legitimized "contacts" as a transitive verb.). Wolfe will not leave his house on business, that is, accommodate himself to the world's needs. He is a center around which the action revolves, a center of will and meditation, not a center of power or activity. He provides a paradigm for Christian ministry which, while reticent and reserved, is there in vast presence when needed. He has no need for advertising techniques or public relations programs. He is there and needed because there is something wrong in the world (murder and other criminal extremes). He models a ministry which is not here to be loved, not designed to inspire affection. It is its function that is admirable. It is massive, central, important — a genius, in fact. But you don't have to like it.

In all this there is an implied criticism of a church which has succumbed to public relations agents who have mounted Christian pulpits to make the church attractive, to personalize her, to sentimentalize her. Wolfe, as Christian ministry, levels a rebuke against that kind of thing.

It follows that there is disdain for defensive explanations — a Barthian avoidance of "apologetics" to a world which seeks assurance of his reliability and effectiveness. To that kind of inquiry he says: "I can give you my word, but I know what it's worth and you don't. Before I went to a lot of trouble to establish my good faith I would need satisfaction on a few points myself" (*Over My Dead Body*). The church's ministry is cheapened when it tries to defend itself or make itself acceptable in terms the world can understand.

Church Prototype

Wolfe's ecclesiastical nature is furnished with an environment in which to work by the brownstone house on West 34th Street laid out to correspond to a church. The dining room is the chancel, a place reserved for the best food and the finest conversation, word and sacrament. ("Which he loves most, food or words, is a toss-up" — *Gambit*.) The kitchen is the sacristy. The office, where the people and the ministry encounter one another, is the nave. The "front room" in which guests are placed prior to a decision on how they are to be involved, is the narthex. But the house is never simply lived in. There is no domesticity, no spilling over of activities from one room to another. Each room defines a function. There are no parties, no gatherings of friends for discussion or play. Christian ministry is thereby prevented from being interpreted as an exercise in human relations, or a kind of pious improvement on human amiability.

The imagery of Christian ministry is further elaborated in two rituals which dominate Wolfe's life. The first ritual involves the care and raising of orchids. Two periods each day, from nine to eleven in the morning and from four to six in the afternoon, are spent in the plant rooms on the roof caring for orchids. These morning and evening periods are not to be interrupted. "In all weathers and under any circumstances whatever his four hours a day on the roof with the orchids . . . were inviolable" (*League of Frightened Men*). Orchid-tending is a symbol for prayer and meditation, morning and evening.

No outsider can ever understand how Wolfe can give such regular and important blocks of time to nurturing new hybrids and cultivating fresh blossoms. He carries on some correspondence with other orchid raisers about his activities. But it is not something over which he makes small talk. At the same time he makes no secret of what he is doing, and often as he descends from the top floor (the "upper room") he brings a blossom and places it on his desk, a sign of "the hard work that makes all other work easy" (Kenneth Rexroth's description of meditation).

Prayer is not an activity that is determined by demands from the world. It is not ordered by outside expectations. It is absolutely non-utilitarian, like the orchid, the least useful and most delicate of flowers. Still, it takes priority over all else.

The second set of Wolfe's rituals concerns meals and constitutes a symbol of the church's ministry in worship. All meals are meticulously prepared. The greatest art goes into them. Wolfe's cook, Fritz Brenner, is skilled and knowledgeable. When the church gathers for worship, there is to be no such thing as casual, "fast-food" service.

It is significant that no business is discussed over Wolfe's dinner table. Worship is not something you do in the background while your mind is on something else. It is important in its own right, not fuel for something "practical." Anything of interest may be discussed at the meals except the work at hand. Prayers and sermons in Christian worship must not be propaganda, not a platform for getting something done. Archie refers to ". . . the charming gusto of Wolfe's dinner conversation — during meals he refused to remember that there was such a thing as a murder case in the world" (*League of Frightened Men*). "Practical sermons" are out. Against the background of the everyday excellence of the meals Sunday stands out: "It was now routine for Wolfe to spend Sunday morning in the kitchen with Fritz, preparing something special" (*Murder by the Book*).

Ministerial Colleague

The symbolism of Christian ministry is not complete in Nero Wolfe himself. He has an indispensable colleague, Archie Goodwin, who symbolizes the aspect of the church's ministry usually designated by the word "witness." Only in combination, Wolfe and Archie, is the Christian ministry symbol adequate. It is Archie who narrates the tales; apart from him we would know nothing, for Wolfe has neither need nor inclination to talk about himself. Jacques Barzun has noted that "Archie is (as close-reading critics would discover from his name) an arche-type." The church's ministry is not only a center for recollection, an ordering of power, a concentration of will: it also does things. Archie is that aspect of the church's ministry which gets involved in the world. He gets in fights, is quick with repartee, knows his way around the lobbies, taxi cabs, and saloons of the world. He is good at listening and good at getting information. He is good at reporting back to Wolfe. But he doesn't give a lot of opinion, nor feel compelled to make himself the main character of the story he is telling.

He frequently doesn't know why he is delivering messages or gathering evidence, but he is, nevertheless, responsive to orders. Not that he always does it with good grace. In fact, when asked to do things without knowing why he is doing them, he displays considerable irritation. He wants to understand the whole plan and is miffed when Wolfe doesn't let him in on the inner workings of his own mind. Sometimes he is full of doubts about Wolfe even though the genius has proved himself adequate every time in the past. And yet, full of alternating doubt and irritation, he obediently goes about his work as "witness" (in word and deed). Wolfe needs him and could not, in fact, function without him, for it is his words and actions he uses to arrive at his solution.

Archie's independent spirit frequently brings him to the brink of quitting, but he always reconsiders (repents) and is soon back at work as Wolfe's man. But he doesn't just take orders. When he finds himself in a situation for which he has no instructions, the rule is that he is to operate on his own: "Whenever Wolfe sent me on an errand without specific instructions, the general instruction was that I was to use my intelligence guided by experience" *(Gambit)*.

The parallels with Christian witness are strong. The witness operates blindly much of the time. He is commanded to testify to love, justice, and health in a world where hate, injustice, and disease are everywhere. He never does understand the logic of the whole. And he experiences both doubt and irritation in not having an inside look into the "mind of the maker."

Archie's creative part in the work is to keep Wolfe working. ("Of all the things I do to earn my pay, from sharpening pencils to jumping a visitor before he can get his gun up, the most important is riding Wolfe, and he knows it" — *Homicide Trinity.*) He also knows that the only way he can do it is to come up with a murder case. Petty crimes don't interest him. But murder, which brings to focus all the energies of good and evil, calls forth his best energies. In a similar way the Christian ministry is only interested, ultimately, in sin. There are a great many things in the world that are interesting in which the Christian ministry is not interested. It specializes in sin and sinners. The Christian witness feeds back into the church an agenda for action, presenting it with the sin problem and goading the church to do something about it.

Yin/Yang

Wolfe and Goodwin (the yin/yang of Christian ministry) are provided a foil in Inspector Kramer of the New York City police. The

Wolfe/Goodwin combination is a symbol of the Christian ministry as over against Kramer, a type of humanist ministry of good works — trying to do the right thing, well-intentioned, but, in the end, ineffectual. Kramer wants to do what Wolfe/Goodwin want to do, namely, solve the problem of murder: find out what is wrong with the world and do something about it. But the style is completely different. Kramer is all activism. He puts an army of workers to the task of fingerprinting, tailing, gathering evidence, and following clues. He creates a tremendous amount of bustle, has a large budget to work with, and, in routine things, does very well. Wolfe acknowledges that side of his worth, and even depends upon it at times. But invariably Kramer must come to the brownstone for help.

The contrast is clear. The world has good intention, but no mind, no spirit of detection. One can't imagine Kramer spending two minutes, let alone two hours, in the plant rooms. He is *busy*. He *does* things. The church's ministry, on the other hand, *is* — a life of being and becoming. For it knows that "the just shall live by faith."

In the attempt to understand just what Jesus meant in his sentence ". . . other sheep I have, which are not of this fold" (John 10:16), speculation has ranged from identifications as prosaic as first-century Samaritans to fantasy-tinged guesses of inhabitants on other planets or galaxies. It is at least plausible to see it as a reference to the "sheep in Wolfe's clothing" who models the church's ministry for the secularized world of the twentieth century.

140

Kittel among the Coffee Cups

Every Tuesday from 11:30 to 2:00 o'clock a group of Maryland pastors engages in a disciplined exegesis of Scripture as a first step in sermon preparation. Very little is done (usually nothing) regarding actual sermon construction. The focus is on exegesis: a deliberate, sustained effort to read Scripture accurately and theologically.

The host pastor puts on a pot of coffee and each brings his or her own sack lunch. About thirteen men and women from several denominations participate in the group. The group has been in existence now for ten years. While there is some change in personnel there has been surprisingly little variation in style and purpose. It is something like the woodsman and his ax Thomas Mann wrote about. Sometimes the helve would wear out and he would replace it; sometimes the head would wear out and he would replace it; but it was always the same ax.

Dietrich Ritschl in his excellent book on preaching, *The Theology of Proclamation* (John Knox, 1960), encouraged the use of "coworkers" in sermon preparation. The pastor, he said, should get elders, deacons, youth, or any interested persons, to meet with weekly to choose a text and study it together. Their questions, needs, and insights would shape the course of exposition. With that kind of preparation the sermon would not be just the preacher speaking to the people; the split between clergy and laity would be healed and

---

Originally published in *The Princeton Seminary Bulletin*, October 1973.

the sermon be much more an act of the people of God (pastor *and* people) in worship. His thesis was that "the whole church is called to participate in the office of proclamation which is held by Jesus Christ alone . . ." (p. 7). Ritschl, though, did not intend that such a group should constitute the whole of sermon preparation. He identified something more basic: "The primary task is a rediscovery of exegesis . . . exegesis is the preacher's weekly work, or else he is not a faithful minister" (p. 182).

What Ritschl failed to suggest was the use of co-workers in exegesis, the act he identified as "the primary task." It may have been sheer coincidence, for none of the Maryland pastors had read the book at the time, but they were during this same period (the 1960s) developing a "co-worker" approach to the task of exegesis by meeting together weekly and learning how to assist and challenge one another in the exegetical task. Convinced that solid exegesis is necessary, and realizing that they were not doing it on their own, they developed a supportive fellowship to carry it out.

I

A lectionary is used as a basis for the selection of texts. The lections are varied seasonally: Gospel lessons are used in Epiphany and Lent; Epistle lessons in Eastertide; Old Testament lessons in Pentecost; Gospel lessons in Advent and Christmastide; Epistle lessons in Epiphany and Lent; etc.

Each participant in the group assumes leadership in turn. The entire group does preparatory work, but the leader is expected to have worked harder than the rest. He analyzes the passage, does word studies, reviews the history of interpretation of the passage, offers exegetical comments, moving then to possibilities for exposition in the context of congregational needs. The text is explored and debated. The mix of mind provided by the group turns up quantities of exegetical material — some relevant and some irrelevant — accessible for the later work of exposition.

When the group disperses at about two o'clock there are still five days left to put the exegetical work of the group to use in personal sermon preparation.

I once asked the members of the group why they came so

faithfully, for there is a high degree of consistency in attendance. Surprisingly, all the responses mentioned something other than the exegetical work. Yet exegesis is the purpose around which the group is structured. They mentioned personal support, a sense of being part of a professional community, the congeniality of an accepting group which also had integrity so that it was possible to share both personal and parish problems in confidence.

The group does move, with fair frequency, from exegesis to a kind of informal support therapy. A pastor may show up full of anger about something involving church leadership and break up a close exegetical analysis with something quite irrelevant to the discussion. The group easily drops its exegetical work for the next thirty or forty minutes in order to deal with the emotions. Or a pastor suffers personal loss and is pastored by the rest of the group. There is a mixture of professional and personal investment that quite consistently pays off.

II

Still, all agreed that it would not be wise to drop the rigorous concentration on biblical exegesis. An illustration was offered: six persons take a trip in an automobile to a destination, say, a thousand miles away. The purpose of the trip is to arrive at the destination. But during the trip they are pleasantly surprised to find some companions in the car who are delightful conversationalists. The highway is through countryside packed with natural beauty and they find that they are fortunate to have drivers who are not so obsessed with the "goal" that they can't stop and look at an occasional meadow or mountain. All the time the trip is in progress the six are both enjoying the scenery and the persons with whom they are traveling. After arriving at the destination there is an interview in which each of the six is asked what was the most important part of the trip. One would mention a jutting mountain peak, another some flowers that were unusually colorful, another the stimulating conversations of the traveling companions. It would be understandable if no one would answer the question by saying simply and obviously, "getting here was the most important part." Personal impressions and experiences would appear to be the most rewarding aspects of the journey. And yet if they had never arrived at their destination there would be a good bit of irritation and grumbling about the futility of the whole thing. And no one would be likely to repeat it.

The illustration is appropriate to the group: biblical exegesis is, in fact, the destination of the group and everyone takes it seriously. Each is part of the group for that reason. Each takes a turn at the responsibility of being "driver" and makes sure the destination is finally achieved. But that doesn't mean that the car isn't stopped for a few minutes if somebody wants to get out and look around.

Interestingly, the group does not assimilate new members easily. Or, to continue the previous illustration, hitchhikers have a hard time. While there is a surface courtesy extended to the visitor, those who have weathered the entrance rites have noted that it takes several months before they feel at home. Much of this can be explained in terms of strong in-group dynamics. But some of the reason is because the newcomer has a difficult time believing that these pastors are all that serious about *exegesis*. As a "hitchhiker," the visitor doesn't come in sharing the same goal commitment; expectations are at the level of Rotarian bonhomie, support therapy, or "getting sermon ideas." It takes a while to adjust to serious exegesis and many, not feeling such a need or sharing such a purpose, quietly drop out.

The effectiveness and cohesiveness of the group result from a common concept of pastoral ministry which takes preaching seriously, knows that good exegesis is necessary for it, and accepts the need of peers for discipline and motivation. The pastor is put into a position where he or she is most visible to most people when in the pulpit during the Sunday morning hour of worship. And yet there is very little in either the life of the congregation or the life of the culture to affirm the conviction that preaching is, in fact, central to pastoral ministry, and a great deal to say that it is trivial. A group of peers, who take seriously the goal of preaching and the disciplines required to make it strong, over the long haul builds up a reservoir of affirmation.

III

The group has demonstrated that preaching requires community at both ends, in its exegesis and exposition. In exposition the need for a community is self-evident. A solitary preacher in the act of preaching is an absurdity — listeners are a presupposition for preaching. But if a congregation is necessary for exposition a community is no less necessary for exegesis. For as long as there were Christian presuppositions in society, a kind of consensus among the people that preaching was central, there was no problem. While doing the exegetical work in preparing a sermon, the pastor felt supported by the expectations of the people. They nurtured the pastor's exegetical work by their assumptions. The culture was on the side of the exegete. Today's pastor doesn't have that support. Even if there is a large congregation to preach to on Sunday, there is no community support during the week challenging the pastor to think, pray, and prepare for the act of preaching. The world is activist and the culture is secular. The presuppositions of the people are inconsiderate of the exegetical work that makes preaching viable.

A series of articles in a contemporary theological journal was entitled "From Text to Sermon." Several preachers describe the process they go through in making a sermon. In each case the work of exegesis is arduous, exacting, and indispensable. It is remarkable, though, that not one of them refers to any kind of community as part of exegetical work. The work of sermon preparation is conceived in each instance as an individual task — the solitary preacher laboring in the study. But that kind of exegetical work, involving skill with the biblical languages, an acquaintance with the theologians, and the patience to follow sound hermeneutical procedures, is not likely to take place with parish pastors week by week, year in and year out, working by themselves. It does, though, take place among the pastors described here who meet every week with a cup of coffee in one hand and Kittel in the other.

There were in Israel, during the times when Yahwism was threatened with extinction, groups called b*ne hanabim* ("sons of the prophets"). We encounter them at several places in the southern part of the kingdom of Israel in the ninth and tenth centuries B.C. We don't know exactly what they did; we do know that they provided a *milieu* out of which prophecy could be expressed, communities which made it possible for the office of prophet to be sustained among God's people.

Biblical preaching is under a similar threat today. The preacher rides no wave of enthusiastic expectation in preaching. Exegesis, the basic requirement for biblical preaching, is not encouraged. But just because the culture doesn't provide a friendly *milieu* for the hard exegetical work behind preaching is no reason for the pastor to do without it. One can be created simply by inviting some colleagues to lunch. For the cost of a pound of coffee pastors can create a school of exegesis that will feed their self-esteem, encourage their vocations, and provide fresh insights into the most hackneyed text.

Mastering Ceremonies

Most pastoral work takes place in obscurity, deciphering grace in the shadows, blowing on the embers of a hard-used life.

Pastors stay with their people week in and week out, year after year, to proclaim and guide, encourage and instruct as God works his purposes (gloriously, it will eventually turn out) in the meandering and disturbingly inconstant lives that compose our congregations.

This necessarily means taking seriously, and in faith, the dull routines of life. It means witnessing to the transcendent in the fog and rain. It means living hopefully among people who from time to time get flickering glimpses of the Glory but then live through long stretches of unaccountable grayness. This is hard work and not conspicuously glamorous.

But there are frequent interruptions in this work in which the significance blazes all of itself. The bush burns and is not quenched. Our work is done for us, or so it seems, by the event. We do nothing to get these occasions together: no prayer meeting, no strategic planning, no committee work, no altar call. They are given — redolent with meaning and almost always, even among unbelievers, a sense of reverence. These interruptions of the ordinary become occasions of ceremony and celebration: weddings, funerals, baptisms, dedications, anniversaries, graduations, events in which human achievements are honored.

Originally published in *Leadership,* Spring 1987.

Instead of deficiency of meaning, which characterizes so many lives and for which people compensate in frenzy or fantasy, there is an excess: the ecstasy of love, the dignity of death, the wonder of life, the nobility of achievement.

These occasions burst the containers of the everyday and demand amplitude and leisure in which to savor the fullness. No love was ever celebrated enough, no death ever mourned enough, no life adored enough, no achievement honored enough. People set aside time, clear space, call friends, gather families, assemble the community. Almost always, the pastor is invited to preside.

But when we arrive, we are, it seems, hardly needed, and in fact, barely noticed. One of the ironies of pastoral work is that on these occasions when we are placed at the very center of the action, we are perceived by virtually everyone there to be on the margins. No one would say that, of course, but the event that defines the occasion — love, death, birth, accomplishment — also holds everyone's attention. No one inquires of the pastor what meaning there is in this. Meaning is there, overwhelmingly obvious, in the bride and groom, in the casket, in the baby, in the honored guest.

The pastor is, in these settings, what the theater calls "fifth business" — required by the conventions but incidental to the action, yet, in its own way, important on the sidelines. This is odd, and we never quite get used to it, at least I never do. In the everyday obscurities in which we do most of our work, we often have the sense of being genuinely needed. Even when unnoticed, we are usually sure our presence makes a difference, sometimes a critical difference, for we have climbed to the abandoned places, the bereft lives, the "gaps" that Ezekiel wrote of (22:30) and have spoken Christ's word and witnessed Christ's mercy. But in these situations where we are given an honored place at the table, we are peripheral to everyone's attention.

Where Is the Spotlight?

At weddings, love is celebrated. The atmosphere is luminous with adoration. Here are two people at their best, in love, venturing a life of faithfulness with each other. Everyone senses both how difficult and how wonderful it is. Emotions swell into tears and laughter, spill over in giggles, congeal into pomposity. In the high drama that pulls families and friends together for a few moments on the same stage, the pastor is practically invisible, playing a bit part at best. We are geometrically at the center of the ceremony, but every eye is somewhere else.

At funerals, death is dignified. The not-being there of the deceased is set in solemn ritual. Absence during this time is more powerful than presence. Grief, whether expressed torrentially or quietly, is directed into channels of acceptance and gratitude that save it from wasteful spillage into regret and bitterness. The tears that blur perception of the living, including the pastor, clarify appreciation of the dead.

At the baptisms and dedications of infants, the sheer wonder of infant life upstages the entire adult world. The glory that radiates from the newborn draws even bystanders into praise. In the very act of holding an infant in the sacrament of baptism or the service of dedication, the pastor, though many times larger, stronger, and wiser, is shadowed by the brightness of the babe.

At anniversaries and graduations, ground breakings and inaugurations — the various community occasions when achievements are recognized and ventures launched — the collective admiration or anticipation produces a ground swell of emotion that absorbs everything else. Every eye is focused on, and every ear is tuned to, the person honored, the project announced, the task accomplished, the victory won. The pastor, praying in the spotlight and with the amplification system working well, is not in the spotlight and barely heard.

And so it happens that on the occasions in our ministry when we are most visible, out in front giving invocations and benedictions, directing ceremonies and delivering addresses, we are scarcely noticed.

The One Thing Needful

If no one perceives our presence the way we ourselves perceive it — directing operations, running the show — what is going on? We are at the margins during these occasions. No one came to see us. No one came to hear us. We are not at all needed in the way we are accustomed to being needed.

No one needs us to tell the assembled people that things of great moment are taking place. No one needs us to proclaim that this is a unique event, never to be repeated, in which we are all privileged participants. All this is unmistakably obvious and not to be missed by even the stiff-necked and uncircumcised of heart.

So why are we there? We are there to say *God*. We are there for one reason and one reason only: to pray. We are there to focus the brimming, overflowing, cascading energies of joy, sorrow, delight, or appreciation, if only for a moment but for as long as we are able, on God. We are there to say *God* personally, to say his name clearly, distinctly, unapologetically, in prayer. We are there to say it without hemming and hawing, without throat clearing and without shuffling, without propagandizing, proselytizing, or manipulating. We have no other task on these occasions. We are not needed to add to what is there; there is already more than anyone can take in. We are required only to say the Name: Father, Son, Holy Ghost.

All men and women hunger for God. The hunger is masked and misinterpreted in many ways, but it is always there. Everyone is on the verge of crying out "My Lord and my God!" if only circumstances push them past their doubts or defiance, push them out of the dull ache of their routines or their cozy accommodations with mediocrity. On the occasions of ceremony and celebration, there are often many people present who never enter our churches, who do their best to keep God at a distance and never intend to confess Christ as Lord and Savior. These people are not accustomed to being around pastors and not a few of them politely despise us. So it is just as well that we are perceived to be marginal to the occasion. The occasions themselves provide the push toward an awareness of an incredible Grace, a dazzling Design, a defiant Hope, a courageous Faithfulness.

But awareness, while necessary, is not enough. Consciousness raising is only prolegomena. Awareness, as such, quickly trickles into religious sentimentalism or romantic blubbering, or hardens into patriotic hubris or pharisaic snobbery. Our task is to nudge the awareness past these subjectivities into the open and say *God*.

The less we say at these times the better, as long as we say *God*. We cultivate unobtrusiveness so that we do not detract from the sermon being preached by the event. We must do only what we are there to do: pronounce the Name, name the hunger. But it is so easy

150

to get distracted. There is so much going on, so much to see and hear and say. So much emotion. So much, we think, "opportunity." But our assignment is to the "one thing needful," the invisible and quiet center, God.

We do best on these occasions to allow the sermonic advice of the Rebbe Naphtali of Ropshitz: make the introduction concise and the conclusion abrupt — with nothing in between.

Such restraint is not easy. Without being aware of it, we are apt to resent our unaccustomed marginality and push ourselves to the fore, insisting we be noticed and acknowledged. We usually do this through mannerism or tone: stridency, sentimentality, cuteness. We do it, of course, in the name of God, supposing we are upholding the primacy of the one we represent. This is done with distressing regularity by pastors. But such posturing does not give glory to God; it only advertises clerical vanity. We are only hogging the show, and not very successfully, either. For no matter how resplendent we are in robes and "Reverends," we are no match for the persons or events that gave rise to the occasion to which we were asked to come and pray.

In Golden-Calf Country

But there is another reason for keeping to our position on the margins of ceremony and celebration. This is golden-calf country. Religious feeling runs high, but in ways far removed from what was said on Sinai and done on Calvary. While everyone has a hunger for God, deep and insatiable, none of us has any great desire for him. What we really want is to be our own gods and to have whatever other gods that are around help us in this work. This is as true for Christians as for non-Christians.

Our land lies east of Eden, and in this land Self is sovereign. The catechetical instruction we grow up with has most of the questions couched in the first person: How can I make it? How can I maximize my potential? How can I develop my gifts? How can I overcome my handicaps? How can I cut my losses? How can I live happily ever after, increase my longevity, preferably all the way into eternity? Most of the answers to these questions include the suggestion that a little religion along the way wouldn't be a bad idea.

Every event that pulls us out of the ordinariness of our lives puts a little extra spin on these questions. Pastors, since we are usually present at the events and have a reputation of being knowledgeable in matters of religion, are expected to legitimize and encourage the religious dimensions in the aspirations. In our eagerness to please, and forgetful of the penchant for idolatry in the human heart, we too readily leave the unpretentious place of prayer and, with the freely offered emotional and religious jewelry the people bring, fashion a golden calf-god — Romantic Love, Beloved Memory, Innocent Life, Admirable Achievement — and proclaim a "feast to the Lord" (Exod. 32:5). Hardly knowing what we do, we meld the religious aspirations of the people and the religious dynamics of the occasion to try to satisfy one and all.

Calvin saw the human heart as a relentlessly efficient factory for producing idols. People commonly see the pastor as the quality-control engineer in the factory. The moment we accept the position, we defect from our vocation. People want things to work better; they want a life that is more interesting; they want help through a difficult time; they want meaning and significance in their ventures. They want God, in a way, but certainly not a "jealous God," not the "God and Father of our Lord Jesus Christ." Mostly they want to be their own god and stay in control, but have ancillary divine assistance for the hard parts.

There are a thousand ways of being religious without submitting to Christ's lordship, and people are practiced in most of them. They are trained from an early age to be discriminating consumers on their way to higher standards of living. It should be no great surprise when they expect pastors to help them do it. But it is a great apostasy when we go along. "And Moses said to Aaron, 'What did this people do to you that you have brought a great sin upon them?'" (Exod. 32:21). Aaron's excuse is embarrassingly lame, but more than matched by the justifications we make for abandoning prayer in our enthusiasm to make the most of the occasion.

Our Real Work

Our churches and communities assign us ceremonial duties on these occasions, which we must be careful to do well. There are right and wrong ways to act and speak, better and worse ways to prepare for and conduct these ceremonies and celebrations. No detail is insignificant: gesture conveys grace, tone of voice inculcates awe, demeanor defines atmosphere, preparation deepens wonder. We must be diligently skillful in all of this.

But if there is no will to prayer in the pastor — a quietly stubborn and faithful centering in the action and presence of God — we will more than likely end up assisting, however inadvertently, in fashioning one more golden calf of which the world has more than enough. What is absolutely critical is that we attend to God in these occasions: his Word, his Presence. We are there to say the Name, and by saying it guide lament into the depths where Christ descended into hell, not letting it digress into self pity. We are there to say the Name, and by saying it direct celebration into praise of God, not letting it wallow in gossipy chatter.

Our real work in every occasion that requires a priestly presence is prayer. Whether anyone there knows or expects it, we arrive as persons of prayer. The margins are the best location for maintaining that intention. Our vocation is to be responsive to what God is saying at these great moments, and simply be there in that way as salt, as leaven. Most of our prayer will be inaudible to those assembled. We are not praying to inspire them (they are inspired enough already) but to intercede for them. The action of God is intensified in these prayers and continued in the lives of the participants long after the occasion. The ceremonies are over in an hour or so; the prayers continue. This is our real work: holding marriages and deaths, growing lives and lasting achievements before God in a continuing community of prayer.

Teach Us to Care,
and Not to Care

I want to talk about our Christian vocation. After we become Christians, there comes a time, sometimes shortly after, sometimes long after, when we realize that something has happened to us that requires vocational expression.

We come to the place where it is not enough to be saved — we want to share the salvation life. We take on responsibilities inherent in the saved life and find ourselves assigned to positions in our neighborhoods, in our communities, where the ways of God and men and women intersect. People show up at these crossroads lost, discouraged, fatigued, and confused. The task of Christians assigned duty at these intersections is to give direction to people on the way, encourage and exhort them, provide information about the weather and the road conditions and serve up refreshments. It is an incredibly busy place, traffic hurtling this way and that, and there are a lot of accidents, a lot of injuries, and therefore much caring to be done.

It goes without saying that Christians care. Baron von Hugel used to say, "Caring is the greatest thing. Christianity taught us to care." Christians care and if they don't, they don't stay in business very long, or they don't stay credible very long. This word care is at the heart of our community traditions. *Cura animarum,* the cure of

Originally published in *Crux* 28, no. 4 (December 1992).

souls, is a phrase which occurs over and over again in our history. It combines meanings that have gotten pulled apart. If you live in a culture like ours, things fall apart, and this is one of the places where meanings have fallen apart. The word *cura* combines our words cure and care. Cure is nurturing a person towards health; care is being a compassionate companion towards a person in need. Cure requires that we know what we are doing. Care requires that we be involved in what we are doing. Applied knowledge is necessary, but it is not enough. Empathetic concern is necessary, but it is not enough. *Cura* combines both these dimensions, the curing and the caring. But getting this word right in a dictionary definition does not mean that we have got it, does not ensure right practice, which is obvious when we look around us.

There is a huge irony here. We know more about caring than any other generation that has ever lived on the face of the earth. We have more men and women professionally trained in the skills of caring and committed to professional lives of caring, and yet the reports coming back day after day from the field — people telling stories of what has happened to them in the hospital, church, with the social worker, at school — document an alarming deterioration of care on all fronts.

Instead of being cared for, people find themselves abused, exploited, organized, bullied, condescended to, ripped off. There is nothing new in this, of course. People in need of care show up in a weakened condition and are therefore vulnerable, and such vulnerability always seems to arouse the killer instinct in a few individuals, who use their professional roles as cover to indulge themselves in one or several of the deadly sins. For thousands of years now, bitter stories have been told of the rapacity of priests, physicians, nurses, and counselors, as they move smilingly through our communities in their sheep's clothing. Dante and Chaucer, between them, told the stories that pretty much cover the rascality dimensions in our caring work. So there is not much more to be said on those aspects of our care or mis-care and there is nothing much more to be done, except set a few watchdogs to see if we can catch the bad ones at it.

But I want to talk about a different part, a different aspect of the failure or the deterioration of care. It is not quite as epidemic, perhaps, as what we see in our culture at large. I want to talk about something more endemic to the Christian community, something more subtle and far more likely to involve the well-intentioned than the ill-intentioned. In order to do something about it, it is not enough just to get rid of people who do it badly. Something more like a renovation of our imagination is required, a revisioning of who we are and what we are doing when we care. We need to recover the largeness, the health, the essential sacredness of all of our vocational living, that is, this Christian life as it becomes lived out into the community in relationship to others.

Let me take a few steps back and get a running start on this from a different direction. I want to take a text from T. S. Eliot: "Teach us to care, and not to care." It comes from a poem that he wrote after his conversion, "Ash Wednesday." The prayer is imbedded in the experience of conversion to the Christian way. Eliot qualifies as a preacher to be reckoned with in these matters because he both lived through and articulated in prophetic oracle much of what we are dealing with. In the poem that made him famous, "The Wasteland," he showed the chaos and aridity of a world without God, without community, without traditions. It was the world that Nietsche campaigned for under his slogan "God is dead," but Eliot not only articulated this in his poem, he lived it. The wasteland was within him, as well as written out in his poem, "The Wasteland."

On this waterless, treeless ground, he lived day after day, year after year. His marriage consigned him to continual humiliation and guilt. His alienation from family and country cut him off from emotional nurture and an organic sense of place. And then he became a Christian. His conversion was a scandal among the cultured despisers, a betrayal of the new religion of sophisticated despair for which he had written the canonical scriptures. He worked his emerging Christian faith and hope now into new lines of poetry, even more skillfully than he had his un-Christian scepticism and despair. He wrote "The Wasteland" proclaiming the death of God and the emptiness of the world, was converted and wrote "Ash Wednesday," praying this prayer that we are using as a text, and then went on to write the greatest Christian poem of our century, "The Four Quartets," in which he gathers up the shards of experience, these pieces of truth and broken lives, and weaves them in poetry and prayer into a marvellous, powerful poem. He takes the experience of the street corners, where we have been assigned duty, intersections where all these collisions, accidents, wreckages occur among God-ignorant and soul-denying drivers, and he puts together a world which, because it is a world which God has both created and redeemed, is not a wasteland, but a garden, a rose garden, in fact.

A rose garden replaces the wasteland as the metaphor for the world in which we are living. No matter how frequently and learnedly the journalists and scholars report that the world in which we are living is a wasteland, it is not. It is unfortunate that everyone knows Eliot as the poet of "The Wasteland" and very few know him as the poet of the "Four Quartets." They want to skip his conversion; they want to leave all of that out. But if we submit ourselves to his prophetic-poetic imagination — there is a nearly Isaianic power in it — a power capable of shifting our perceptions so they can take in the reality of the world in which we are living.

The primary reason that we are in trouble in our caring, that our lives of caring are in a deteriorated condition, is that we carry them out on the mistaken assumption that caring takes place in a wasteland. If we are going to free ourselves of this mistaken presupposition, we must relearn the world. And since Eliot explored this wasteland as thoroughly as anyone in our century and in the process found his way through prayer and penitence into a garden, he seems to me to be the best of guides and his text a focused prayer: "Teach us to care, and not to care."

So, "Teach us to care." We begin with a realization of our poverty: We do not know how to care. What we have been prayerlessly engaged in and glibly calling care, is not care. It is pity, it is sentimentality, it is do-goodism, it is ecclesiastical colonialism, it is religious imperialism. Caring, noble and commendable as it seems, is initiated by a condition that can, and often does, twist it into something ugly and destructive. That condition is need. A child cries out, a woman weeps, a man curses, a youth, as we say, "acts out." More often than not, one of us — a Christian who has discovered a vocation to care, either professionally or amateurly, it does not matter — is there. We help. So far, so good. The child's pain, the woman's tears, the man's anger, the youth's confusion are all real enough and need to be responded to. If someone is there and willing to care it is sheer blessing.

But there is another element in this scenario that is frequently missed and when missed, silently and invisibly squeezes all the cure out of care. The element is sin. The child with a bruised knee is a

157

sinner. The woman cursing her abuser is a sinner. The man lamenting his failed vocation is a sinner. The youth stumbling over the hypocrisies of society is a sinner. The condition that calls us into the action of caring, the condition of need, disarms us by its apparent innocence, since the cry, the curse, the tears, and the confusion are mostly uncalculated and spontaneous.

The urgency and innocence of the care-evoking situation obscures an element of the condition that we must not leave in obscurity and that is this: We human beings learn early and quickly to acquire expertise in using our plight, whatever it is, to get those around us to do far more than get us through or over the conditions. We learn how to use the conditions of need as leverage in getting our own way. Not our health, not our maturity, not our peace, not justice, not our salvation, but our way, our willful way. This impulse to make oneself the center, to shrewdly, or bullyingly manipulate things and people to the service of self is what we, at least in our theology textbooks, call sin. *Incurvatus in se* was Augustine's phrase for it, life curved in upon itself.

We are created to be open. To be open to God, to open out towards our neighbors. We can only be whole and healthy in so far as we do this. When we are in need, when first-hand experience documents our inability to be whole beings on our own, the first thing that can happen is that we will become more authentically human. Need rips gashes in our self-containment and opens us to the neighbor. Need blows holes in our roofed-in self-sufficiency and opens us to God. But not necessarily.

For the self-willed self does not give up easily. It makes a persistent and determined stand to use these need-generated openings not to move out, but to pull whoever is trying to help it, into its service, put the neighbors to its use. If unwary, the person providing care is co-opted into feeding selfishness, which is to say, sin.

There is a great irony here — that so much of our caring nurtures sin. The only group of people in our society who show any sign of acknowledging this is parents of young children.

Parents know that there is nothing less innocent than childhood. After a few weeks, months at the most, of responding unquestioningly to every sign of need, mothers and fathers start getting smart, start filtering the requests, cross-examining the wails. If they don't, they realize in a few years, and with a sense of dismay, that it might be too late to do anything about it, because as they have been bandaging knees, wiping away tears, buying designer jeans, running interference for break-away emotions, they have at the same time been feeding pride, nourishing greed, fueling lust, and cultivating envy.

But outside the circumstances of child rearing, there does not seem to be much awareness of this deviousness. The moment any one of us says, "Help me!" and discovers how quickly others are in attendance on us, making us the center and confirming our importance, a vast field for the exercise of sin — that is, getting our own godless and neighborless way — opens up. It is really quite incredible the amount of illness, unhappiness, trouble, and pain that is actually chosen, because it is such an effective way of being in control, of being important, of exercising God-like prerogatives, of being recognised as significant, without entering the strenuous apprenticeship of becoming truly human, which always requires learning the love of God, practising love of the neighbor.

The reason the awareness of this deviousness is so dim among us is that as a wasteland society, we do not take into account the reality of sin. There is no sin in the wasteland. There is no God in the wasteland. There is deprivation, or poverty, or bad luck, but there is no sin. Christians have less excuse than others in being naive or ignorant about sin since we go through life with a book in our pocket, or at least within reach, that is both insistent and convincing on the subject. But no one has much of an excuse.

Sin is, as G. K. Chesterton once pointed out, the only major Christian doctrine that can be verified empirically. But because of this failure to take with full seriousness the nature and presence of sin, a great deal of caring is simply collaboration in selfishness, in self-pity, in self-destruction, in self-indulgence — all the seemingly endless hyphenations that the self is able to engineer. We wake up one morning and realize that we have poured ourselves out for these needy people and they are not getting any better. And we know that something is wrong in our caring, so we pray: "Teach us to care. I've been trying to care in a wasteland, and I've been doing it all wrong. I need to learn it all over again. Teach us to care."

As Christians who begin to sense a vocation, a reaching out, knowing that this life matters now to other people, the most central thing that we are doing is to teach them to pray. This is our genius as Christians, this access to God, this life of intimacy with God. This is why we are Christians, to live in this healed, loved way. If we do not use the occasions of need, of caring, as a school for prayer, we abdicate our most central concern. None of us can do this all by ourselves; caring is a community act, a lot of people are involved.

Caring is complex and we need all the help we can get, but the Christian presence needs to be a praying presence, and when we pray "Teach us to care," the reports that start coming back, the lesson plans that start coming back, all have to do basically with prayer. This wound of the self that calls for help, this self that is closed in upon itself and now is open just a little bit, is an opening through which we can listen to and answer God. For the wound is more than a wound. It is access to the outside, to God, to others. The Christians standing at the intersection where all this carnage is going on are the ones who know that this wound is more than a wound, it is access. The wound must not be bandaged over as fast as possible; it is there to be a listening post, a chance to exit the small confines of a self-defined world and enter the spaciousness of a God-defined world.

I do not mean simply praying for people, although that is involved. I mean teaching them to pray, helping them to listen to what God is saying, helping them to form an adequate response. Teaching people to pray is teaching them to treat all the occasions of their lives as altars on which they receive his gifts. Teaching people to pray is teaching them that God is the one with whom they have to deal, not just ultimately, and not just generally, but now and in detail.

Teaching people to pray is not especially difficult work — anyone of us can do it, using a few psalms and the Lord's Prayer — but it is difficult to stick with it, for we are constantly interrupted with urgent demands from family and friends to, as they say, "do something." And it is difficult to get the person who has asked for help to stick with it because there are a lot of other people in the intersection, offering short-cut approaches for providing care, short-cutting God and promising far quicker results. It is difficult for all of us to stick it out, for often in the confusion and noises of wasteland traffic, it is hard to stay convinced that sin and God make that much difference.

But difficult or not, this is our calling. Whatever else we are doing is with our hands, with our feet, with our minds — bandaging, directing, giving. This is the core of what we are doing, getting them in touch with God, with neighbor, receiving love, grace. If we do not use these occasions of need to teach people to pray, we cave in to the pressures of care in which there is no cure.

Sometimes one incident becomes pivotal in your life to wake you up to these things. For me it was Brenda. She was in the hospital; I was her pastor. I went to see her. She was a social worker, mother of two sons, wife, faithful in her worship. I had been her pastor for five or six years. I asked her what brought her to the hospital. Well, she was in for tests, things were not going right, doctors could not figure out what was going wrong. I prayed a perfunctory prayer and left.

I came back a few days later and asked her what had happened and she said that the tests didn't show anything and the doctors thought she ought to see a psychiatrist, they thought something other than her body was causing the trouble. She said, "I think they're probably right." Following my usual script, I would ordinarily have said, "Brenda, would you like to talk to me about it?" Along with many pastors of my generation — this was the sixties, the decade of counseling and psychology — I had received good training, found I had an aptitude for it, and loved the dynamics of the therapeutic encounter.

There were no psychiatrists or therapists in our community. I was soon counseling not only my parishioners, but many of their friends as well. It was good work. I found I liked being valued by the community in ways I never was as a mere pastor. But the work was also exhausting. At that moment beside Brenda's bed, I did not think I could handle one more set of complex emotions. I knew she expected me to express my care for her by being her counselor, but at that moment I was just too tired, and I ducked. Instead of offering myself as a counselor to her, I used prayer as an escape hatch and got out.

Then I began feeling guilty. I had let her down. I did not care. After a couple of weeks, my guilt got the better of me and I called her and said, "Brenda, this is Pastor Peterson." We exchanged a few commonplaces and then I said, "Is there anything I can do for you?" There was a fairly long pause that made me really nervous. Then she said, "Yes, there is. I've been thinking a lot about it. Would you teach me to pray?"

That was the last thing I expected. I had been a pastor at this time for seven years, and it was the first time anyone had asked me to teach them to pray. I had expected to do this when I became a pastor, but when no one seemed interested, at least not to the point of asking, I began to respond to what they were asking. They were asking me to help them with their marriages, their kids, their emotions, their parents, questions about the Bible, and so I did. I was caring for them on the terms that they set for me. God was not ignored in the work; I offered prayers for help and healing, but the problems of these people, the needs for which they requested help, needs which I often helped them identify, became the agenda. Need-oriented, problem-driven, solution-expectant. And I was usually able to work God in somewhere or other. But more often than not, I was entering and accepting the world as a wasteland, a world where need, not God, was sovereign, and had become an unwitting collaborator in reinforcing their self-centered worlds, amnesiac on the nature of sin. Since they were not sinning conspicuously — stealing, committing adultery, robbing the bank — I dropped my guard.

Brenda's request, "Would you teach me to pray?", returned me to the country of my origins; God-oriented, mystery-attentive, obedience-ready. My central task among these people was not to help them solve their problems, but to help them to see how their problems could help solve them, serve as stimulus and goad to embrace the mystery of who they were as human beings, and then offer to be companion to them and teach them the language of this world in which we are God-created, Christ-invaded, Spirit-moved, the language of prayer.

I have given you a story from my own life, but pastors have no corner on this. This is the Christian vocation; this is what Christians do. The prayer in our text is "Teach us to care." Brenda asked me to teach her to pray, and by doing so taught me to care. When care is restored to our lives in its true and proper context, the presence and the action of God, our caring then becomes an extension of our prayer, instead of just being tacked on to our caring. When this happens, our caring is detached from the controlling context of sin-twisted needs, self-serving ploys, this cultural-spiritual wasteland that Eliot describes so well, the wasteland that drains all the cure out of care.

And, "Teach us not to care."

The prayer "Teach us to care" is balanced by the prayer "Teach us not to care." In the business of caring there is something we need to learn how to do, but there is something also that we need to learn not to do. What we learn not to do is just as important as what we learn to do. A major contributing cause to this deterioration of care that we are all part of is the widespread refusal to learn not to care by accepting limits and respecting boundaries.

All through the traditions of caring (this is not only in Western, but also Eastern cultures) there are frequent counsels to reticence, to detachment, to holding back, to letting go. "Don't do too much." But our times do not honor such counsel. We have so much knowledge to apply and so much technology with which to apply it, that not to use it, not to exploit it to the hilt, is unthinkable. We are hell-bent on ploughing full speed ahead and damn the torpedoes. We are so sure that a little more knowledge will make us more effective, that a breakthrough in technology will usher in a new level of competence, that a larger budget will provide the resources for success, that to not do something when it is possible to do anything at all, escapes our imagination.

But the reason for the counsel to reticence is that the act of caring, responding to a person in need, takes place in an environment that is already surging with life, prodigal with energy, vitality, beauty. This life, creation in all of its aspects, is exceedingly complex and far past the capacity of our understanding. You realize that we are far more ignorant of the world than we are knowledgeable of it. Despite all of our explorations and discoveries, all this information that is before us, all this understanding of how it works, there is still far more that we do not know than what we do know. And of all the parts of the creation we have come across in our travels, this part we call human is the most marvelous, most complex, most mysterious.

We know a lot about our bodies, our minds, our emotions, our souls, digestive systems, guilt and forgiveness, kidney functions, love, faith, moral strength, schizophrenia, growth hormones, growing in Christ, fetal development, character formation, synapses in the brain, lesions in the heart, but when we stand before the human being, any human being, most of what is taking place is beyond us. And for that reason, we had better not start poking around in what we do not understand, lest we destroy something precious. There is much that is wrong in the world and in the people around us, but there is far more that is right. Everything wrong takes place in an environment that is incredibly, dazzlingly alive, stunningly beautiful.

The primary act of the Christian in all of this is to worship. When you and I go to church on Sunday morning and hear someone say to us, "Let us worship God," we stop in our tracks: sit down, stand or kneel, and shut up for an hour, except to sing a few hymns, or say "Amen." We are worshiping, becoming aware of what we have been in all the time, but were too busy or distracted to notice.

No one as far as I know has ever commented on the incalculable good that is done every week by thousands and thousands of pastors calling people into churches and saying, "Let us worship God," and getting people off the streets for an hour. Crime rates plummet, accidents decrease, pollution diminishes just because we quit caring for an hour. We are not doing anything, we are not in charge. That is most significant in worship: our eyes open, our mouths drop, we just look and listen. We are not exactly catatonic, we say, "Praise God" or "Thank you," sing a little. But there is no usefulness to any of it, we are not doing anything. As William James once said, "There's no cash value to it." We are not caring, we are responding to Eliot's prayer, "Teach us not to care."

So we enter places of worship from time to time, weekly usually, places of not doing, not saying, not caring, so that we can see what is going on, hear what is being said. The most important thing going on right now is what God is doing. We get in the way, we talk too much. The most important thing being said right now is something God is saying, marvelous things are being done and said right now. Look. Listen.

We Christians are scattered through the society, standing on street corners, intersections, all over the place. We are the ones who have a chance to say, "Oh, look. Listen to that." If we just barge in and start doing something or other, we only contribute to the noise, the frenetic activity. What God has done and is doing is far more significant than anything you or anyone else will ever do. What God has spoken and is speaking is far more important than anything you or anyone else will ever say.

If we are not constantly brought to an awareness of this huge God-dimension, trained in attentiveness to this immense God-presence, we will act and speak out of context, as if we are in a wasteland. But there is no wasteland. We are in a garden, a rose garden. No matter how purely motivated we are, we will finally do more damage than good if we do not operate in response to God rather than the environment. We live on holy ground. We inhabit sacred space. This holy ground is subject to incredible violations. This sacred space suffers constant sacrilege. But no matter. The holiness is there, the sacredness is there. If our lives, and in this case, our caring lives, are shaped in response to the violations, to the sacrilege, and not out of the holy, our lives are shaped wrongly. We are responding to the wrong environment, a false environment, a wasteland environment. We are called to be gardeners, not garbage collectors.

A number of years ago, my wife and our three children were in Yellowstone National Park, the first of our national parks. I often think of our parks as sanctuaries, parallel to our churches. The churches are sanctuaries for the cross, the covenant, salvation. The parks are sanctuaries for the creation. They are places for protecting creation from exploitation, places we can look on the earth and the fullness thereof, be in adoration of the Creator and in awe of his creation. Yellowstone was the first place on this continent to be set apart in this way.

I have always felt a personal involvement in the formation of this park because Cornelius Hedges, a Montana lawyer, was in on it. It was his idea, in fact. He got Teddy Roosevelt to come out and see the country, camped with him on a little triangle of land, a little island between the Fire Hole and the Madison Rivers, and convinced Roosevelt that this had to be done, that it was important to preserve its wildness and naturalness against chainsaws and bulldozers. As a schoolboy in Montana, I attended Cornelius Hedges School. Through the years with this story in my imagination, I took on the persona of Cornelius Hedges, who took great pride in forming this creation sanctuary.

As my family and I were walking in a mountain meadow in Yellowstone Park, there was a little boy of four or five about 30 yards out in the meadow picking fringed gentians — exquisite alpine flowers. Now you know that it is against the rules to pick flowers in national parks. My children knew this; they had learned the Sierra Club motto: "take nothing but pictures, leave nothing but footprints." They knew that verse as well as John 3:16 (one of them told me a few years ago that he used to think it was from Scripture). So here is this little kid out in the meadow, picking the flowers; I see him and I'm outraged — sacrilege taking place on holy ground. I yell at him, "DON'T PICK THE FLOWERS." He just stood, wide-eyed, innocent — and terrified. He dropped the flowers and started crying.

You can imagine what happened next. My wife and children, my children especially, were all over me. "Daddy, what you did was far worse than what he did! He was just picking a few flowers and you yelled, you scared him. You ruined him. He is probably going to have to go for counseling when he's forty years old." My children were right. You cannot yell people into holiness. You cannot terrify people into the sacred. My yelling was a far worse violation of the holy place than his picking a few flowers. Later I had plenty of opportunity to reflect on this, reminded, as I frequently was, by my children.

I do that a lot, bluster and yell on behalf of God's holy presence, instead of taking off my shoes myself, kneeling on the holy ground, and inviting whoever happens to be around to join with me. Plato insisted that all authentic philosophy — and we can extrapolate to theology — has its beginning in a sense of wonder. Existence is vastly beautiful, wonderfully good, majestically true. We can only get off on the right foot by beginning in adoration. All authentic anything has its beginning in a sense of wonder. And caring must begin with a sense of adoration and wonder. If we do not begin in adoration, we begin too small. If we begin by formulating a problem, by iden-tifying a need, by tackling a necessary job, by launching a program, we reduce the reality that is before us to what we can do or get others to do.

If we measure the world and the people in it according to our knowledge of it, we leave out most of the data. The most significant data is the God-data. How can we hope to do anything that is healing and whole and blessed if we are out of touch with our environment, unaware of the real world?

So in embarking on our tasks of caring for these troubled souls, these sick bodies, these disordered communities, we need frequent interruptions, someone to say, "Let us worship God" or some equiv-alent of that, calling us to attention before the environment as it really is, the environment we have ignored in our hurry to get across the street while the light was still green. We begin paying attention to the God-created dimensions in the people around us that we missed in our determination to make them socially acceptable.

"Lord teach us not to care so we can see and hear what you and some of your servants are doing and caring." There are no holy places in the wasteland. That's a given. If we think we are caring in a wasteland, we are going to go at it with everything we've got, all the time. There is nothing to wonder about. In a wasteland anything we do is an improvement on what is there. But if we are in a rose garden, this garden created by God, no matter how dishevelled it is, no matter if beer cans have been thrown into the rose bushes, it is still a rose garden, and there is more to look at than will ever exhaust our wonder and our adoration.

So as Eliot leads us through prayer and poetry into the rhythms of God's creation, a redeemed creation, a creation which is always being shaped by these powers of the cross and a sacrificed Christ working his will in the world, we begin to look around. We do not quit doing things, but we are not so quick to do them on our old presuppositions. God is gracious and gives us responsible tasks to carry out in the garden. But if we lose our sense of the holy, if we lose perception of the sacred, we will only contribute to the deterioration of care. The sad thing, the alarming thing, is this vast deterioration of care which takes place in Christian communities. We have lost the sense of prayer, lost the sense of the sacred. We have gone to work with the best wills in the world, but ignorant of our environment; we think we are working in a wasteland when we are working in a rose garden. Instead of making things better, we are trampling the roses and making things worse.

Teach us to care, teach us to use all these occasions of need that are the agenda of our work as access to God, as access to neighbor. Teach us to care by teaching us to pray, to pray so that human need becomes the occasion for entering into and embracing the presence and action of God in this life. Teach us to care by teaching us to pray so that those with whom we work are not less human through our caring but become more human. Teach us to care so that we do not become collaborators in self-centeredness, but rather companions in God-exploration. Teach us to use each act of caring as an act of praying so that this person in the act of being cared for experiences dignity instead of condescension, realizes the glory of being in on the salvation, and blessing and healing of God, and not driven further into neurosis and the wasteland of self.

And, not to care. Teach us to be reverential in all these occasions of need that are the agenda of our work, aware that you were long beforehand with these people, creating and loving, saving and wooing them. Teach us the humility of not caring, so that we do not use anyone's need as a workshop to cobble together makeshift, messianic work that inflates our importance and indispensability. Teach us to be in wonder and adoration before the beauties of creation and the glories of salvation, especially as they come to us in these humans who have come to think of themselves as violated and degraded and rejected. Teach us the reticence and restraint of not caring, so that in our eagerness to do good, we not ignorantly interfere in your caring. Teach us not to care so that we have time and energy and space to realize that all our work is done on holy ground and in your holy name, that people and communities in need are not a wasteland where we feverishly and faithlessly set up shop, but a garden, a rose garden in which we work contemplatively.

Suffer us not to mock ourselves with falsehood.

Teach us to care and not to care.

Teach us to sit still, even among these rocks. Amen.

Unexpected Allies

Pastoral work is demanding, and I need lots of help. Fortunately, a lot is offered, much of it in the form of books. Theologians and counselors, scholars and consultants write for me. I am informed by their knowledge, guided by their counsel.

But I get my best help from writers who did not set out to help me. My most valued allies in ministry are those who write novels and poems. I think I know why. The act of creation is at the heart of life, whether in biology or in faith.

Pastors wake up in the middle of this creative work every morning. We also wake up amid many uncreative, behind-the-scenes responsibilities. These routines are the most visible parts of my life. I prepare sermons, visit people, administer programs.

Most books directed my way try to help me in these visible areas. But I also need help in the invisible parts — the creative center. Creation and re-creation — making lives to the glory of God — is the core of the gospel, of the Spirit's work, of pastoral work.

Often, however, this center is moved to the periphery, and "creative" means nothing more than "interesting" or "innovative." Who is there to keep me aware of the very nature of creation, the work that goes into it, the way it feels?

My allies are the novelists and poets, writers who are not *telling* me something, but *making* something.

Originally published in *Christianity Today,* February 1, 1985.

*　　*　　*

Novelists take the raw data of existence and make a world of meaning. I am in the story-making business, too. God is drawing the people around me into the plot of salvation; every word, gesture, and action has a significant place in the story. Being involved in the creation of reality like this takes endless patience and attentiveness, and I am forever taking shortcuts. Instead of assisting in the development of a character, I hurriedly categorize: active or inactive, saved or unsaved, disciple or backslider, key leader or dependable follower, leadership material or pew fodder. Instead of seeing each person in my life as unique, a splendid never-to-be-duplicated story of grace, unprecedented in the particular ways grace and sin are in dramatic tension, I slap on a label so I can efficiently get through my routines. Once the label is in place I don't have to *look* at him and her any more; I know how to *use* them.

Then I read Fyodor Dostoevsky, William Faulkner, Anne Tyler, or Walker Percy and see how an artist committed to creative work approaches the most ordinary and least promising human: the unexpected depths in the ordinary, the capacities for good and evil in the apparently conventional!

Rebuked in my shallow efficiency, I return to the person that I in disgust or boredom had dismissed from my prayers and preaching, ready again to be witness and servant in the messy, unmanageable world of the Spirit's creation.

*　　*　　*

Poets are caretakers of language, the shepherds of words, keeping them from harm, exploitation, misuse. Words not only mean something; they *are* something, each with a sound and rhythm all its own.

Poets are not primarily trying to tell us, or get us, to do something. By attending to words with playful discipline (or disciplined playfulness), they draw us into deeper respect both for words and the reality they set before us.

I also am in the word business. I preach, I teach, I counsel using words. People often pay particular attention on the chance that God may be using my words to speak to them. I have a responsibility to use words accurately and well. But it isn't easy. I live in a world where words are used carelessly by some, cunningly by others.

It is easy to say whatever comes to mind, my role as pastor compensating for my inane speech. It is easy to say what either flatters or manipulates and so acquire power over others. In subtle ways, being a pastor subjects my words to corruption. That is why I frequently spend a few hours with a poet friend — Gerard Manley Hopkins or George Herbert, Emily Dickenson or Luci Shaw — people who care about words, are honest with them, respect and honor their sheer overwhelming power. I leave such meetings less careless, my reverence for words and the Word restored.

How significant that the biblical prophets and psalmists were poets. It is a continuing curiosity that so many pastors, whose work integrates the prophetic and psalmic (preaching and praying), are indifferent to poets.

I don't read novels to get sermon illustrations. I don't read poems for quotable lines. I read them to feel the act of creation, to associate with those doing with words what the Spirit is doing with lives.

This world of making is the pastor's essential home. But it is a difficult and sometimes lonely habitation. There is so much more backslapping camaraderie among the explainers and exhorters.

I am saddened when friends tell me, "I'm swamped with 'must' reading; I don't have time for novels or poetry." What they are saying is that they choose to attend to the routines and not to the creative center.

There is no "must" reading; we choose what we read. What is not fed does not grow; what is not supported does not stand; what is not nurtured does not develop. Artists are not the only people who keep us open and involved in this essential but easily slighted center of creation, but they are too valuable to be slighted.

Novelists, Pastors, and Poets

Anyone of us, waking up in the morning and finding ourselves included in that part of the creation called human, sooner or later finds ourselves dealing with language, with words. We are the only creatures in this incredible, vast creation doing this. Language is unique to us human beings. Turnips complete a fairly complex and useful life cycle without the use of words. Roses grace the world with an extraordinary beauty and fragrance without uttering a word. Dogs satisfy tens of thousands of us with faithful and delightful companionship without a word. Birds sing a most exquisite music to our ears, lifting our spirits, giving us happiness, all without the capability of words. It is quite impressive really, what goes on around us without words: ocean tides, mountain heights, stormy weather, turning constellations, genetic codes, bird migrations — most, in fact, of what we see and hear around us, a great deal of it incredibly complex, but without language, wordless. And we, we human beings, have words. We can use language. We are the only ones in this stunning kaleidoscopic array of geology and biology and astronomy to use words. We share a great deal with the rest of creation. We have much in common with everything around us, the dirt beneath our feet, the animals around us, the stars above us, and we recognize links in this family identity. But when it comes down to understanding our humanity, who we are in this vast scheme of things, we find ourselves attending

Originally published in *Crux* 26, no. 4 (December 1990).

to language, the fact that we speak words, and what happens to us when we do.

When a person becomes a Christian, interest in language doubles because not only do we use words, but we find that God uses words as well. The one who reveals God to us is named *Word.* This human nature of ours with its mysterious and unique capacity for language is paralleled in the nature of God. God speaks. In the term we use to refer to our interest in God, *theology,* the two words are set along side each other and then combined; *theos* meaning God and *logos* meaning word. *Theos* is capable of *logos. Logos* is characteristic of *theos.* Then the significance of this parallel hits us: We are capable of speech; God reveals himself in speech. In the complete revelation of God, the Word became flesh. We who are already flesh become words, speak words, and as we do, we become human. Language is what we have in common. In the very act of speaking, regardless of the words we use, we are in on something that is divine. One consequence of this is that those of us who speak to and with Christians have a more than ordinary commitment in the uses of language. Words are a precious gift; language is a marvelous thing. We require, and then acquire, reverence before the sheer fact of language. "God himself is with us, let us now adore him and with awe appear before him. God is in his temple, all within keep silence and bow before him with reverence."

It is a particular cause for dismay when those who use language violate it. Blasphemy, the use of language to defile, has always been abhorrent to lovers of words and the Word. Lies, the use of language to conceal or manipulate rather than to reveal and free are known to be as dangerous to the human condition as termites to a barn. If we let it go the foundations are destroyed and the structure crumbles. Gossip and cliché are also a violation of language. Words used carelessly, impersonally, and thoughtlessly are aspects of sacrilege. We live in a wind tunnel of gossip and cliché these days, so Christians, especially Christians who use words in leadership need to take special care to reverence language and use it accurately.

One obvious way to maintain reverence and accuracy is to keep company with the masters of language: the novelists and the poets. I want to talk about one novelist and one poet who have kept the language true and supple and fresh for me. The novelist is James Joyce and the poet is Jeremiah.

Novelist

The first book on pastoral care that meant anything to me personally or vocationally was *Ulysses,* James Joyce's novel. Two-thirds of the way through this meander of a narrative, I saw what I could be doing, should be doing, in my rounds as a pastor going into homes, going into hospitals, meeting people, talking with them on the street. Before *Ulysses,* I never looked on this part of my world as particularly creative. I knew that it was important and I accepted that it had to be carried out, whether I felt like it or not, but except for occasional epiphanies, it was not very interesting. Nearly everything else I did — preaching, praying, writing, teaching, administering — put far greater demands on my mind and imagination and spirit, pulled the best out of me and pushed me to my limits. But making small talk with someone around the water fountain, calling on a lonely woman, visiting a man in the hospital, sitting with the dying — these were more or less routine functions that I just did. I did them satisfactorily with a modest investment of tact, compassion, and faithfulness. Faithfulness was the big thing, just showing up.

So it was, until I read *Ulysses.* At about page 611 an earthquake opened a fissure at my feet and all my assumptions of ordinariness dropped into it. All those routines of pastoral care suddenly were no longer routines.

Leopold Bloom, the Ulysses of James Joyce's story, was a very ordinary man. There was no detail in his life that was distinguished, unless it was his monotone ordinariness. Dublin, the town where he lived, was a very ordinary town with nothing in it to set it off, unless it was its depressing ordinariness. A colorless, undistinguished human being in this colorless, undistinguished town provides the contents of the novel. James Joyce narrates a single day in the life of the Dublin Jew, Leopold Bloom. Detail by detail, Joyce takes us through a single day in his life, a day in which nothing of note happens. But, as the details accumulate, observed with such acute and imaginative (pastoral!) care the realization begins to develop that, common as they are, these details are all uniquely human. Flickers of recognition signal memories of the old myth, Homer's grand telling of the adventure of the Greek *Ulysses,* as he travelled all the country of experience and possibility and finally found himself home.

I woke up. Joyce woke me up to the infinity of meaning within the limitations of the ordinary person on an ordinary day. Leopold Bloom, buying and selling, talking and listening, eating and defecating, praying and blaspheming, is mythic in the grand manner. The twenty-year voyage from Troy to Ithaca that Homer's Ulysses took is repeated every twenty-four hours in anyone's life if we only have eyes and ears for it.

Now I knew my world; *this* is the pastor's work. I wanted to be able to look at each person in my parish with the same imagination, insight, comprehensiveness with which Joyce looked at Leopold Bloom. The story line is different, for the story being worked out before my eyes, if I can only stay awake long enough to see it, is not the Greek story of Ulysses, but the gospel story of Jesus. The means, of course, are different. Joyce was a writer using a pencil, and I am a pastor practicing prayer, but we are doing the same thing: seeing the marvelous interlacing of history, sexuality, religion, culture, and place in a particular person, on a particular day.

I saw now that I had two sets of stories to get straight. I already knew the gospel story pretty well. I was a preacher, a proclaimer of the message. I had learned the original languages of the story, been immersed by my education in its long development, and taught how to translate it into the present. I was steeped in the theology that kept my mind sane and honest in the story, and conversant in the history that gave perspective proportion. In the pulpit and behind the lectern, I read and told this story week after week after week. I loved doing this, loved reading and pondering and preaching these gospel stories, making them accessible to people, people in different cultures, living in different weather, under different politics. This is glorious work, privileged work. This is the work that I expected to do when I became a pastor, and for which I was adequately trained.

But this other set of stories, these stories of Leopold Bloom and Buck Mulligan, Jack Tyndale, Mary Vaughn, Nancy Lion, Bruce Mac-Intosh, Olaf Odegaard, Abigail Davidson — I had to get these straight, too. The Jesus story was being reworked and re-experienced in each of these people in this town, this day. And I was here, to see it take shape, helping it to take shape, listening to the sentences form, observing the actions, discerning character and plot. I determined to be as exegetically serious when I was listening to Eric Matthews in Koine American as I was when reading St. Matthew in Koine Greek.

175

I wanted to see the Jesus story in each person in my congregation in just as much local detail and raw experience as James Joyce did with *Ulysses* in Leopold Bloom and his Dublin friends and neighbors.

The Jesuit poet, Gerard Manley Hopkins, gave me a text for my work,

> For Christ plays in ten thousand places,
> Lovely in eyes, lovely in limbs not his
> To the Father, through the features of men's faces.

From that moment until now, visits to homes and to hospitals, conversations on the street, calls on the lonely, sitting with the dying, have been primary occasions for getting time for this work, access to these stories. A lot more than tact, compassion, and faithfulness are required now. There is a lot more than just "showing up." I find myself listening for nuances, making connections, remembering, anticipating, watching how the verbs work ("is that an imperfect, an aorist, a perfect?"), watching for signs of atonement, reconciliation ("is that justification that is being worked on right now?"), sanctification. I am sitting before these people as Joyce sat before his typewriter, watching a story come into existence.

Confinement by illness or weakness to a single room, from which most of the traffic of the world is excluded and to which most of the fashion of the world is indifferent, provides limits that encourage concentration and observation. While some people call that boring, most writers try to put themselves in a boring environment so they can concentrate on what is within. Too much action outside your window will not do, you will never get anything written. These sick rooms, these rooms of the dying, restrict our attention so that we pay attention to what is right there before us.

Over the course of years, most of the families in a pastor's congregation have illness or confinement or death of some kind or another. Since my Joycean conversion, I no longer consider my visits at these times duties of pastoral care, but rather, occasions for original research on the stories being shaped in their lives by the living Christ — stories in which I sometimes get to put a sentence, or maybe a period, or sometimes only a semi-colon. I go to these appointments with the same diligence and curiosity that I bring to a page of Isaiah's oracles, or to a tangled argument in St. Paul.

There is a wonderful text for this work in St. Mark's Gospel, "He is risen . . . he is going before you to Galilee, there you will see him as he told you" (Mark 16:6, 7). I have acquired the habit of quoting this silently, previous to any visit or any encounter. "He is risen . . . he is going before you into Galilee, there you will see him as he told you." Every time I show up, I have been anticipated; the risen Christ got there ahead of me. What is he doing? What is he saying? What is going on? I enter a room now not wondering what I am going to do or say, but what the risen Christ has already done, already said. I come in on a story that is in progress, something that is resurrection, already going on. Sometimes I can clarify a word, sharpen a feeling, help recover an essential piece of memory, but always dealing with what the risen Christ has already set in motion, already brought into being.

When we listen to writers talk about their writing, what we hear them saying is that they do not so much make up a story as have it come to them. They write things they never knew, or at least never "knew" that they knew. Images and plots enter their awareness, an arrival from somewhere else. They become writers, real writers, when they cultivate openness to these mysterious comings and goings. They become listeners to these presences. This is the grounding for all creative work.

It is also the grounding for spirituality. We use words to bring into awareness, to provide images and vocabulary to what the risen Christ is doing in these lives. To how many Leopold Blooms in Dublin did James Joyce give back their Ulysses story? To how many people in my congregation can I bring to awareness of their Jesus story?

Pastor

Words are the means by which the gospel is proclaimed and the stories told. Not all words tell stories that proclaim the gospel, but they can. Our awareness that all language derives from the Word now pushes us into awareness that all words can return to the Word and bear witness to it. But words often get severed from the Word. Novelists have been important teachers in showing me, a pastor, how to reconnect them, making a story, pulling them out of the chaos of commercial advertising, of gossip and cliché, creating something that has integrity and wholeness to it, teaching a gospel story, a Jesus story.

In a kind of rough-and-ready sorting out, words can be put into two piles: words used for communication, and words used for communion. Words for communion are the words used to tell stories, to make love, nurture intimacies, develop trust. Words used for communication are used to buy stocks, sell cauliflower, direct traffic, teach algebra. Both piles of words are necessary, but words for communion are the pastor's specialty. If we approach people as masters of communication, we are as out of place as a whore at a wedding. We are not here to sell intimacy. We are here to be intimate. For that we use words of holy communion.

When my daughter Karen was young, I often took her with me when I visited nursing homes. She was better than a Bible. The elderly in these homes brightened immediately when she entered the room, delighted in her smile, asked her questions. They would touch her skin, stroke her hair. On one such visit we were with Mrs. Herr, who was in an advanced state of dementia. She was talkative and directed all her talk to Karen. She told her a story, an anecdote out of her childhood that Karen's presence triggered. When she completed the story she immediately began at the beginning and did it again, word for word and then again and again and again. After twenty minutes or so of this I became anxious lest Karen become uncomfortable and confused about what was going on. So I interrupted this flow of talk, anointed the woman with oil, laid hands on her, prayed, and left. In the car and driving home, I commended Karen for her patience and attentiveness. She had listened to this repeated story without showing any sign of restlessness or boredom. I said to her, "Karen, Mrs. Herr's mind is not working the way ours is." And Karen said, "Oh, I knew that, Daddy; she was not trying to tell us any*thing*, she was telling us who she *is*."

Nine years old and she knew the difference, knew that Mrs. Herr was using words not for communication but for communion. Her father, who should have known better, was nervous because there was not any communication going on. This is a difference which our culture as a whole pays very little attention to, but that pastors must pay attention to.

There is an enormous communications industry in the world that is stamping out words like buttons. Words are transmitted by television, radio, telegraph, satellite, cable, newspaper, magazine. But the words are not personal. Implicit in this enormous communications industry is an enormous lie: if we improve communications we will improve life. It has not happened and it will not happen. Often when we find out what a person "has to say," we like him or her less, not more. Better communication often worsens international relations. We know more about each other as nations and religions than we ever have before in history, and we seem to like each other less. Counselors know that when spouses learn to communicate more clearly, it leads to divorce as often as it does to reconciliation.

The gift of words is for communion. We need to learn the nature of communion. This requires the risk of revelation — letting a piece of myself be exposed, this mystery of who I am. If I stand here mute, you have no idea what is going on with me. You can look at me, measure me, weigh me, test me, but until I start to talk you do not know what is going on inside, who I really am. If you listen and I am telling the truth, something marvelous starts to take place — a new event. Something comes into being that was not there before. God does this for us. We learn to do it because God does it. New things happen then. Salvation comes into being; love comes into being. Communion. Words used this way do not define as much as deepen mystery — entering into the ambiguities, pushing past the safely known into the risky unknown. The Christian Eucharist uses words, the simplest of words, "this is my body, this is my blood," that plunge us into an act of revelation which staggers the imagination, which we never figure out, but we enter into. These words do not describe, they point, they reach, they embrace. Every time I go to the ill, the dying, the lonely, it becomes obvious after a few moments that the only words that matter are words of communion. What is distressing is to find out how infrequently they are used. Sometimes we find we are the only ones who bother using words this way on these occasions. Not the least of the trials of the sick, the lonely, and the dying is the endless stream of clichés and platitudes to which they have to listen. Doctors enter their rooms to communicate the diagnosis, family members to communicate their anxieties, friends to communicate the gossip of the day. Not all of them do this, of course, and not always, but the sad reality is that there is not a great deal of communion that goes on in these places with these ill and lonely and dying people, on street corners, in offices, in work places, in schools. That makes it urgent that the Christian becomes a specialist in words of communion.

Poet

Most societies have honored poets because of the general importance of words. Martin Heidegger used to call philosophers "shepherds of being." I think of poets as "shepherds of words," watching over them, binding them up when they get injured, going after them when they get lost, knowing them by name, in love. It has always seemed to me that pastors, who have so much to do with words, should be more fond of poets than they are. It surprises me when pastor friends are indifferent or hostile to poets. More than half of our Scriptures were written by poets. If the form in which something comes to us is significant — and it is — then poetry and poets are a force to be reckoned with for anyone who has responsibility to conveying the Christian message in any way for this Word made flesh.

The first thing that a poet does is to slow us down. We cannot speed-read a poem. A poem requires re-reading. Unlike prose which fills the page with print, poems leave a lot of white space, which is to say that silence takes its place alongside sound as significant, essential to the apprehension of these words. We cannot be in a hurry reading a poem. We notice connections, get a feel for rhythms, hear resonances. All this takes time. There is a lot to see, to feel, to sense. We sit before the poem like we sit before a flower and attend to form, relationship, color. We let it begin to work on us. When we are reading prose we are often in control, but in a poem we feel like we are out of control. Something is going on that we cannot pin down right away and so often we get impatient and go read Ann Landers instead. In prose we are after something, getting information, acquiring knowledge. We read as fast as we can to get what we want so that we can put it to good use. If the writer is not writing well — that is, if we cannot understand him quickly — we get impatient, shut the book and wonder why someone does not teach him or her to write a plain sentence. But in poetry we take a different stance. We are prepared to be puzzled, to go back, to wait, to ponder, to listen. This attending, this waiting, this reverential posture, is at the core of the life of faith, the life of prayer, the life of worship, the life of witness. If we are in too much of a hurry to speak we commit sacrilege. Poets slow us down, poets make us stop. Read it again, read it again, read it again.

The poet I am using alongside the novelist James Joyce is Jeremiah. Jeremiah is one of the great poets of not only our faith, but of the world's life. He begins the book that is called by his name with a poem:

> And the word of the Lord came to me saying,
> "Before I formed you in the womb, I knew you,
>   and before you were born I set you apart,
> I appointed you as a prophet to the nations."
> "Ah, sovereign Lord," I said, "I do not know how to speak,
>   I am only a child." But the Lord said to me,
> "Do not say 'I am only a child,'
>   you must go to everyone that I send you to
>   and say whatever I command you,
> do not be afraid of them for
> I will be with you and will rescue you,"
>   declares the Lord.
> Then the Lord reached out his hand and touched my mouth
>   and said to me,
> "Now I have put my words in your mouth.
> See, today I appoint you over nations and kingdoms,
> to uproot and tear down,
> to destroy and overthrow,
> to build and to plant."
>
> The word of the Lord came to me, "What do you see,
>   Jeremiah?" "I see the branch of an almond tree," I replied.
> The Lord said to me, "You have seen correctly for I am
>   watching to see that my word is fulfilled."

From that poem on the opening page of Jeremiah I want to make some observations. Jeremiah is a classic poet, doing things that poets do that impact all of us who use words. He is not only a prophet; he is a poet, caring for words, caring for language, showing us how language works.

The first thing that I note here is that the word is first, word is

181

primary. "Before you were born I knew you, before you were born I consecrated you. I appointed you as a prophet to the nations." Previous to Jeremiah, God is shown as knowing, consecrating, appointing. These are all verbal actions. The word is previous to everything else. Before we are conceived and shaped in the mother's womb we are spoken into being. The word is first. Before sun, moon, stars, (in Genesis) there is word. Before trees and flowers and fish, word. Before governments and hospitals and schools, word. If word gets displaced from its "firstness," its primacy, everything goes awry. If the word is made second or third or fourth, we lose touch with this deep, divine, originating rhythm to creation. If the word is pushed out of the way and made a servant to action and program, we lose connection with these vast interior springs of redemption which come out of the word, the Word made flesh. If the word is treated carelessly, casually, we wander away from the essential, personal intimacies that God creates by the use of word. That is why we have "ministers of the word" who take seriously what it means to have a word. The poet helps us attend to the nature of that ministry, that it is wordcare, wordservice, serving this word, this God Word.

When Jeremiah heard God's word, he answered it. He said, "Ah, sovereign Lord, I do not know how to speak, I am only a child." It was kind of an apologetic answer, but it was an answer. He did not just stand there like a dummy. The word is not a label that you put on a box in order to identify the contents of the world or its people. It is not a piece of information. The word is personal. When the word is really heard it calls forth an answer. Suddenly something has been created — Jeremiah. He has a name, he is someone, God is addressing him, and he begins to answer him, "Ah, sovereign Lord." We can ponder the fact of God from morning to night for the rest of our life and never have our life changed. We can take tests and eat meals and play games for our whole life and never change other than biologically. But when the word is spoken and answered, something new is created — not just God out there speaking the universe into being, not just me sitting here stewing in my own juice, but a *relationship* full of energy, change, development, love. Jeremiah does not believe that yet; he does not see what is going on. He is modest and does not see how a word of God could have anything to do with his word, "I am only a youth — I cannot speak, I cannot use the same kind of language that God uses, the language I use has no connection with the language that God uses." But God says it does. He says, "we are speaking the same language, Jeremiah, do not say that you are only a youth." There can be conversation between the God who speaks worlds into being, speaks our lives into being, and a man or a woman who uses words to get a second helping of potatoes, or to tell a check-out clerk that she was overcharged $3.50 on the broccoli. These words are compatible — God's word and our word.

Poets do what we do not think can be done; they put together two sets of words that do not seem compatible, that do not fit, and then show how they are part of the same conversation — God speaking, me speaking. At least part of what it means to be in the image of God is to have language, to be able to speak and listen to words that link these mysterious interiors of our lives with this vast mystery of who God is.

Then the Lord put forth his hand and touched Jeremiah's lips, the place where words are formed and the action starts. Energy flows from these word actions, word utterances. Three pairs of words, six verbs, pluck up, break down, destroy, overthrow, build, plant. Each originates in word. It is so easy to lose connection with this reality. We let ourselves be intimidated by force, by might, money, horsepower, nuclear power.

We should look at one more thing in Jeremiah the poet, another aspect of poetry; maybe it is the most important. "The word of the Lord came to me saying 'Jeremiah, what do you see?' I said, 'I see a rod of almond.' Then the Lord said to me, 'You have seen well for I am watching to see that my word is fulfilled.'"

The word God gives us to speak is confirmed in the world that God made. Words are analogous to matter, the word God gives to speak is confirmed in the world God creates. There is a congruence between word and world. The congruence is often destroyed by sin, by rebellion. The task of the poet is to bring them back together. Jeremiah uses a pun and a vision to accomplish this in his poem.

God asks Jeremiah what he sees. Jeremiah looks out the window and says, "I see an almond branch." I am guessing that it is spring. The almond branch is a blossom of white flowers similar to our apple trees blossoming white fragrant clusters of petals. "I see a flowering almond branch." God replies with a pun, "You have seen well, Jeremiah, for I am watching over my word to perform it." We cannot reproduce the pun in English. In Hebrew it sounds like this, "what do you see Jeremiah?" "I see a *shaqed* (almond branch)." "Right, Jeremiah, I am *shoked* (watching) my word to perform it." Do you see what is going on here? Every person who uses words wonders at times if anything happens with them. Are they congruent with what God is doing in this world? Every spring for the rest of his life Jeremiah would see the almond branch *(shaqed)* burst into blossom, and hear "I am watching over my word to perform it" *(shoked)*. These words are watched over, kept, confirmed, validated. "No word shall return unto me void." This is what poets do; they draw us into an experienced congruence of word and form. Every time he sees *shaqed,* he hears *shoked.* The deep, internal organic divine connection is restored between word and world, between what is said and what happens.

For those of us who use words — pastors, teachers, witnesses of all kinds in the service of Christ — we need to believe in this connection between word and sacrament, between what we see and what happens. That blossoming almond branch in three or four months becomes a cluster of nuts. Words are not just pretty words, they *become* something because God is watching over his word to perform it. He is the shepherd of the word, he is not going to let one of these words get away. Words are never mere words; they get under our skin, shape our lives, make us from the inside out. When the word is spoken, preached, taught, said, sung, prayed, meditated, that is not the end of it. God continues to watch over this word, tending it, caring for it. And we watch him, we watch God watch over the word. Not, however, as spectators at a ballgame, but as shepherds of a flock, parents of a child, as lovers, friends, watching for the signs of grace, watching for movements of joy, watching for the evidence that once again this word is becoming flesh.

Novelists and poets can be our allies in helping us respect words and show us how they work into our lives. As you listen to the stories around you and listen to the words before you, know that the word of God is present in all these words we speak and can become flesh.

Pastors and Novels

It was an offhand remark in a casual conversation. I mentioned to a pastor acquaintance that I was reading *Middlemarch* again. "Again," he said, "why would your bother reading it even once?" I detected condescension in his tone as we went on, "I'm too busy to read such stuff — when I read, I read *seriously*." Right then we were joined by another who brought a report on the sixth inning score in the World Series game being played at that moment. My serious friend had some most serious opinions on the issues hanging in the balance in that contest, and *Middlemarch* slipped through the cracks. I was relieved. I had the feeling that if the conversation had continued, I would have been shown up to be a pastor lacking in seriousness, a very trivial pastor indeed.

I often find myself slow-witted in conversation, easily bested in repartee. Later, though, in the sanctuary of my study, I write and take my revenge. And even though the one person to and for whom I am writing will, in all likelihood, never read what I write, there is considerable satisfaction in getting the last word. The last word in this instance is that reading a novel is among the more serious activities available to a pastor. Pastors who neglect to read novels lack seriousness, or at least one aspect of it. Read scripture, certainly; theology, of course; commentaries, diligently; and novels, by all means.

Originally published in *Theology, News and Notes,* December 1991.

I am setting out vocational, not personal, reasons for pastors to read novels, reasons that have to do with the kind of work we do and the conditions in which we do it. Pastors proclaim the story of God's salvation in Christ to specific people in a particular place. The proclamation part of our work is for the most part unchallenged. The world, even when it ignores us, expects us to take our place in pulpits each Sunday and preach. It would wonder what was wrong if we didn't. But the world conditions in which we carry out this work can, if not vigorously countered, silently kill the leaf and blossom in our work like acid rain in the forest.

World conditions, a steady and relentless drizzle of acid rain, strip us of story, identity, and place. But it is the *story* of salvation to specific *people* in a particular *place* that compose the conditions of our work. If the gospel proclamation is rendered storyless and addressed to "Occupant" in "Anywhere, USA," the pastoral distinctiveness of this ministry is rubbed out. Meanwhile any number of fiction writers work away day after day, year after year countering these conditions, showing the story-shape of all existence, insisting on the irreducible identity of each person, and the glory of this piece of geography.

Anyone serious about the distinctive conditions of the pastoral calling, *story, person, place,* will welcome these novelists as friends and spend time in their company. Not all writers of fiction, of course, qualify as allies. There are discernments to be exercised, but a considerable number take their stand with us against the pastor-debilitating world conditions.

Story

Existence has a story shape. The most adequate rendering of the world in words is by storytelling. It is the least specialized and most comprehensive form of language. Everything and anything can be put into the story. And the moment it is in the story it has meaning, participates in plot, is somehow or other significant. The biblical revelation comes to us in the form of story. Nothing less than story is adequate to the largeness and intricacy of the truth of God and creation, or of the human and redemption.

One of the verbal effects of sin is either the destruction or obfuscation of story, the fragmentation of story into disconnected anecdotes, the reduction of story to gossip, the dismemberment of story into lists or formulae or rules. Most of the words that come before us today are delivered by television, newspaper, and magazine journalists. There is no story in them beyond the event, the speech, the accident. There is nothing that connects to the past, reaches into the future, plumbs the depths, or soars to the heights. Instead of connecting with more reality, the words disconnect us, leaving us in a litter of incident and comment.

Every time someone tells a story and tells it well and truly, the gospel is served. Out of the chaos of incident and accident, story-making words bring light, coherence and connection, meaning and value. If there is a story, then maybe, just maybe, there is (must be!) a Storyteller.

Wallace Stegner has served as one of the premier storytellers in and for my life. I grew up in the West in a kind of anarchist/populist atmosphere. We sat loose to authority and had no sense of continuity with the past. The town I grew up in was only 40 years old when I arrived in it. I had no sense of tradition. The Scandinavia of my grandparents was half a world away, and the Kootenai and Salish Indians who were native to the valley I grew up in were not ancestors in any living sense.

People moved around a lot, looking for a "better deal." We moved ten times during my growing up. Experiences were intense and sometimes glorious, but they weren't part of anything large or historic, and my understanding of the gospel was thereby reduced to the temporary and the "better deal."

In his novel, *The Big Rock Candy Mountain*, Stegner makes a story out of the materials of my life. He grew up a couple of hundred miles from me (but thirty years earlier) in a town not unlike mine. As I read his novel about the American/Canadian west and its people, I recognize in it most of the people I grew up with, and also the feelings I had, the language I learned and used, the wanderlust and loneliness, the rootless and religionless poverty/prosperity. As an adult, I was in danger of rejecting it all in favor of something more congenial to what I understood as a Christian culture. Stegner's storytelling put the materials of my experience, the land and weather, the slang and customs, the jerry-built towns and makeshift jobs, into a story. He made a cosmos out of it, showed this country and people as capable of plot and coherence as anything in Homer's Greece or St. Mark's Galilee.

It is significant, I think, that it was not the pastor in my congregation or a professor in my seminary who did this for me, but a novelist who convinced and continues to train my imagination to take in everything around me and realize that it is worth attention of an Author. It is not only for myself that I need this help, but also for the people around me, the men and women to whom I am a pastor. They also experience themselves as unworthy of the attention of an Author, not interesting enough or important enough to be included in a plot. And so, lest I inadvertently be conditioned by the world to take on a journalist's view of these people, i.e. good for an hour or so of attention, but only if they happen into an accident or win a prize, I read novels frequently and seriously, to deepen and retain the habit of story in my conversation and proclamation.

Person

The persons to whom this gospel story is proclaimed are, each of them, one-of-a-kind. "There are no dittos among souls," Baron Friedrich von Hugel was fond of saying. As schoolchildren we learn to marvel that no two snowflakes are the same, no two oak leaves identical. From snowflakes and leaves we gradually move on to grasp the intensification of the unique that takes place in the human being. As much as we have in common with other parts of the creation, when it comes to being *human* there is nothing quite like us. And as much as I have in common with all other humans, when it comes to being *me,* I am far more different from everyone I meet than alike. A true hearing of the gospel always takes in the specifically personal. "I have called you by name" is an essential element in the economy of salvation.

Meanwhile, world conditions are constantly at work eroding the high profile specifics of each person into a flat and featureless generality, identified by label: Introvert, Elder Material, Ectomorph, Unsaved, Anorexic, Bipolar, Single Parent, Diabetic, Tither, Left-brained. The labels are marginally useful for understanding some aspect of the human condition, but the moment they are used to identify a person, they obscure the very thing that we as pastors are most interested in, the unprecedented, unrepeatable soul addressed by God.

Every time someone is addressed by name and realizes that in the address they are being treated as one-of-a-kind, not as a customer, not as a patient, not as a voter, not as a Presbyterian, not as a sinner, the gospel is served. Saving love is always personally specific, never merely generic. Christ's mercy is always customized to a discrete history, never swallowed up in abstraction.

Anne Tyler provides me with eyes to see past the labels, ears to hear beneath stereotyping clichés. She creates characters in her novels that are always just a little quirky, not quite fitting into society. When I meet people like that in my parish, I am always a little impatient and try to fit them into categories that I am familiar with, so I won't have to take the extra time to get to know them. I have, after all, a lot to do. The church has programs for a variety of needs, and people are supposed to fit into the categories. Most people are so used to fitting into categories supplied for them by hospitals, schools, shopping malls, and social services that they raise no objections when the church treats them similarly. But insofar as they acquiesce, they lose capacity to realize what God is most interested in working in them: sanctity, which means becoming more your created/redeemed self, not less, not being reduced to what will fit into a program, not being depersonalized in the cause of efficiency.

As I let Anne Tyler show me how character is formed, I learn to treat my parishioners with respect, with reverence even, and just as they are, not insofar as they fit into what is convenient for me and useful to the organization. When I hesitate over details that make this man odd and somewhat of an embarrassment in the coffee hour after worship, Anne Tyler trains me to take in the oddness and love him not in spite of but because of it. These irregularities that make this woman unsuitable as a role-model in our youth ministry, Anne Tyler trains me to see as occasions for the grace of our Lord, not obstructions to it.

All good novelists do this for us, develop characters in ways that show us this person unlike any other before or after, and that the human condition is capable of endless variations, and that each variation is a marvel. But Anne Tyler, for me, is the contemporary master: her unforgettable characterizations of Morgan in *Morgan's Passing*, of Macon in *The Accidental Tourist*, of Maggie in *Breathing*

Lessons, have been a major source of energy in identifying, without condescension and without ridicule, characters that keep showing up in my congregation. She gets me to know them by name and not by label. She gets me to say their names in such a way that they realize they are precious, just as they are, in God's sight, and have a place in salvation that no one else will ever occupy.

Whenever I find myself getting irritated and impatient with some sinner who doesn't fit in, I reach for another novel by Anne Tyler and sign up for retraining in character recognition and personal naming.

Place

The work of salvation is always local. Geography is as much a part of the gospel as theology. The creation of land and water, star and planet, tree and mountain, grass and flower provides ground and environment for the blessings of providence and the mysteries of salvation. The covenant always has the creation for its context. Nothing spiritual in our scriptures is served up apart from material. Creation, Incarnation, sacraments, all these are integral to the gospel. When God fashioned a universal gospel for "all the world," he became incarnate on a few square miles of Palestinian hills and valleys. An accurate street address is far more important in the proclamation of the gospel than a world map.

But world conditions are not congenial to this honoring of locale. Ordinary place, the place of residence and work, is dismissed with the terms such as "backwater," "hick town," "out-of-the-way," "regional," "provincial," and "the sticks." Places that are honored are places to visit such as Bermuda or places to be entertained such as Disney World. Exotic scenery and exciting diversion give value to place, but place as such is limitation and confinement, a place to be stuck. So successful is the devil and his angels in convincing us that God's creation is a millstone on the neck of our spirituality that we resort to the most unlikely expedients to confer value on our place: a house containing the bed George Washington slept in, a battle fought 200 years ago, the victorious reign of a football team. When world conditions so debase our imaginations into a devaluation of place, we no longer have a context for faith in Jesus Christ. Faith is reserved for the far-off exotic, or faith is confined to the occasional ecstasy. It would never occur to us that the actual place we live and labor is adequate to support large spiritual enterprises like salvation and sanctification.

And so it is necessary that a love of the locale be recovered: this street, these trees, this humidity, these houses. Without reverence for the locale, obedience floats on the clouds of abstraction. Every time a rock is named, a flower is identified, a house number is located, a street is walked, noticing the details, observing the texture and color, insisting on the immediate particularity, the gospel is served, for space is cleared and location provided for yet another spin-off of the Incarnation, most of which came to its definitive form in small towns and on county roads.

Pastors are in charge of the gospel *in locale,* a limited and bounded area (although the automobile has extended the lines considerably). We are particularly vulnerable to devaluating place because we are used to trafficking in large ideas, proclaiming the gospel to all the world and telling the stories of courageous missionaries across the seas, in tension with parishioners who examine the daily paper for bargains and calculate their social security benefits. They keep each other up to date on the adulterous goings on of Mr. Auchinclos in the third house down from the corner. But if we lose touch with the immediate locale, we lose touch with the only place these people will ever have a chance at the abundant life in Christ.

Novelists are particularly good at keeping us in touch with the locale. I use them to keep myself in touch with my locale. I watch how careful they are with the actual details of fragrance and color and shape — the things people buy, what gets dropped in backyards, what can be seen in a curbside gutter in the beauty of broken glass.

Wendell Berry is more or less a specialist in considerations of place. He not only writes a particular place into being, which all skilled novelists do, he goes on to wonder about it, commenting on the glory of the very dirt under our feet, *local* dirt. He does this in an age when the earth is being ravaged by people who refuse to honor it as a place to live but only as a resource to exploit. His novels, *Nathan Coulter* and *A Place on Earth,* have been personally powerful antidotes to the world conditions. He draws me into noticing how precious place is, how sacred the ground that is given to us by the Creator to tend and nurture, and that all place is local somewhere or other. Place is never "in general." He honors the delicate spiritual interactions that take place between human and humus. Place is not simply empty space in which we can work our will. It has its own created nature, which must be treated with respect lest we violate what God designated as good and our ancestors experienced as holy. As Wendell Berry writes out his awareness of a few dozen acres of Kentucky hill country, my appreciation of the local weather and ground in my parish sharpens and deepens. These are the conditions in which I and my parishioners commit our sins and receive forgiveness. This is where some days praise springs up, and on others despair thickens. I immerse myself, again, in the smells and sounds of this place, and I am prevented, for a while at least, from grand abstractions and standoffish condescensions.

Novelists are not, of course, necessary to keep pastors attentive to *story* and *person* and *place*. Many pastors seem to get along fine without them. Reading the Bible itself, this extraordinary story-person-place saturated book, ought to do it. But the world conditions, which insidiously eat away at these fundamentals of our reality, are so pervasive and hard to detect that it seems derelict not to make use of such skilled and pleasant companions as present themselves between the covers of a novel.

CONVERSATIONS

A Conversation with
Eugene Peterson

By Michael J. Cusick

In a Christian publishing culture where marketing potential, charisma, and the latest recipe for self-improvement are often more valued than things substantial, Eugene Peterson cuts an ordinary figure at best. But in the world of spirit, integrity, art, and imagination, Peterson stands high above the crowd.

Known for years as a pastor to pastors, more recently he has become a pastor to the English-speaking world with the release of The Message: The New Testament in Contemporary English *(NavPress). In this fresh paraphrase of Scripture, Peterson's exegetical deftness meets headlong with poetic brilliance, forged in the fire of nearly thirty years of pastoring.*

"The pastorate," says Peterson, "is one of the few places in our society where you can live a truly creative life." Indeed, this man has been creative. With eighteen books, numerous contributions to others, and dozens of journal and magazine articles to his credit, his writing career has been nothing short of prolific. No minor accomplishment for a man who at the

"A Conversation with Eugene Peterson" by Michael J. Cusick was originally published in *Mars Hill Review*, a journal of essays, studies, and reminders of God, issue 3 (Fall 1995): 73-90. Copyrighted article reprinted with permission of *Mars Hill Review* (1-800-990-MARS).

same time pastored Christ Our King Presbyterian Church in Bel Air, Maryland, for twenty-nine years.

In order to devote more time to writing and teaching, Peterson retired from the pastorate in 1991. He currently is Professor of Spiritual Theology at Regent College in Vancouver, British Columbia.

Mars Hill Review: You are Professor of Spiritual Theology at Regent College. How is spiritual theology distinct from traditional theological studies?

Eugene Peterson: Spiritual theology has to do with living the Christian life instead of thinking about it. It has a long history both pre- and post-Reformation. It has an academic tradition hooked into it — prayer, spiritual direction, and theological underpinnings of how one understands the faith. Up until the time of the Reformation, theology was just theology. Theologians prayed and they thought. There was no split between living the Christian life and thinking about it. But then the rise of scholasticism and the polemics of the Reformation came about and the two became separate. The systematic theologian became an academic and the spiritual theologian became the chaplain. In Roman Catholic schools there was always a strong leadership in spiritual theology, in worship and prayer. In Protestantism, it pretty much dropped out of sight and left it up to the individual to take care of his or her own prayer life.

People often say, "Why the adjective — isn't all theology spiritual?" Actually, here at Regent you are as apt to get spiritual theology in a Hebrew course as in one of my courses on spirituality. The aim is to integrate them both so that all of your thinking becomes prayerful.

MHR: To what do you attribute the resurgence of spirituality and intense interest in spiritual direction?

EP: Part of it is just the end of the so-called modern era. It's not enough to think. Rationalism just doesn't work. And activism doesn't work. So the evangelical church is trying to recover its holiness. We have started paying a lot more attention to the older traditions of prayer, spiritual direction, and liturgy. We're not reducing them to being something individualistic you do in your quiet time.

So I think it's a sense of thinness that we have. We're realizing we have left out something that is very essential. Whenever there is any kind of a movement like evangelicalism which starts out with an incredible amount of energy, the momentum of that energy carries it for a long time. But it's not carrying it now. Suddenly, people are feeling thin, impoverished, and realizing our spiritual ancestors had rich resources that we need to recover. Fortunately, we are recovering them.

MHR: Has the failure of the modern counseling movement to offer something transcendent to people set the stage for this increased interest in spiritual direction and formation?

EP: I think that's part of it. The counseling movement, even within the church, became heavily psychologized and almost exclusively therapeutic. If you had a problem, you went to a counselor. So people ended up dealing with problems. And in most cases counseling lost its moorings in the biblical revelation.

But spiritual direction, in a sense, doesn't begin with a problem. You shouldn't have to have a problem before you start dealing with spiritual things. Spiritual direction deals much more out of health and an identity of Christian holiness. So yes, I think it's an obvious response to the failure to transcend.

MHR: As you refer to holiness here, as well as in your writings, you offer a refreshing picture that doesn't seem like the typical evangelical definition. How do you define holiness?

EP: Holiness is the Christian life mature. It's gathering all the parts and pieces of your life into obedience and response to God, and living with some energy. Holiness is a blazing thing, an energetic thing. Part of the reason the modern church has lost its taste for holiness is that it has become engineered. Although we're really firm about the fact that justification is by faith, holiness is by disciplines, work, arranging. So it has become hedging around the rules, hints, regulations, and technology. Therefore, it has become very boring and claustrophobic.

197

MHR: Do you mean boring and claustrophobic as opposed to what is conveyed in The Message *— that holiness is something that naturally grows out of your life as you enjoy relationship with God?*

EP: Yes, but I wouldn't say that holiness naturally grows out of your life. I would say it's the work of the Holy Spirit in your life. It's a work in which there is conscious and intentional participation and obedience. It's living the life of the Spirit under the same theological conditions that you live the life of faith or justification. It's very Trinitarian. Unfortunately, we have lost that Trinitarian wholeness, a sense of relational wholeness. I think it's a result of the culture and the fragmentation of the culture, how we specialize in different things. As Protestants we get nervous about anything that didn't stem from the last revival.

MHR: How has our loss of relational wholeness affected the church?

EP: It's made the church very busy — because if you don't have a sense of a large context in God, you get frantic. There's a lot to do and you'd better get at it. It's also affected the church in depersonalizing relationships. We are now defined by our function. You are a good Sunday School teacher or a zealous missionary, so the activity that you generate becomes a substitute for Trinitarian spirituality.

The Trinity is a very active concept. If you lose that you just end up with doctrines — a doctrine of God, a doctrine of justification, all propositions that you continually have to reactivate in your life.

Traditional Christian spirituality is not taking bits and pieces of doctrine and putting them to use — it's entering into the life of God that is already in motion. There is already movement in the Trinity. It's a matter of shifting your image of what's going on. Are we in a spiritual bazaar where we are picking out verses and texts that we can use, or are we in a home that is ordered by Father, Son, and Holy Spirit, where we can enter into what's already going on? We can learn to be obedient, participate, receive affection and give it. But it's not our home; we're not the ones in charge of it.

MHR: Can some of what's been lost be recovered with a reclamation of the doctrine of the Trinity?

EP: We're never past recovery. The church is always finding itself in some place or other whereby it needs to be rescued, and we currently need to be rescued from this excessive, commodity-oriented culture. Everything is thingified, and we become thingified. There is a lot of recovery of the doctrine of the Trinity going on right now, but it probably hasn't gotten down to where it's shaping pastors and leaders and teachers yet.

MHR: Regent College calls itself "the un-seminary." What do you think of seminaries today?

EP: Regent started out as a school for the laity. It was to be an international school for Christian graduate studies. Along the way, students started to say, "We want to be able to prepare for pastoral leadership at Regent." Because of the wonderful faculty that is here, people have been attracted from all over the world to study at Regent. Then pressure grew to have an M.Div. degree, and we've had one now for over ten years. But there is a strong sense at Regent of resistance to the professionalization of the clergy. So there's a constant attempt to keep parity between the marketplace and the church and parachurch ministries. They both stand on a parity called of God. So when the school advertises as an un-seminary I think it is trying to make a statement that says, "This is not a trade school where you come to learn to be an ecclesiastical leader of some kind. It's a place where you're immersed in the Christian mind, the Christian spirit, so that you can be equipped to be a pastor, or an architect." I just completed a course this last weekend in Ministry and Spirituality, with one hundred people in the course. Half of the students were laity and half were in church-related vocations.

MHR: What a wild concept! To equip people to live for God in their vocation, wherever it may be. You once said that if you were to start a seminary, you would spend the first two years studying literature. Would you elaborate on that?

EP: Even now, in all of my courses, students read poetry and novels. In my course in spirituality they write reviews of the books *Middlemarch, The Power and the Glory,* and Walter Wangerin's *Book of the Dun Cow.* The importance of poetry and novels is that the Christian life involves the use of the imagination — after all, we are dealing with the invisible. And, imagination is our training in dealing with the invisible — making connections, looking for plot and character. I don't want to do away with or denigrate theology or exegesis, but our primary allies in this business are the artists. I want literature to be on par with those other things. They need to be brought in as full partners in this whole business. The arts reflect where we live. We live in narrative, we live in story. We don't live as exegetes.

MHR: To use your words again, "Existence has a story shape to it." Is that what you mean?

EP: Yes, we have a beginning and an end, we have a plot, we have characters. We are not journalists — rather, we accumulate meaning. If we put it in the larger framework, God has a story. The Scriptures are given to us in the shape of a story. I spend a lot of time in what I write, what I teach, and what I preach, calling attention to this storiedness of our lives. It's pretty natural — most people tell stories, especially in other cultures. My African students have been doing it all their lives. But there's something about North America and evangelicalism that wants to package things into a neat little formula.

MHR: Do you consider yourself a narrative theologian?

EP: I welcome all this emphasis on narrative theology, but the trouble with a label like "narrative theologian" is that the narrative theology movement has lost, or never had, the internal workings of Spirit. It finds its meaning in the story — but Jesus is the story, he's the fascination. In their excitement of seeing how narrative works, many of them have dropped all theological dimension. I don't see a whole lot of gain in that.

MHR: You speak of the importance of artists and the arts, but it seems there is such a lack of artistry in the Christian community. How can we encourage an expansion of the arts — music, literature, drama, sculpture?

EP: Here on the campus at Regent we always have art exhibits, with works of art brought in from artists all over Vancouver. There is also

200

a good deal of fresh music brought in. Regent is a very open place for the arts. I think we are encouraging it. It seems there are a lot of the arts going on in the church too, but they just don't get high visibility. It seems there is more of an openness to the arts.

MHR: Tell me about the Chrysostom Society that you are part of. How did it come into being?

EP: Richard Foster, Calvin Miller, and Karen Mains got together because they were very isolated in their craft of writing. They felt as writers that nobody cared if they wrote or not. And nobody cared if they wrote well. Publishers cared if they wrote or not, but only on their terms. So this group felt it was important just to get together, write together, and believe in each other as practitioners of a craft to the glory of God. They sat down and wrote down fifteen or twenty names of people who would want to do that. It was a very random kind of thing. I don't think there was much of an election process, but [my wife] Jan and I were invited. I didn't go the first year because I was on sabbatical, but the second year I went very tentatively because I didn't really feel the isolation. I was a pastor. Calvin Miller was the only other pastor, Walter Wangerin had been a pastor, but most of them felt the isolation more. Some of them are teachers, editors. But after I had been there for the first several days, I knew I wanted to be a part of it. Nobody else had ever treated me as a writer. It meant something to me to have the affirmation from peers who cared whether I wrote well or not. They didn't ask questions about how many books or contracts I had going. They just asked, "Are we writers to the glory of God?" We meet every year for four days. They have become wonderful friends.

MHR: What does "Chrysostom" mean?

EP: Chrysostom was a man, a third-century pastor in Asia Minor. I think Chrysostom was a nickname because it means "golden mouth." He was an orator, a great preacher. Nobody in the group liked the name. But Richard Foster kept calling it the Chrysostom Society, and nobody came up with anything better.

MHR: While on the subject of words, you wrote: "I work with words. In pastoring I work with people, but not mere words or mere people, but words and people as carriers of Spirit. The moment words are used prayerlessly, and people are treated prayerlessly, something essential seems to leak out of life." What does it mean to be prayerful with people and words?

EP: It's right at the heart of our theology. In the beginning was the Word. The Word was with God. The revelation comes by Word. And all these words are personal, there is no abstract word. God is himself incarnating himself by word. Language is the way in which we reveal ourselves to one another — it's the primary means of deepening and continuing intimacy. The minute language becomes functionalized, there is sacrilege going on.

MHR: What do you mean "when language becomes functionalized"?

EP: It becomes functionalized when it is used just for information or in getting someone to do something for you. Or, in getting someone to buy something. As Christians we get caught up in that culture, and we start using language, albeit necessarily, in its lowest sense. The primary sense in which we were given language is for revelation, for blessing. We've left our heritage — our theology, our Scriptures — and we've taken these same words which began in holiness, a Trinitarian kind of holiness — a relational holiness — and we think just because we have the right words such as, "Jesus saves," or John 3:16, we can use them any way we want. But we can't. They have to be spoken in the way they were revealed, at least in the same posture and tone. I think it's time for a great recovery of language. We have to recover the nature of our language because words are holy.

People are the same way. As I look at you, I can see that you are in the image of God. I've got to be aware of that. If I'm not, then you become a way for me to get a better job. When you are no longer of use to me, you're out of here.

MHR: You're implying, then, that we ought to be far more intentional with our words?

EP: Yes, but I wouldn't want it to sound as if you have to be calculating or shrewd. When you are taking words seriously, when you respect language, you can be quite spontaneous. That's why I used the word prayerful. If the words are coming from who you are, and from the relationship you have with God and your friends, you can be quite spontaneous with your words. So if you put the idea of being intentional far enough back, I agree with you. It starts with how you perceive language to function and how you conceive people to be. But if when you say "intentional" you mean a kind of obsessing whether you should say something, then I would disagree. Words come out of relationship and prayer — a life of prayer, not just saying your prayers.

MHR: Could you talk a bit more about the idea of "a life of prayer" as opposed to saying our prayers?

EP: Prayer is a life that you are immersed in. It is the interiorness of our life in relationship to the God who has spoken to us — so deep within us there is a dialogic reality. God spoke life into being, and we answer it. That is the way our life is: As our life enters this lively word, this revelation, prayer is living our life *now* in response to that. Prayer cannot be confined to a certain period of time. It is only nurtured in those disciplines, and we realize certain aspects of it during those times.

At one point I realized that when I'm spending time in the external act of prayer — where someone could see through a knothole and say I was praying — I'm not really praying then; I'm just getting ready to pray. When I get up off my knees or out of my chair at eight o'clock, that's when I start praying. That other time of saying my prayers is just the time I spend getting ready to pray. It's getting rid of the distractions and making pre-decided things about the day that give me room so that I'm not swallowed up by everybody else's agenda.

When I was growing up, my parents often invited missionaries to our family home in Montana so they could rest and recover. I was around fifteen years old or so when a certain man came to visit us one summer. He was a Frenchman named John Wright Follett — a small, birdlike man who had never married. He was a teacher of quite some acceptance in the Pentecostal movement in the thirties and forties, and because his name was a household name in our circles I was in awe of him. When I met him he was probably seventy years old.

One day he was lying in a hammock with his eyes closed and I wanted to talk to him. I told my mother I wanted to talk to him and she said, "Just go up and talk to him. It's okay." I timidly approached the hammock and said, "Dr. Follett, how do you pray?" He didn't open his eyes at all. He just grunted and said, "I haven't prayed in forty years!" That stunned me. I walked off totally puzzled. Since then I have realized the wisdom of the man. You see, anything he had told me I would have imitated. I would have done what he said he did and thought that's what prayer is. He risked something to teach me what prayer was, and I'm glad he did. Prayer wasn't something he did — it was something he was. He lived a life of prayer. It took me about six or seven years to understand what he had done. But it was sure better than wasting time trying to imitate what he did.

MHR: Tell me about The Message *and how it came into being.*

EP: It started with a phone call from Jon Stine, who is now my editor at NavPress. He said, "Remember *Traveling Light*, the book you wrote on Galatians? Well, I cut out all the paraphrased parts, Xeroxed them, stapled them together, and I've been carrying this around for ten years showing it to all my friends. I'm just getting really tired of Galatians. Would you paraphrase the whole New Testament?"

Well, it took me a year to do Galatians. So I thought, how could I ever do the whole New Testament? Jon called me three or four months later when, in the meantime, for unrelated reasons, I had decided to resign from my parish. Jan and I decided it was time to leave the pastorate, mainly so I could spend more time writing. After that decision, while we were still with the congregation, Jon called again. I realized I could do it at that time — but personally I didn't think I could do it. Maybe I could do Paul, because Paul is easy in a sense. He gets tangled up and you can untangle him. But I didn't think I could ever do the Gospels. I agreed to do ten chapters of Matthew, at which time Jon would show it to his colleagues to see what they thought. The first few chapters were really bad — I was just plodding along. But when I hit chapter five, the Sermon on the Mount, something kicked in and I suddenly had that sense of, "This is what I do." It was then that I thought I was onto something.

To tell you the truth, the whole time I was writing *The Message* and sending Jon what I wrote, I thought he would tell me to quit. You see, the writing and paraphrasing didn't really seem like different work to me because I had been doing this all my life. It's what I do. Because I love language and love words, I have always read my Bible in Hebrew and Greek as an adult. So I was always trying to get those languages into American English, especially in my preaching and teaching. But I was always in a small congregation and nobody there thought it was all that great. As I was doing *The Message* I often had the feeling of harvest. It was as if I wasn't even working at it, because I was just taking what had been growing and developing. In some ways it was easy, like walking through an orchard and picking apples off a tree.

MHR: The harvest being the result of a lifetime of pastoring people, and your academic background?

EP: Yes, but it goes back even before either of those. I've realized that I was prepared for this from a very early age because my dad was a butcher. We always lived close to his butcher shop, and I was always there, I literally grew up there. My mother made me a butcher apron every year. And because my dad wore a butcher apron, and smiled, and people loved to come into our shop, I always thought of him as a priest. I knew the story of Samuel, Eli, and Hannah. And I always figured that as Samuel grew up he wore a butcher apron just like mine. I thought that's what a priestly robe was.

So I always had this sense of sanctity and holiness in the workplace. The working place was the place and the language that you talked about God in and prayed in. It was a whole new place. We had a preacher who specialized in Leviticus and the temple and all that went on there. So I knew what went on there — they killed animals, and there was a lot of blood and guts and flies. So all the worship stuff that I would hear in church, I would just translate into our butcher shop with my dad who was a priest. We were in a small, western town and there were a lot of misfits and oddballs, so language was colorful. I didn't grow up with sophisticated language.

MHR: So you never grew up with a mind-set that the Bible was a ceremonial, Elizabethan kind of book?

EP: That's right, it never was. But when I became a Presbyterian pastor, all these people came into church on Sunday mornings and left 80 percent of their vocabulary behind them. How could they hear the gospel in this reduced, nice language, much of which they learned in college? I knew I had to get a language that they used all the time. I did it for thirty years as a pastor. The tone and the rhythms of my language had to be congruent with the text, which started out as street language.

MHR: *To hear how the hand of God was on your life even as you were a boy, and how your early days in your Dad's butcher shop affected how you would translate the Scriptures later in life — that is a powerful picture of providence.*

EP: I really believe that. I can see so many things now, like the fact I was being prepared to do *The Message* when I was four years old. *The Message* has been so well received, and it surprises me completely. I had no idea, never even an inkling, that this would happen. I've started thinking, "How did that happen?" I never sat down to do it — it just happened. There was a sense in which it was effortless. I worked hard and put in long hours, but it wasn't as if I were trying to do something I didn't know how to do.

MHR: *Some of the words used to describe* The Message *are "breathtaking," "captivating," "It will stop people dead in their tracks." How do those descriptions make you feel?*

EP: I guess people get enthusiastic and extravagant. But it seems to me people are surprised *The Message* is *so* ordinary. They didn't know God was speaking to them where they were, that He entered their lives where they were. We have this idea of a dichotomized life — a religious life and a secular life. Well, here's something secular and people are caught by surprise. If that's what they are talking about, then I'm pleased. But I think it's the ordinariness of *The Message* that surprises people.

MHR: *It seems that it is the ordinariness that is so powerful to people. One pastor has said he hopes* The Message *will "smash through our comfortable thinking about the Bible." Why do you suppose we have become so comfortable with the Scriptures?*

EP: I think it's partly our sin. One of the devil's finest pieces of work is getting people to spend three nights a week in Bible studies.

MHR: *I'm sure that's going to surprise a lot of readers!*

EP: Well, why do people spend so much time studying the Bible? How much do you need to know? We invest all this time in understanding the text, which has a separate life of its own, and we think we're being more pious and spiritual when we do it. But the Bible is all there to be lived. It was given to us so we could live it. Most Christians know far more of the Bible than they're living. They should be studying it less, not more. You just need enough to pay attention to God.

MHR: *You say we treat the text as if it has a life of its own. Many would say that it does have a life of its own — yet obviously you mean something else.*

EP: I think I would want to say it a different way. We treat the text as if it is in a separate world of its own, apart from our lives. Yet this text reveals God lovingly at work in the world. And the intent of the text is to draw us into that world of God's action. Study is normally an overintellectualized process — it takes us out of relationships. So I guess I'm just not pleased with all the emphasis on Bible study as if it's some kind of special thing that Christians do, and the more they do the better. It needs to be integrated into something more whole.

MHR: *So, there's a very natural interplay between the text and our lives.*

EP: Yes, but then again, as long as we're ignorant of the Scriptures we won't have a clue as to what God is doing. We do need to recover the large world of the Bible. What I see happening is that when people read the Bible, they reduce the world to something they call Bible study. But the world of the Bible — the world revealed in Scripture — is a much larger world than anything you get in the newspapers or history books. If we're doing Bible study right, we ought to get a glimpse of that. But the way Bible studies are often conducted, it ghettoizes the people doing them.

MHR: You wrote The Message *for "disaffected outsiders and bored insiders." Who are those people?*

EP: Outsiders don't think the Christian faith has anything that has to do with them. They think Christianity is for religious people. And since they aren't religious, they're not going to open the Bible. There are also a lot of people who have been intimidated by Christians and don't feel themselves up to snuff. They think that unless they pass a prerequisite stage, they can't understand what's going on. There's an enormous amount of ignorance about God and the Scriptures. Some of it is perpetuated by this intimidation. It's as if you have to have a special introductory course before you can know what's going on. The bored insiders are those I meet all the time. They've heard the Scriptures over and over, and they've lost touch with the reality of these words.

Here again is part of the providence you mentioned. I had a congregation that was a mix of both outsiders and insiders. There were people who had grown up in the church and had been there all their lives. It was a kind of conventional thing for them. I also had people who had never heard anything Christian. I couldn't say the name *Abraham* and expect people to know who I was talking about. So I had to learn how to say it because I had all these outsiders who didn't know anything about religion or Christianity. They forced me to let their language be the language of my preaching and teaching. I had to learn that. But if you're an insider, it's really easy to get dull ears — and I wanted to wake those people up. It's what preachers ought to be doing every Sunday — and it's what I've been doing all my life.

MHR: I understand you're currently working on paraphrasing the Old Testament. How is that progressing for you?

EP: I just finished Song of Songs, which was the last of the wisdom literature I had to do. I think Song of Songs was the hardest thing I've done yet. I'm doing it in chunks, and I put this one off until last. I think it went really well. My apprehension was that we've lost a language of sexuality. We either have euphemisms or we have vulgarities. But that sweet, erotic innocence of the Song of Songs — where can you find that? I didn't know if there was a language left for that. I feel good about what I did there.

A Conversation with Eugene Peterson

MHR: I understand you're more comfortable with the Semitic language of the Old Testament. Is the translation work easier and more natural for you than the New Testament?

EP: I think so, but it's hard to tell at this point. I did my graduate school training in Semitic languages. So technically I know more about Hebrew, but I've been reading Greek for thirty-five years and feel equally at home with it. But there is a real sense of at-home-ness that is coming to fruition as I work through the Old Testament.

MHR: Are there plans to publish The Message *as an entire Bible someday?*

EP: Yes, if the Lord doesn't return too soon! I just wrote out a schedule for my editor. I hope to have it done in six years. I have it broken down into four sections, with two years per section. I just finished the wisdom literature. I'll do the history books next, then the prophets, then the Pentateuch. I think I have a schedule that will work well. The New Testament was done in about a year and a half. It was too much, with many long days where that's all I did. When I finished I said I would never keep that pace again. Then NavPress asked if I would do the Old Testament and my first reaction was, "No! I can't live that way." But as the responses started coming in, I realized what was happening. After about six months I thought, "Lord, maybe this is my work." I prayed long and talked about it for a long time. It was an incredible commitment. But I made the decision that this is my work now.

This might sound strange, but I'm a writer and writers like to write. Yet *The Message* isn't writing — it's translating. When you write you may work for an hour or two on a sentence, and suddenly it's there. You feel that nobody's ever quite done it like that before and they're never going to do it again. There is a sense of "A-hah! I did that." But I never get that with *The Message*. I'm always second rate to Paul, second rate to Mark and John. I remember telling Jan once just after I had finished *The Message,* "I'm so tired of coming in second." I didn't want to do it anymore.

MHR: It sounds very humbling. And yet you're keeping pretty good company with Paul, John, and the others.

209

EP: That's right. But my work on the Old Testament means I'm not writing a lot of things I've wanted to write. I'm still writing some things. But I've realized that this is my work. This is what I've been given to do. So I'll do it.

MHR: *You've already had a prolific career. What has it been like to do such a major project and now be known as the man who paraphrased the Bible? Is that a weight to carry?*

EP: To be honest, I'm not aware of it. You say things about being prolific and I know you're not making it up, but I have almost no internal sense of it. In a way, I feel fortunate it wasn't my idea. It wasn't something I had been planning or plotting out. I just did it and it was done.

MHR: *J. B. Phillips was reported to have struggled with depression as a result of the acclaim of his translation of* The New Testament in Modern English. *Has* The Message *affected you personally?*

EP: Phillips's depression started pretty early after he did it. And he also had a history of depression even before his translation work. He was treated so badly. People really came down hard on him, saying he shouldn't have done it. I think that sent him into a tailspin and had a major effect on him. I wouldn't say it has had that effect on me, except as a distraction. But we've solved that problem somewhat, because I don't take any speaking engagements now. I don't go anyplace. I just stay here at Regent, teach my classes, and see my students and colleagues. Jan is writing several letters a week and answering phone calls, turning down the speaking invitations that would destroy me if I accepted them. There is something very depersonalizing about traveling and speaking. I find it very destructive to the soul. I've always been in a small congregation, and all my work has always been done in a place of intimacy. When it started that I was being talked about instead of addressed, used as a speaker or something, I found it very alien and hurtful. So we made this decision about three or four months after I came here. As a result, I feel very protected.

MHR: *How have you responded to your critics?*

210

EP: I've been very fortunate in that I've had very little criticism. One person took me on and made a campaign out of it for a while. I didn't do anything about it, though — NavPress handled it all. They were very courteous and attentive to his concerns and criticisms. I have a team of scholars who check everything I do, and they responded to him very well. I wasn't impervious to it, but they handled it very well. As I understand what happened, the man who had waged the campaign was barraged by people saying, "Don't do that."

When we published *The Message,* I knew about J. B. Phillips, and I knew about Kenneth Taylor, who wrote *The Living Bible.* Taylor really had a hard time, to the point that he received death threats. It was horrible for him. I thought, "Let's just go to the South Seas for two years and hide out until it's all over."

MHR: *What about criticism at the level where people are uncomfortable with some of the startling language, the rawness and reality of it?*

EP: I haven't gotten much response to that, and I don't think NavPress has. Once in a while somebody writes a letter, but that's only occasional. I've been pleasantly surprised because I get wonderful letters. One woman who wrote was eighty-seven years old. She said, "I'm a King James Bible person, but I've got all these nephews and nieces who won't read the Bible. I thought maybe I could give them *The Message,* so I got a copy and checked it out. I want you to know that I'm never going to read it myself, but I checked it against my King James and I think it's okay. It was right every time, so I'm giving it to all my nephews and nieces."

MHR: *You should put her on your advisory board!*

EP: It was such a dear letter. And she assured me two or three times she wouldn't be reading it herself.

MHR: *You've written a lot about being subversive in the pastorate and spiritual leadership. And you are a poet. Are poetry and the arts subversive?*

EP: Yes — poetry and the arts are subversive. They come at things indirectly. They aren't usually frontal. They sneak in on you, and they're quiet.

211

Spiritually speaking, the self is constantly construing itself against God. That's the nature of our sin — we want to be our own gods. So we have all these layers of defensiveness that often take the form of pieties. Religion is the major defense we have against God. So how do you take people who are heavily defended against God by religion and get through the defenses? You do it by subversion. You get around the defenses. That's what a parable or a proverb does. Jesus did very little that was direct. People were always scratching their heads and saying, "What does he mean?"

On another, lesser level, culture develops ideologies to protect people from reality. So how do you get past the ideology? Suppose someone says, "All black people are inferior," and you have been living that ideology all your life. How do you get behind that? You usually don't do it with argument or by being rational.

MHR: You've written that "Jesus was the master of indirection." Are evangelicals too direct with the gospel, too frontal?

EP: I'd hesitate to say we're too frontal because that's part of proclamation — the kingdom of God is here, repent, believe the gospel. But, yes, we need to do a lot more indirection. That's basically what a poet or a novelist does. I wouldn't say we need to do less frontal work with the gospel. We just need to do more of the subversive stuff.

MHR: I read an article where you wrote, "Every time someone tells a story and tells it well, the gospel is served." Do you mean that we need to put the gospel into different forms other than, "Here are the steps to be saved?"

EP: I think the key word in what I said is *served*. I didn't mean the gospel is proclaimed every time someone tells a story. When stories are told people begin to get a sense that life has value and meaning, and that they are significant. Then they start looking for the significance, asking, "Where's the meaning? Where can I find significance?" But until people begin to realize their embeddedness in creation and in suffering, that they aren't just accidents along the way, they really don't hear the gospel story. So, the important word is *served*.

If you were standing on a street corner, and some lonely person

212

came by, you could ask, "How are you?", and they might start telling you. If you listen to them, in five minutes, part of their life has come into being again. Your letting them tell their story provides them with a context to receive Jesus and for the Holy Spirit to work. But if they feel they have no story, then there is no context, no embeddedness.

MHR: So it's more of a doorway into proclaiming the gospel?

EP: It's also a familiarizing with the way in which the gospel norma-tively comes to us. It comes through the story of Jesus, not through the doctrine of Jesus. He was born, he lives, he dies, he rises again — it's all story. It's very important to keep the story and not just distill ideas out of it.

MHR: Evangelism is a word you're not comfortable with in light of how it's often used. What is evangelism to you?

EP: I'm not comfortable with it in its bullying sense. I'm very com-fortable with it in its etymological sense. Evangelism is believing and living as if this really is good news, as if it's incredible news, and we have something to say. Evangelism also means that we learn to say it the way Jesus said it and not just the way we want to say it. We have to learn his methods as well as his truth, so that we learn to treat people with dignity.

I heard a terrible story the other day from one of my students who had just come from Rwanda. As she was working among the dying, bleeding, and massacred, she was going through the bodies putting a mark on the foreheads of those who needed and could benefit from medical treatment. A team of doctors was following behind her to give the care and treatment. But there was one man, a fellow missionary, who was selling tracts to these people. She said, "What are you doing!" He answered, "It's surprising how many of them have a penny or a dime on them. It's amazing how much money these people have." It sounds unbelievable. Yet if you think ten seconds, you know you've seen this in yourself. Maybe in not quite as dramatic a way, but you've seen it in yourself.

Evangelicals need to learn how to do evangelism from Jesus, not from a handbook. I have a student who is a pastor in Hong Kong.

He's writing a dissertation for me on evangelism in Hong Kong. Everyone in Hong Kong is panicked because of 1997, when mainland China will begin to rule. They know they've got to evangelize the place before then. So they are using every public relations and technological method available. But in their minds, there are no *people* in Hong Kong. No sinner there is a person, but rather a target. This pastor is extremely upset with the depersonalization of the whole city in the name of evangelism.

MHR: And that kind of depersonalization contradicts the whole idea of incarnation.

EP: Yes, it does. The primary thing we're dealing with is that God is doing something. It's not just that he exists, it's that he's doing something. That's why we say we believe in the Holy Spirit, because we believe he is doing something. If God is doing something, the most important thing I can do is look for it, watch for it, and respond to it.

All this charging into the fray and "doing something for Jesus" is getting in the way. We are distracting people from what God is doing. You hear all these things where people are caught up on some bandwagon, not really paying attention to anything at all. By the time you get to be my age, you've grown very skeptical about anything where there is a great amount of enthusiasm, because next week there will be a new bandwagon.

I don't think I'm a quietist in any way, encouraging people to be spectators. In fact, it's very energizing when you start responding this way. It's also very freeing, because you're not working from anxiety, but from grace.

MHR: What would you like to be remembered for?

EP: (Laughing) Michael, that's not a good question!

MHR: Why not? You don't like to talk about yourself, do you?

EP: I would want to be remembered that I was a good husband, a good father, a good pastor. I would want to be remembered in terms of the people I've lived with.

MHR: *I think your answer is a powerful one. A lot of people might think, "He did* The Message, *he wrote sixteen books, he was a pastor. . . ." But you know that's all meaningless if those closest to you weren't loved. If you knew you were giving your last sermon or message, what would be some of your themes?*

EP: I think I would want to talk about things that are immediate and ordinary. In the kind of world we live in, the primary way that I can get people to be aware of God is to say, "Who are you going to have breakfast with tomorrow, and how are you going to treat that person?" I don't feel like I'm part of the big vision, or the catchy slogan. I just want to pay attention to what people are doing, and help them do it in acts of faith and prayer. I guess I'd want to say, "Go home and be good to your wife. Treat your children with respect. And do a good job at whatever you've been given to do."

Haphazardly Intent:
An Approach to Pastoring

In his eighteen years as pastor of Christ Our King Church in Bel Air, Maryland, Eugene Peterson has done a lot of thinking about successful pastoring: What is it? Who does it? How is it done?

The answers? Eugene doesn't know if there are hard and fast answers, but he agreed to talk about the problems in Leadership's interview. In the process we get glimpses of successes and failures, his frustrations, satisfactions, and, yes, the continuing struggles. In short, we get a picture of the way he does it.

Eugene developed his approach to pastoring from scriptural study (his book Five Smooth Stones for Pastoral Work, *Eerdmans, illustrates his method) and personal experience.*

Publisher Harold Myra, Editor Terry Muck, and Assistant Editor Dan Pawley found Eugene particularly enlightening, not only for his ministerial strategies, but also for the personal aspects of his life. He's a man who reads mysteries, extracts theological insights from classic novels, runs marathons, and goes for long hikes in the woods with his wife.

Originally published in *Leadership*, Winter 1981.

Haphazardly Intent: An Approach to Pastoring

You see yourself as a pastor, not an administrator. How did you develop that view of your pastoral role?

One of the worst years I ever had was in the early days of this church. Our building was finished, and I realized I wasn't being a pastor. I was so locked in running the church programs I didn't have time to be a pastor. So I went to the session one night to resign. "I'm not doing what I came here to do," I said. "I'm unhappy, and I'm never at home." The precipitating event was when one of my kids said: "You haven't spent an evening at home for thirty-two days." She had kept track! I was obsessive and compulsive about my administrative duties, and I didn't see any way to get out of the pressures that were making me that way. So I just said, "I quit."

How did they react to that?

They wanted to know what was wrong. "Well," I said, "I'm out all the time, I'm doing all this administrative work, serving on all these committees, and running all these errands. I want to preach, I want to lead the worship, I want to spend time with people in their homes. That's what I came here to do. I want to be your spiritual leader; I don't want to run your church." They thought for a moment and then said, "Let *us* run the church." After we talked it through the rest of the evening I finally said, "Okay."

I'll never forget what happened because of that talk. Two weeks later the stewardship committee met, and I walked into the meeting uninvited. The chairman of the group looked at me and asked, "What's the matter? Don't you trust us?" I admitted, "I guess I don't, but I'll try." I turned around, walked out, and haven't been back since.

Although now I never go to committee meetings, it took a year or so to de-program myself.

Don't you have to be moderator of the session, though?

Yes, I do moderate the session. And I tell other committees that if they want me to come for a twenty-minute consultation on a specific problem I'll be happy to do that. But I haven't been to a committee meeting now, except in that capacity, for twelve years.

CONVERSATIONS

You've been in Christ Our King Church now for eighteen years, and for the last twelve, your elders have successfully run the church. To what do you attribute that?

I suppose the mutual trust. They don't always do it the way I want them to, but when I decided I wasn't going to run the church, I also had to decide that if they were going to run it, they would have to do it their way, not mine. They listen to my preaching, are part of the same spiritual community, and know the values being created and developed; so I trust them to run the church in the best way they know how. Sometimes I do get impatient, because it's not the most efficient way to run a church; a lot of things don't get done.

Why is that? Because they are volunteers?

Partly. Some of the leaders aren't fully motivated. A congregation elects elders and deacons and sometimes chooses them for the wrong reasons. Some are only marginally interested in the life of the church, so they have neither the insight nor motivation to be productive. I can either give them the freedom to fail, or else step in and train people to be exactly what I want them to be. I've chosen to let them alone.

You're saying your first priority has to be your pastoral ministry? And that some other good things, such as making the administration of the church more efficient, must be left to others? There's nothing you can do about it because your priority is your ministry?

That's right.

Walk us through one of the inefficient things you allowed to happen, even though many leaders would see it as an administrative lapse.

I recall the case of a woman who was working in a voluntary capacity coordinating several closely related programs. When she started out, she was excited about it and did a good job. But as time went on, she dipped into other things and began doing her job indifferently. I was dealing with her as her pastor on family problems, and I felt it was important for me not to criticize her administration or ask her to resign. So I didn't do anything.

Matters became worse. I had many phone calls and listened to many complaints. I said, "I'd like to improve the situation, but I can't promise anything." I just waited with it and kept on being a pastor to her. I felt that to keep from compromising my position as pastor to her, I had to let the programs in a sense fail that year and suffer with poor administration. Now, many pastors wouldn't have permitted that, and for their ministry styles it might have been correct for them to step in and administratively handle the situation. I'm not against that kind of efficiency by any means, but I need to know what I'm good at. I have to pay the price of being good at certain things and not be a jack-of-all-trades.

Are you saying it's all right for pastors to sharply differ in how they run churches?

Definitely. I was Bill Wiseman's associate pastor in White Plains, New York. He has personal integrity and is highly skilled in all areas of pastoral work. He did more than any other person to enable me to be a pastor, especially in the administrative and managerial aspects. He runs a tight ship; things like structure and efficiency are very important to him. However, our styles of ministry contrast markedly. He now has a church of 5,000 members in Tulsa, Oklahoma, and he would go crazy running a church the way I do.

Later on, I realized my real gifts were not in administration; that what I really wanted to do was spend most of my time in personal ministry to my congregation.

Do you have any full-time staff?

No, we have a man who has been a pastor, and who works with us just on Sundays as a youth pastor. We also pay our choir director and organist; and we have a sexton who works about twelve to fifteen hours a week. There's no paid secretarial staff — just volunteers.

Volunteer secretaries? How has that worked?

Wonderfully! The idea came to me while I was reading a Dorothy Sayers mystery. Peter Wimsey is out trying to solve a murder, and he's having a difficult time getting information. Nobody will talk to him because he's an outsider. So he searches for someone who would know the community, locates an elderly spinster, and hires her as a typist. Then he has her employ a typing pool, and these ten to fifteen people are his links to the community.

I thought, "That's exactly what I need." So I asked a woman who I thought was competent in these areas to be the church office coordinator. We found two people for each weekday to work from nine to two o'clock, and informed the congregation of the new office hours. We divided up the office work to specific days and defined the responsibilities for each person. We have to plan a little bit ahead; we can't get things done immediately. But the plus part is that we really developed a lot of ministry. They do a lot of listening, they're in touch with many people, and they tell me things that are going on. They are important to the running of the church.

Do these ideas make a difference in how your people view the church? Do they draw the community together?

Community to me means people who have to learn how to care for each other, and in one sense, all efficient organization mitigates against community, for it won't tolerate you if you make mistakes.

This is not the situation in the church. We have inefficiency on our church office staff, but efficiency is not nearly as important as being patient with people and drawing them into a mutual sense of ministry. It's the way we operate; everything doesn't have to be "out today." If work is planned well enough, there's room for things to wait. Sometimes I need people to just answer the phone or do telephoning for me. I'll say, "Why don't you call so-and-so? She's lonely and bored; see if she can come in one day and help us." Sometimes that's just the thing needed to draw people back into a sense of ministry and community. They arrange for my home visitation from a list I give them. It's important and they know it's important.

Tell us about your home visitation program.

I've never done visitation systematically. Sometimes I'll read about somebody who goes through the whole church list in the year and sticks to a rigid schedule. I've never done that. I do home visitation on a sense of need, when I know there's something special going on in someone's life. Birth, death, loss of job, relocation, or trouble in the home are good indicators for me to visit. I go and talk with them, listen to their problems, find out where they're at, and pray with them. That's the advantage of pastoral work — it can respond to all the little nuances of community life and participate in them. There's a line in a poem about a dog going along the road with haphazard intent. Pastoral life is like that. There's a sense of haphazardness to it, for me anyway, because I don't want to get locked into systems where I have to say, "No, I'm too busy to do that; I can't see you because I have this schedule." But the haphazardness is not careless; there is purpose to it. I like to keep the freedom where I can be responsive to what's going on with my people.

It's fascinating the way you use literary allusions. Why should a pastor have time to read Dorothy Sayers? Isn't that a waste? Shouldn't you be deep into theology?

I read because I love to read. Novels are food for me. I need to be immersed in that kind of reality to keep my head straight and be in touch with things that are going on. Sometimes I read detective stories; they're kind of a spiritual tonic for me. When I really feel clogged and sodden, when everything is complicated, when I can't sort myself out, I'll go off for two days and read detective novels. I have to do it on the sly — that is, I have to keep my work going. I'll make the phone calls, see the people, make the visits, but then I race back to some corner and devour another story.

But, Eugene, don't you feel guilty?

Yes! But some time ago I finally became resolved to the fact that I'd never get over the feeling of guilt. My father was a butcher by trade, and when I was young, he would seldom permit me to just sit around. I always had to be doing something. When I'd be home reading a book, he would come into the room and say, "Gene, why aren't you doing something!" So I grew up feeling guilty about reading a book.

Sometimes when I'm reading, my wife Jan will say, "But shouldn't you visit so-and-so?" I kind of kiddingly say, "I'm really doing theological work." One day I wrote an article about Rex Stout called "Wolfe in Sheep's Clothing" in which I showed how Nero Wolfe and Archie Goodwin were really a type of ministry — a theological underpinning in pastoral work. It was fanciful, but I worked out all the details and sent it to a Christian magazine with a note to the editor saying I hoped he'd take it seriously, because if he didn't, all my credibility with my wife would go down the drain. Fortunately, he accepted it.

You mentioned that you also read novels. Which ones have been important to you in your role as a pastor?

First, *The Brothers Karamazov* by Dostoévsky. You have to read that over and over. There's a sense of the theology of destiny and of pastoral vocation in Father Zossima. Dostoevsky's perception of the human condition is essential reading for a pastor. Herman Melville's *Moby Dick*, for Americans especially, is in some ways perhaps the most important theological book ever written. It came at a key time in our history; it showed what we were missing by all of our sentimental optimism, everything-is-going-to-turn-out-okay attitudes. Faulkner articulates so well the sense of sin and redemption in, for instance, *Light in August*.

Flannery O'Connor's stories and novels are also very important. She was a great theologian. A book I think would be important for pastors is the collection of her letters called *The Habit of Being*. One of the things she says is that somebody reviewed one of her books and called her a hillbilly nihilist. She said, "I don't mind the first word, but I'd rather they call me a hillbilly theologian." She was very conscious of the Christian theology she presented through her work.

Walker Percy is helpful for Christian pastors today. Percy has one of the most powerful senses of ministry as a novelist of anybody working, and he senses the desperate straits we're in spiritually and morally. He's a believing Christian and is able to present that reality in his novels *The Moviegoer, Love in the Ruins,* and *The Last Gentleman.*

Is it important for all pastors to read?

No. Others might get the same kind of satisfaction out of completely different activities. I think all pastors must have some way of recharging their batteries, but reading is not the only way to do it.

For example, some people run to recharge their batteries. I

started running two years ago just to prove I could do it. But it wasn't enough for me to just go out there and feel good — I wanted to win races. The first race I entered, a ten-mile race over in Delaware, I finished first and my sixteen-year-old son finished second. It was exhilarating.

Do you use literary allusions in your preaching?

I don't, because my people aren't reading these things. I don't want to throw quotations at them that they're not in touch with.

But if you're reading a novel and you find this graphic illustration — isn't it tempting to relate it to your people?

Yes, but I want to preach the Word of God. Scripture is the only text that's important to me when I preach. I want my congregation to know what the Scriptures have to say about what they're living through. I start my sermon on Tuesday, choose the Scripture, and all week long I'm in dialogue with that Scripture, not just personally, but communally.

When I stand in the pulpit on Sunday, I hope the people hear themselves being addressed in the sermon because I've listened to them; I've asked their questions, cried out their doubts, gone through their boredom.

Don't you sometimes use illustrations from literature?

Sure. I've just been reading *Specimen Days* by Walt Whitman, and I'm going to use the illustration of Whitman in the hospitals during the Civil War. He goes through this terrible carnage. As he enters a hospital ward, he sees amputated arms and legs piled up outside because nobody has time to dispose of them. But he goes into the wards and is cheerful and happy — not insensitive, but bringing in that sense of life and vitality. This is a great passage to teach pastors about pastoral visitation in hospitals.

You've said that preaching should be from the Word. What about the pastoral role in general? Does it come straight from the Word, or has time changed its criteria?

A hundred or so years ago, pastors had a clear sense of continuity with past traditions. You knew you were doing work that had integrity; your life had recognized value and wholeness. Today, that's just not true; we're fragmented into doing different things. On the other hand, in the pulpit you do have that sense of continuity. When I'm preaching I know I'm doing work that has continuity way back to Isaiah. I prepare sermons somewhat the way Augustine and Wesley prepared sermons. I'm working out of the same Scriptures, so I don't feel third rate when I'm in the pulpit.

During the week, however, I do feel looked down upon — when I go to the hospital to visit, for example, I'm a barely-tolerated nuisance. They can talk about the healing-team business all they want to, but . . .

You don't buy that?

Not the healing team. The doctor, nurse, and pastor are a part of the healing team, but they don't look at you that way. I'm an amateur, they're the experts. And, in a sense, that's true. In the modern hospital it's a different kind of healing center than anything the church has experienced, and we don't fit there — we're outsiders. Other factors contribute to this feeling of uselessness, too. When you have serious problems running your church, what do you do? You call up a company and have them send out somebody to show you how to run a duplicating machine, or you take a course in church management. And who teaches you? Somebody from the business community. All through the week it seems we're intimidated by experts who are teaching us how to do our work — but they don't know what our work is. They're trying to make us respectable members of a kind of sub-organization they're running, and as a consequence, we develop a self-image that's healthy only on Sunday. I think pastoral work should be done well, but I think it has to be done from the inside, from its own base. That base, of course, must be the Bible; that's why I immerse myself in biblical materials. In my book *The Five Smooth Stones* I elaborate on this.

What does that title refer to?

Five Old Testament books — Song of Songs, Ruth, Lamentations, Ecclesiastes, Esther — each of them is an instance of pastoral work.

Song of Songs gives a model for directing prayer; Ruth is a story about visiting and counseling; Lamentations deals with grief and suffering; Ecclesiastes is an inquiry into values, the nay-saying sermon; and Esther is the story of community building. These aren't the only areas of pastoral work, but they are five important resources that provide for my pastoral ministry a great sense of continuity with traditional biblical principles. Today's pastor has to go back to similar scriptural truths. Nothing else will suffice. Modern success models can't match the effectiveness and self-worth provided by Scripture.

So you've found your pastoral role model in Scripture?

In the process of this study, I found I really like being a pastor; that's my vocation, pastoral work. Through the whole process, I discovered what God has called me to do and the gifts he had given me in order to do it. In my younger years, I often found myself doing things that were not my ministry. I finally learned to say, "No, I'm not going to do that anymore." I say no often. I disappoint many people, mostly people in the community and in my denomination. They have expectations they want me to fulfill, and I don't.

Let's speak in terms of the outward signs of success. Assume for a moment you've been approached by the search committee of a large church. They don't tempt you with traditional success lures such as a bigger salary or a bigger church — they appeal to your ministry values. Here's an opportunity to minister to 3,000 people, when your present congregation is only 300. Look at all these people you could be touching. This isn't necessarily the American success speech, but the ministry success speech. How do you respond?

That's simple. If you speak to 5,000 people and are not speaking out of your own authenticity, your own place where God has put you, you won't be any more effective as a servant of God. I don't think the number of people who hear you speak means a whole lot. What's important is that you do a good job wherever you are.

I hate suburbia; I detest it. I don't like the architecture, the homes, or the culture. Many times I've said, "Lord, why am I here?" My congregation doesn't share any of my interest in literature. We're not at the same place. But this is where I am. If you feel one of your goals or ministries is to build a spiritual community, then that's where it needs to be built. I've accepted this as my place for as long as I'm supposed to be here. That could be for the rest of my ministry or it could be until next year.

What would trigger a change?

That's difficult to say. Several times I've been at the place where I felt I was ready to leave. I just wasn't working well and was not fulfilled. Each time I've said, "I'm going to make sure this isn't a normal restlessness," and I've plunged back in and come out okay. Let me illustrate:

The last couple of years I've felt as though I've been losing momentum. I quit doing many things I used to be enthusiastic about. I felt my life becoming more inward. My deepest interest is in spiritual direction, and since our community contains many psychiatrists and counselors, I quit counseling so I could spend more time alone in study and prayer. But then I found large gaps had begun to form in my congregation's life. I had underestimated the community needs, and I really wasn't providing community leadership. I felt my people deserved more from their pastor than they were getting. I thought maybe I belonged in a church with a staff that could be assigned the tasks of parish programs, and I could study more and maintain a ministry of personal spiritual direction and of preaching.

I talked with a friend about this for three days. He listened thoughtfully and then said, "I don't think you need to leave, you just need somebody to be a director of parish life." The minute he said that, I thought of Jane. She's a woman of about thirty-five who came to me last spring saying she was in a transitional stage, wondering where the next challenge was for her. She had organized programs for the community, done a superb job administering them, and now was relatively idle. When I asked her if she would be director of parish life, a big grin came on her face. She said, "Let me tell you a story." Her husband was an elder, and two years ago was in the session meeting when I shared this problem about my leadership. After that meeting Fred had come home and said, "You know what Eugene needs? He needs you." It took me two years to recognize that. And now Jane is at the place in her life where she is ready to assume this role of parish director. She needs to be in ministry and is filling some of the gap left by my withdrawal. I'm free to study more and be more sensitive to spontaneous needs within the congregation. In a sense, I had gone through a period of failure to discover grace.

What is your evaluation of the church growth movement?

It's said to a lot of pastors, "You don't have to go along the rest of your life in a rut. You can do it differently and you can do it better." It has excited and awakened many pastors and given them some tools to work with. It's been a positive adrenaline boost to many churches. The worst thing about it is that the whole process and all the formulas are very easily distorted, and by a flick of the wrist it can turn into something very bad. There are people doing it really well, yet others do a poor imitation. The fact is that some ministries are not meant to exist in a burgeoning place. There are ministries meant to be small, in small places, with a few people. Growth, certainly, but not always in terms of quantity.

Is your church growing in numbers?

Slowly. My pastoral goals are to deepen and nurture spiritual growth in people, and to build a Christian community — not collect crowds.

Could it grow faster?

Well, it could. If I did certain things we could double our membership. We could organize house-to-house visitation, advertise, bring in special speakers, create programs for the community that would tune in to some of their felt needs, or develop an entertainment-centered musical program. We could do all of those — but we'd destroy our church.

Why would that destroy it? Why don't you get 350 new people you can preach to on Sunday?

Because I'd have to quit doing what I need to do — pray, read, prepare for worship, visit, give spiritual direction to people, develop leadership in the congregation. I have to work within the limits of my abilities while I continue maturing in them.

227

CONVERSATIONS

Aren't you neglecting the unchurched people of your community?

We're not the only church in Bel Air, and I'm not the only pastor. Few places in America are unchurched. Am I going to trust the Holy Spirit to do his work through other churches in my community, or am I going to think that if we don't do it, it's not going to get done?

A great deal of arrogance develops out of the feeling that when we have something good going, we have to triple it so everybody gets in on it. Many different ministries take place in the community and in the world, and it's bad faith on my part to assume the Holy Spirit isn't just as active in them as in my ministry.

Some people would probably say at this point, "All right, you've been in your church for eighteen years; yet you obviously have very little sensitivity for the need of evangelism. If every church acted like yours, how would the world be evangelized?"

My answer is that the Lord has many other people. I have to learn how to use my gifts. I'm not an evangelist, I'm a pastor. Some people in my congregation are evangelists and do a good job. I'm not much good to them; I don't know how to direct them. Another pastor would be able to do a better job with them. I believe evangelism is an essential work, but that doesn't mean I should make it the entire focus of my church. My gifts lie in other areas.

Many pastors want to focus their ministries, but when they try, pressures from various groups in the church who want other things keep them from it. They become reactors to their church environment.

That's true, and the pressures are real. I don't think anybody can do it alone. It helps to have colleagues who are experiencing the same things, friends you can share with.

Do you have a close group of colleagues?

I meet with a group of twelve pastors of various denominations every Tuesday from 11:30 to 2:00 for prayer and Bible study. Since we all use a lectionary, we preach from the same passage. Our discussion relates to our pulpit ministries — we exegete the passage, discuss it and suggest ways we might preach from it. We're all committed to preaching, so we don't talk about church programs, problems, or how to run the church. When someone is going through personal difficulty, we scrap the agenda and deal just with that. But we don't let anything else intrude.

How does this sharing of ideas affect your preaching?

It gives it depth. It insists on a certain discipline and gives it priority; you can't put preaching off until Saturday. I've had rare weeks when all the sermon preparation I did was in that weekly meeting. Everything fell apart that week, with deaths and other crises, but I was able to stand in the pulpit and have a respectable sermon.

A while ago you pointed out that preaching is in some ways much more difficult now than it was a century or two ago. What has changed to produce this effect?

Preaching a hundred years ago was a kind of literate and sophisticated conversation between pastor and people. The people knew the Bible as well as the pastor did, and they all shared the same culture. Today most people are biblically illiterate; they enter the Sunday morning service unsettled, not with maturity and wholeness, but ripped apart by all kinds of things. The Sunday morning congregation is a hospital, and you just can't do the same things done years ago.

You know it's a hospital because you've been involved with people, you've seen trauma and pain first-hand during the week?

Yes, you know — the alcoholic, the adulterer, the family whose kid just ran away from home. It's all sitting right in front of you. Saturday nights I go to the church, walk through the sanctuary for an hour, and think ahead to Sunday morning and the diversity and chaos represented. It can be discouraging. It's something that Alexander Whyte, one of the great preachers of the last century, didn't have to face. He stood in the pulpit and his sermon was a conversation with the people who were well versed in Scripture and who read the same books. He made his people read books. He took them into *Pilgrim's*

Progress, William Law, Saint Theresa, Dante. He was their school-master as well as their minister.

The people I preach to watch television, listen to the radio, take night courses, and go to special seminars for their work. They're just bombarded. They don't need me to say, "You must read this book." I need to say, "Let's worship God," and then lead them into Scripture and make that a privileged time in their lives. But on the other hand, there's an electricity in preaching; you're suddenly breaking into the humdrum, technological, rat-race world, and you have something really fresh, a new dimension to share. That's exciting.

What counsel would you give to pastors who are in struggling situations, or who are in small churches, and are judging themselves as failures?

That's tough to answer. I'm convinced many pastors are actually doing a really good job.

But they don't necessarily believe they are?

They don't know it — that they are preaching and counseling and leading well. They don't expect to be perfect, but they're doing a good job. I guess it goes back to the other themes we've talked about. A person has to be content to do what he is good at and offer it constantly to the Lord. If you keep trying to do what you're not good at, you're bound to fail. Nobody from the outside knows what the work of a pastor is, so they keep asking us to do things — things we're not good at — and then we end up feeling guilty for not doing a good job.

But doesn't every pastor have to be an administrator, even if that's not his gift?

Every pastor has to make sure administration gets done. If you can't see to it that it does get done, you're in trouble. Pastoring in the twentieth century requires two things: One, to be a pastor, and two, to run a church. They aren't the same thing. Every seminary ought to take their pastoral students and say, "Look, God has called you to be a pastor, and we want to teach you how to be pastors. But the fact is that when you go out to get a job, chances are they're not going

230

to hire just a pastor, they're going to hire somebody to run the church. Now, we'll show you how to run a church, and if you master what we're telling you, you can probably do it in ten to twelve hours a week. That's the price you're going to pay to be in the position of pastor."

What are some of the things you do to pay that price?

I return telephone calls promptly. I answer my mail quickly. I put out a weekly newsletter. I think that's essential. When the parish newsletter comes out once a week, the people sense you're on top of things; they see their names and what's going on. It's good public relations.

Couldn't you do this with the Sunday bulletin?

No, because too many people would miss it. Every week our one-page newsletter assures the congregation everything is under control. If you want to keep your job, people have to believe the church is running okay.

How does a pastor develop communication with his congregation?

I'm not quite sure how it's taken place with me. Leveling with your elders is important. Many times during my ministry I told my elders how I felt, what I was going through, my sense of ministry, what was important to me, and what I felt I wasn't doing well. Twelve years ago I quit, because I just didn't think I could meet the expectations I set up for myself. I assumed they had the same expectations, but I was wrong. They didn't want me to burn out.

What else can a pastor do?

Periodically confer with the leadership of your church and say what is really on your mind. They have a right to the kind of pastor they feel they need. Maybe the combination isn't right. I think there has to be that sense of expendability. I've been surprised at how responsive the people in my congregation have been when I've shared these things.

231

How does that communication begin? Who can pastors talk to? There certainly isn't time in a board meeting.

I haven't solved that problem, but for the most part, I think it's spontaneous. Several times in my ministry when I felt things weren't going well, I've selected people from the congregation and asked if they would meet with me three or four times. "I'm not quite sure what is going on with me," I've said, "but I'm concerned about the ministry of the church. I want to be the best pastor I can, and I'm confused. Would you let me talk to you?" I've made these groups small, five or six people who are in leadership positions, and they are always people who are in touch with the congregation. Sometimes I just need to share my concerns. But sometimes these people have given me solid direction, too.

A number of churches have a group that meets monthly to be a sounding board for the pastor, to really hear his concerns, and perhaps to be an ombudsman for him. How would you feel about setting up such a group?

I'd feel good about that!

In your weekly meeting with your local ministers, what are the biggest problems you hear?

Family and marital problems. I'd say these are the most painful things in terms of pastoral crisis. Another one, which doesn't have the same sense of acuteness, is the feeling of inadequacy. When pastors don't have large congregations or don't receive affirmation from their people, it's very difficult for them to provide creative spiritual leadership. In fact, considering the little affirmation many receive, I marvel that it's done at all. One of the key ministries of lay persons is affirmation of their leaders.

Can you recall times when affirmation boosted your sense of worth?

Yes, although a lot of those things are subtle and small, and they just accumulate. I've been teaching at a Roman Catholic seminary. I've done this for two years, and I'm still a little uneasy. I'm in a foreign territory, so I'm never sure I'm doing a good job. Last week I conducted a class, and I didn't do a very good job. I just didn't teach very well. I spent most of the period letting the class talk about how they were feeling about Scripture instead of giving them content. I have one student, a nun, who has a Ph.D. She is very sharp and knows more about the subject than I do. I'm afraid she feels she's not getting her money's worth. However, she called me up two days after the class and said, "I just want to tell you your class is the best thing that's ever happened to me here. It's nice to see this subject matter not just as academic symbols on the chalkboard, but as part of my personal development as a Christian." That really boosted me; the one person I felt I was letting down told me something was happening to her spiritually. That was great affirmation. I could go for a long time on that.

How do you find ways of getting your own affirmation without being dependent on the compliments of others?

I think it has to do with discovering my need for spiritual nurture and making sure I get it. Prayer is very important for me — I can't function without it.

How does your prayer life work?

In the mornings I spend a couple of hours alone with the Lord. I get up at 6:00 and put a pot of coffee on. Very often I do nothing except pray the Psalms — I've always loved them. They've been the church's prayerbook for a long time. There's an old kind of a monastic nostalgia in me; in some of the monasteries all they did was pray the Psalms. I also read the New Testament, and then after an hour and a half or so I sometimes read something else or write. If I start writing, I often write for a couple of hours.

    Mondays are important. For the first few years of my ministry I never took a day off. There were too many "important" things to do. Now my wife and I leave the house and go hiking in the woods for the whole day, regardless of the weather. We pack a lunch and take our binoculars for bird watching. We've been doing that every Monday for twelve years. It's important for both of us because it's a completely different environment and something we both enjoy doing. In the morning it's a quiet time when we can just be ourselves as well as get in touch with ourselves. At lunch we talk, and then often keep on for the rest of the afternoon.

What role has your wife played in your ministry?

A very prominent and strong one, for it's been a shared ministry. She's a marvelous entertainer, and we have people in our home often. She's a master at making people feel at home, and she's good about caring for them. She's really helped create a sense of community in our church.

I told you that when we arrived, one of our goals was to develop spiritual community. I thought it would be pretty easy: we'd get these people in our home, pray together, sing some hymns, and we'd have it. Well, it just didn't happen. Sometimes we felt we were making progress, but it never really happened. Then a young woman in our congregation died of cancer. She was thirty-one years old and had six children. About a month after she died, the father was discharged from his job and then lost his house. We took those kids into our home. Suddenly things started happening. Food would appear on our doorstep; people would call up and take the kids out and entertain them. It was almost as if we came to a place of critical mass. Then it just exploded, and we suddenly had community in the congregation. It didn't fizzle out either. The hospitality increased and people took an interest in each other. It seemed almost like a miracle, and it took just one incident to trigger it. All our earlier attempts to create community now bore fruit because of the meeting of a need that wasn't part of our strategy.

How can other churches develop community?

It's very difficult to get, and there's not much community in our country. Most of our relationships with each other are based on needs, on roles imposed on us. There's no shortcut to true community. We're immersed in a transactional society where we trade things off, exchange things, and consume things. To get to the point where we're open and vulnerable enough to just be with people is not all that easy. But the thing that is prominent in my mind now is that at our church we did everything we could think of to develop community, and it didn't develop. We did one thing that wasn't part of the strategy, and success, if you want to call it that, came.

An overweening, or overbearing, desire to be successful, it seems to me, inhibits attainment of true community and true success. It prevents us from doing things that are risky, that we can fail at.

Does a long pastorate help in developing community?

It's certainly not the secret formula that ensures success. There are a lot of dangers in a long pastorate.

Such as?

You do what meets the congregation's expectations so you can develop a comfortable society where you're all nice to each other. Or you do good work and the people come to respect you, and then it's easy to quit growing and bask in those past accomplishments. There's also the very real danger of becoming too important to people — your goal is to develop in them a sense of maturity, independence, first-handedness with God.

The other side of the coin is how do you develop community except in a long-term situation? It took about five years before that first incident happened for our church. Only in the last six or seven years have I really felt community is starting to take place.

I can now sense that I'm pastor of a community of people, not just a collection of neighbors.

Subversive Spirituality

For 29 years, Eugene H. Peterson was the founding pastor of Christ Our King Presbyterian Church in Bel Air, MD. At the time of the interview he had just resigned. He described his decision this way:

"Last summer, my son, Eric, was ordained. A moderator of the presbytery asked me to pray the ordination prayer. I anointed him with oil, laid hands on him, and prayed, and while that was going on, I had this extraordinary sense that I was done. I had passed on the mantle to Eric. It took me by complete surprise. My wife and I talked and prayed about it for a long time and finally, about six weeks ago, announced to our congregation that we were resigning."

Eugene has decided to be writer-in-residence at Pittsburgh Seminary for a year and then end up, hopefully, at a school or seminary where he can teach and write. Whatever he does, we hope it will include lots of writing because Eugene Peterson is one of this century's most important writers. Eugene Peterson is bright (people fight over his recommended reading list at seminary), prolific (A Long Obedience in the Same Direction, Traveling Light, Run with the Horses, Working the Angles, Reversed Thunder, Answering God, The Contem-

---

Originally published in *The Door,* November/December 1991.

plative Pastor), *passionate about the gospel, and radical in his understanding of the ministry.*

Eugene Peterson is passionate about life as well. He is very intense and very focused. We're not sure, but we don't think he is known as Mr. Practical Joker in his local presbytery. We asked him if he actually owns a Whoopee Cushion and . . . he didn't seem to know what we were talking about. We think, however, you will understand very clearly what he is talking about in this interview.

Door: How does busyness affect our spiritual lives?

Peterson: Busyness is the enemy of spirituality. It is essentially laziness. It is doing the easy thing instead of the hard thing. It is filling our time with our own actions instead of paying attention to God's actions. It is taking charge.

Door: There is an old Russian proverb that says "Pray to God and keep rowing to shore." It implies that life is both busyness and spirituality. Life doesn't have to be an either/or situation, does it?

Peterson: It *is* an either/or situation. Busyness has nothing to do with activity, and spirituality is not the absence of activity. You either enter into what God is doing or you don't. A busy person is a lazy person because they are not doing what they are supposed to do.

Door: What does that mean?

Peterson: It means that the elder in your church who goes to all the meetings, runs all the committees, and, as a result, doesn't take care of his kids or his wife, is not doing what he is supposed to be doing. Everyone, including the pastor, thinks this elder is wonderful, but his wife and children don't think it's so wonderful.

Door: It seems like most pastors we know are just like you have described. Busy, busy, doing the work of the church.

Peterson: Most pastors want to run a good church and they will do just about anything to make that happen. We pastors have a good nose for the market. We sense when people are getting a little bored and we jazz things up a bit, challenge them with a new project, and we use Sunday morning "worship" as the stage to do that. I'm convinced that most pastors don't give two cents about worship. They really don't. And there's a good reason for it. True worship doesn't make anything happen. It is a losing of control, a weaning from manipulative language and entertainment. It's tough to practice that reality because, given the choice between worship and dancing around the golden calf, pastors know people are going to dance. Pastors sense that if they really practice worship they are going to empty out the sanctuary pretty fast.

Door: We agree that pastors should not be in the entertainment business, so what should they be doing?

Peterson: The pastor's primary work is leading people in worship on Sunday morning, proclaiming the word of God, being knowledgeable in theology and scripture, and being committed to pastoral care which does not have the therapeutic model for its structure. The pastor is the one who is available one-on-one through the week to personalize, to customize, and to deal with the uniqueness of everyone's situation. Pastors pray a lot. Prayer is hard work, but prayer should be the distinctive about us. We should have a deliberate or a conscious, intelligent, personal relationship with God which is articulated in prayer.

Door: It's a lot easier to be busy instead.

Peterson: I hate this professionalization of the church's ministry where the pastor hogs the show all the time. The laity should be committed to doing the real ministry of the church and the pastor should be committed to the spiritual direction of the laity.

Door: We're shocked because we didn't hear you mention a word about the pastor going to committee meetings.

Peterson: I don't go to them.

Door: *That's heretical.*

Peterson: I had a friend — he's dead now — and committee meetings were his forte. He was a pastor at committee meetings and it was his best structure for working. So I don't want to be dogmatic about this, but if a pastor complains about the committee meetings, then he ought to quit going to them. I haven't been to a single committee meeting in 25 years.

Door: *That is amazing. We hear a lot of ministers complain about all the committee meetings they have to attend.*

Peterson: The reason they are going to all those committee meetings is that they don't trust their laity.

Door: *They don't trust their laity?*

Peterson: No. It's an ego problem, really. We have a thousand euphemisms for our ego — spiritual concern, theological wisdom, equipping the laity. All of those phrases can be a euphemism for not trusting the laity.

Door: *Don't the people in your congregation get a little irritated that you never attend a committee meeting?*

Peterson: They love it. They understand that they are in charge. It gives them dignity. Now, understand, I didn't do this cold turkey. People don't know what a pastor does. They know what their doctor does, they know what their lawyer does, so I help them understand what their pastor does. The reason I don't go to committee meetings isn't because I'm too good for them; I don't go because I believe in *them.* Their ministries have just as much validity as mine. I don't think the pastor is the most important person in the church, but the task we are given is very important and we had better do it.

Door: *You mentioned earlier that your model for ministry is spiritual direction. Wouldn't most pastors describe their model for ministry as administration or management?*

239

Peterson: Unfortunately, that is the predominant model for the American pastor.

Door: What would the model of spiritual direction look like?

Peterson: It doesn't have a very exact definition, but classically, it is a friendship or companionship which enables another person to recognize and respond to God in their lives *in detail,* not in generalities. It takes a lot of leisure. You can't do it in a hurry. It requires extensive knowledge of your people. You do this over a number of years, not a number of days. It has no goal in the end. It is not counseling. Counseling has a goal, but there's no goal in spiritual direction.

Door: It sounds so . . . uh . . . non-productive.

Peterson: There is a great story in *Moby Dick.* They are in the whale boat and they are chasing Moby Dick. The sailors are rowing furiously and the sea is frothing, but there is one person in the boat who is not doing anything. He is just sitting there, quiet and still. It's the harpooner, ready to throw the harpoon. Melville has this great line: "To ensure the greatest efficiency in the dart, the harpoonists of this world must start to their feet out of idleness and not out of toil." For a long time the harpoonist appears to be "non-productive." But that is only so that when the right moment comes he can be productive.

Door: So spiritual direction is a slow process that looks idle and inefficient.

Peterson: It's subversive. I'm a subversive, really. I gather the people in worship, I pray for them, I engage them often in matters of spiritual correction, and I take them on two really strong retreats a year. I am a true subversive. We live in a culture that we think is Christian. When a congregation gathers in a church, they assume they are among friends in a basically friendly world (with the exception of pornographers, etc.).

If I, as their pastor, get up and tell them the world is not friendly and they are really idol worshippers, they think I'm crazy. This culture has twisted all of our metaphors and images and structures of un-

240

derstanding. But I can't say that directly. The only way that you can approach people is indirectly, obliquely. A head-on attack doesn't work.

Jesus was the master of indirection. The parables are subversive. His hyperboles are indirect. There is a kind of outrageous quality to them that defies common sense, but later on the understanding comes. The largest poetic piece in the Bible, Revelation, is a subversive piece. Instead of (being) a three-point lecturer, the pastor is instead a storyteller and a pray-er. Prayer and story become the primary means by which you get past people's self-defense mechanisms.

In my book, I say it this way: "I must remember that I am a subversive. My long-term effectiveness depends on my not being recognized for who I am as a pastor. If the church member actually realized that the American way of life is doomed to destruction and that another kingdom is right now being formed in secret to take its place, he wouldn't be pleased at all. If he knew what I was really doing and the difference it was making, he would fire me."

True subversion requires patience. You slowly get cells of people who are believing in what you are doing, participating in it.

Door: This sounds so . . . well . . . opposite of what most people think a successful pastor should be doing.

Peterson: Pastors should not give people what they want just because it brings in customers . . . which it does. The biggest enemy to the Church is the development and proliferation of programs to meet people's needs. Everyone has a hunger for God, but our tastes (needs) are screwed up. We've been raised on junk food, so what we ask for is often wrong or twisted. The art of spiritual leadership is not to tell people that they can't have what they want, but to give them something of what they've asked for and not let it go at that. You try to shift the dimensions of their lives slowly towards what God wants.

Door: Pretty strong words.

Peterson: I can get stronger because I am appalled by how trivially many pastors conduct their ministries. They just do Mickey Mouse stuff all day long.

241

Door: Like . . . ?

Peterson: They go to committees all day long, spend a lot of time in community organizations, do secretarial work, visit for the sake of recruitment, whip up enthusiasm for the next project. We are in a desperate place. There is an urgency about what we are doing which cannot put up with triviality. The task we are given is very important, urgent, and we'd better do it. There really is an apocalyptic dimension to what we do. I believe the New Testament is an eschatological book shaped by a redeemed apocalypticism.

Door: Redeemed apocalypticism? Uh . . . we know what you mean, but for a lot of our readers you'll have to translate that.

Peterson: Everything in the New Testament is written under the pressure of the end. Christ is coming back. Revelation is a flowering of that, but it's all through the New Testament. Unfortunately, the New Testament has been reinterpreted into a kind of moral *Reader's Digest* advice column. It's no wonder there is no sense of urgency. But this is an urgent time and the task of the Christian is to learn how to maintain that urgency without getting panicked, to stay on our toes without caving in to the culture. This is not just a benign culture where everything is going to be fine. Everything is not going to be fine.

Door: How do people learn to live with the tension you've just described?

Peterson: The pastor has to model this for the congregation. People are dying and being killed, getting divorced. We all live in a perpetual crisis community, and the pastor is the one who is there in these moments of crisis, subversively modeling what it is like to live the gospel.

Door: It seems odd that, as a result of your view of the urgency of the hour, you haven't mentioned the word "evangelism."

Peterson: I don't use the word "evangelism" much. It's a ruined word. I have a great concern about evangelism. The very nature of the gospel is that it is to be communicated and shared. But I don't think the gospel is ever going to be very popular. It never has been and it never will be. If we live the Christian faith right, it will not result in full and overflowing churches. There is just no evidence for that any place in scripture or history. If we determine successful evangelism by how many people we bring into the church, then we've got it screwed up from the start. What we have to do is make sure that we are being personal and energetic about sharing our faith — but also being honest. And I think honesty is the hard part.

Door: You've been at your church a long time — 29 years. What do you think about the long-term pastorate?

Peterson: Long-term pastorates cause the minister to grow. You *have* to grow. You can preach and worship and disguise who you are for a few years, but then comes the time when you have to make a decision. Am I going to move to a new place and disguise myself again until they discover who I am, or am I going to become something more? If you decide to stay, you will be forced to become a deeper and more extensive person.

Door: How would you describe your church?

Peterson: It's not a large church — we reported 438 members in the last general assembly. Most of the time it has been much smaller than that — more like 250 to 300 people. But in the 29 years I've been here, we have probably received 2,000 members. That's with no evangelism program. But I want to make it clear that this isn't the only way to have a church, and what I am doing isn't the only way to be a pastor.

Door: Do you have any problem with big churches of, say, 2,000 members?

Peterson: When we started our church, we decided to plan for a church of 500 members. I thought 500 was manageable. We decided that when we got to the place where we exceeded 500, we would start another church. We are at that point now, and we tried to start another church, and the presbytery said no because it is more cost effective to have a church twice our size.

Door: Great reason.

Peterson: Yeah. Now we've got cost-effective people running things. We have to go along with it because I don't believe in flouting my authorities. But let me say something about the 2,000-member church. There is a way to be the Church with 2,000 members — or 5,000 members, for that matter. It requires more pastors, of course, but part of my situation is personal. It would be a mistake for me to pastor a church of that size, but I have nothing against a large congregation.

Door: Have you enjoyed the pastorate?

Peterson: Being a pastor is an incredibly good, wonderful work. It is one of the few places in our society where you can live a creative life. You live at the intersection of grace and mercy and sin and salvation. We have front line seats and sometimes we even get to be part of the action. How could anyone abandon the glory of that kind of life to become a management expert? We are artists, not CEOs. The true pastorate is a work of art — the art of life and spirit.

On Pentecostals, Poets,
and Professors

TSF: How long have you been out of seminary, Eugene?

Peterson: Twenty-six years.

TSF: Was seminary a positive or negative experience for you?

Peterson: Well, for me it was mixed. The seminary I went to was the old Biblical Seminary, a non-denominational school in New York which is now New York Theological Seminary. I hadn't really planned to go to seminary. I grew up in a pentecostal church and it was very anti-intellectual. I was afraid of higher education and I had stretched the limits by going to college. Pastors and people had filled my head with warnings: "You are going to lose your faith; you are going to leave the Lord." But I ended up at seminary, really kind of through the back door because other things fell apart. I didn't know anything about the place, except a college professor got me there. In some ways I was fortunate because I had plenty of intellectual curiosity and motivation. I didn't need anybody to stimulate me intellectually, I just needed a library. Biblical Seminary at that

Originally published in *TSF Bulletin*, March-April 1984.

point was in its decline, and it really didn't have very much going for it in theological studies. But it was a spiritual community and so I found my theological education in a place where prayer was central and important.

TSF: How exactly did that spiritual community operate?

Peterson: There were daily prayers, and a service of prayer. Through the year there were retreat days and there was an encouragement to prayer. Many of the faculty really believed in prayer. It was important to them and they showed it in their own lives. Part of the spiritual community emphasis had to do with the student body. We had many missionaries on furlough. It wasn't a large student body, so these people had influence. The way they lived and prayed made a difference.

TSF: If you were going to seminary today, what type of theological education would you seek?

Peterson: I don't see any seminary that's doing what it seems to me is essential — providing encouragement and direction for the life of faith, training people in the traditions which have always been part of that life, and in the process providing theological structure by which to articulate it. But the whole *guts* of the material have been dropped out and we still have the intellectual, theological stuff but it's out of context. I know there are seminaries that are trying to repair that. But some of the repairs seem to me to be only cosmetic surgery, and I don't know how it's going to turn out.

TSF: You found a balance of spirituality and scholarship among your teachers in seminary?

Peterson: No. I found the interest in the spiritual life, the commitment to the spiritual life. I didn't find the intellectual rigor, which I had to pursue on my own; but, no, I didn't find the balance.

TSF: You were pursuing an academic career?

Peterson: Yes.

TSF: Then you planned to complete a Ph.D. in what area?

Peterson: In Semitic languages. I went to Johns Hopkins and studied with William Albright in the field of Semitics.

TSF: How did you personally try to maintain that balance of scholarship and piety?

Peterson: Well, I don't know, Bill. A lot of this you do by dumb luck. My background, the church, the environment I grew up in, was very intense spiritually, and so I developed through my childhood and adolescence a life which was passionate in terms of spirituality. While much was extravagant and some of it was beside the point, the one thing that was communicated to me was that this Christian life had to do with intensity, with passion, with depth. And so l was spoiled. I never was able to put up with anything that was devotionally dilettante. What I had to fight for was some intellectual rigor. And I didn't find that for a long time. You see, I just had that hunger myself for learning, for knowing. I knew it was possible because I got in touch with some of the old masters who had been dead for a thousand years.

TSF: Who were some of those masters?

Peterson: Well, Augustine was one, Bernard was one, Gregory, Thomas Aquinas. Those were the people who attracted me early. Later I discovered others who were more Protestant and Puritan, but these earlier masters were the ones who inspired me. They were in a sense pre-reformation, they were pre-controversial, and so my pentecostal background had no labels for them. The kind of spirituality that I grew up with had to do with passion and intensity and inwardness — so these masters fit into that style. As I left the culture of the pentecostal church, I was able to leave the stuff that never fit, mainly entertainment — and there is a great deal of charlatanism in that whole business. But somehow because of the home I lived in I escaped that.

TSF: Do you teach now?

Peterson: Yes, I teach in both a secular university and a Roman Catholic seminary.

TSF: Tell me about the seminary teaching.

Peterson: Well, it's been very stimulating to me. I'm working with a community that I have never been close to before, the Roman Catholic community. I've found that in terms of ministry there's not that much difference. We're dealing with the same material. I've been very heartened by the fact that they've wanted me, that they've looked to me for something they are missing themselves — a theology of ministry and an interpretation of Scripture which has spirituality as its base. They have been caught up in this whole secularizing syndrome too — ministry as a career option and Scripture as kind of an academic exercise. They've been very receptive and warmly accepting of an approach to ministry which has spirituality at its core — along with intellectual integrity.

TSF: It seems to me that a lot of students today are viewing seminary as a place to study faith and to work out some types of belief system even though they do not have any kind of special calling or desire to enter ministry. Do you think that's a good trend among Christian students?

Peterson: The students I have for the most part aren't really there to learn. They're there to get a job or get equipped for a job, and it's very discouraging for a professor who gets excited about the material and wants to teach what's there to have the primary concern of most of the students be "how can I pass this course?" I think the motivation you mention is okay. Any place is a good place to get started. But if I'm reading the signs rightly, I don't think the seminaries have adjusted to that desire, so that they are not developing the kind of community that meets that expectation or that need. I don't see anything wrong with going to seminary with that desire, but I think it would be better if the seminary said, "our primary task is to be a spiritual community which develops theological skills." Because thinking about learning theology is not a spiritual task. I had a student at St. Mary's who left his preparation for the ministry several years ago, but continued to maintain his interest in theology. He kept coming to St. Mary's Seminary just because he loved theology even though he didn't go to church and didn't believe in God. And during a course I taught last fall, he came to faith, and he ended the course by making a commitment to both the Christian faith and the ministry. It was the first time he had been in a course which had anything to do with his personal life and his vocation. Now that's hard for me to believe, that someone can go to a theological school for four years and never find oneself addressed at a personal level in order to integrate life with thinking.

TSF: Would you consider yourself an evangelical?

Peterson: Yes.

TSF: Given the state of that term today, could you briefly describe that for us.

Peterson: Evangelical for me, Bill, means two things. One, it has to do with a certain commitment to Scripture and the gospel as life-changing. It also has to do with culture, with a certain culture of the church which comes out of the pietistic, revivalist, sectarian tradition, and often has moved into other parts of the church. That's the church I grew up in, it's the movement I grew up in. Even though I'm part of an establishment denomination at this point, the evangelical church in both the theological and cultural sense is what I'm at home in. I'm not denominationally a part of it, but it is where I find my natural allies and friends and community.

TSF: What future do you see for evangelicalism in this country?

Peterson: Well, I think it's a very positive, strong future because evangelicalism has become, I think, much less sectarian, much less defensive, more confident. Evangelicals no longer understand themselves as a beleaguered band of believers holding the truth, but are really quite confident that they are in the mainstream of things and are willing to become part of other denominations, cross denominational lines. I can be part of a Roman Catholic faculty without any sense of betrayal or leaving the faith or anything like that. So I think it's a very strong position. It's having a fermenting influence on the church.

TSF: Do you see any dangers in the movement?

Peterson: The dangers in evangelicalism seem to me to stem from an unreflective pietism. The pietistic element of the past is not understood in all its depth, so just little parts of it are taken. The dangers also stem from sectarianism which develops a minority mentality of being-against and has a kind of paranoia. I still observe that feistiness, but it seems to me to be less and less. I'm encouraged. The danger is that there is a strength that comes from paranoia. You can marshall a lot of energy if you are paranoid enough, and so as the evangelical movement becomes more ecumenical or open there is a natural danger that it lose its sharp edge. I am not a good enough cultural analyst to know if that's happening. I'm not aware that it is, but I should think theoretically that would be the danger.

TSF: As an evangelical in the Presbyterian Church (USA), what struggles have you had?

Peterson: I haven't had any struggles, I don't think. But I've never felt at home. I've always been an outsider. That's part of my background. I didn't grow up in this, so I've never been part of the club, but that's not their fault. The Presbyterian Church has been very good to me. They've given me a place to work, a congregation to be pastor of, so I've never felt like my sense of being an outsider was their fault. I've never felt particularly at home with the national trends, but I feel very much at home with the historical developments, the whole rootage of the Presbyterian Church, so I'm willing to live through fashions which aren't congenial to me if I sense that the whole basic structure has a good foundation, and I think it does.

TSF: Have you learned any particular lessons working within a mainline denomination that you would like to pass on?

Peterson: The Presbyterian Church is pluralistic. For some people, of course, that's a negative. For me, because I'm a minority person, it's a positive. And if you're a black person in a mostly white world, you're glad when they're pluralistic. And as an evangelical and somebody from a sectarian background, I'm glad that my church is pluralistic.

TSF: Would you encourage more students from evangelical backgrounds to pursue mainline seminary education and ordination?

Peterson: You're asking two different questions. I don't have any opinion about where to go for your education. But it seems to me that it is always better to live out of your own tradition than it is to leave it. That wasn't possible for me. I tried and it didn't work. They didn't accept me; I didn't fit the pentecostal denomination, so I really had to leave. I think it would have been wrong for me to stay because I would have always been a malcontent. I would have always been disrupting things. That takes a lot of emotional energy. I envy people who are in the denomination in which they grew up and are able to build out of those roots and work out of that kind of tradition. I think it gives you a certain strength. So if it's possible, I think you should stay where you were born, but it's not always possible.

TSF: So for students who go off to college and deepen their commitment to the faith through various evangelical parachurch organizations, you would encourage those students to stay within the Presbyterian Church or the United Methodist Church or the United Church of Christ?

Peterson: By all means. Yes.

TSF: What dangers lie in mainline churches as opposed to the independent Bible church tradition?

Peterson: Well, I think there is more danger in the establishment churches assimilating to a bourgeois culture or a church culture. There's more danger in assimilating to a kind of professionalism, a clerical professionalism. In the mainline denominations, congregations generally let you get by with anything you want to do, as long as you are competent. However, evangelical congregations often have well-defined theological expectations and sometimes spiritual expectations and perhaps there's a higher degree of accountability. That's just a hunch I have. On the other hand, the danger in the independent churches is for the pastor to become some kind of a superstar or a dictator, and see oneself as the leader of the church rather than the servant or the pastor of the church. I think it's a very strong danger.

TSF: You read widely. And not strictly within the religious or philosophical field?

Peterson: Right.

TSF: It seems to me that more students today lack a "classical" liberal arts education, and thus they seem to lack that imaginative-creative capacity. How would you suggest a seminarian correct this imbalance? You get your chance, Eugene, to correct all those students who are going to read the TSF Bulletin.

Peterson: The theologian's best ally is the artist. I think we need to awaken an interest in literature which is natural to most people but which gets suppressed. We must see the imagination as an aspect of ministry. What we're really talking about is creativity. We're participating in something that God is doing. He is creating new life. He created life and he's been creating life. Now how does the creative process work? The people who attend to that question most frequently are writers, artists, sculptors, musicians. People involved in church leadership should be passionately interested in how the creative process works — not in how to say things accurately. This great emphasis on how to communicate accurately is a dead-end street. Communicating clearly is not what we are after. What we are after is creating new life. The creative writer isn't interested in saying things as simply or as accurately as possible, but in touching the springs of creativity and letting the imagination work in analogical ways. I think if I were going to set up a seminary curriculum, I would spend one whole year on a couple of poets. I would insist that students learn how to read poetry, learn how words work. We don't pay enough attention to words — we use words all the time but we use them in a commercialized, consumer way. That consumer-oriented use of words has little place in the church, in the pulpit, in counseling. We're trying to find how words work, their own work.

I'm not insisting on any particular poet here. I've just finished reading a volume of poems of William Stafford. I've read Stafford for years, and a book of collected poetry which just came out would be helpful. He's a Christian. His Christianity is indirect and unobtrusive, and he uses words with great skill. I would want to pay attention with people to how that worked, how the creative imagination deals with common experience and learns to express itself rightly. I'd use some poets who've been involved in ministry. George Herbert was a pastor; Gerard Manley Hopkins was a priest. I'd take people who were involved at the core of the gospel and were trying to understand it, but paid attention to the way words worked.

And I would also want to learn from the literary critics. We're involved in the study of Scripture and we've been completely buffaloed by the whole movement of historical criticism which has insisted on looking at Scripture analytically, historically, objectively. You cannot read imaginative literature analytically. You have to be a participant. And the whole revolution in hermeneutics which has taken place in the last thirty years is unattended to by both. Our best allies are the literary critics — people like Northrop Frye, C. S. Lewis in the critical works he does, and George Steiner — people who teach us how to read with our whole selves. It's not enough just to read with our minds. We've got emotions, we've got bodies, we've got histories, we've got jobs, we've got relationships, and we need to come to these texts with our whole beings — with our elbows and knees as well as our brain cells. And some of these men teach us how to do that or show us the way and insist that we follow. That's the way Scripture was read up until the Reformation and through the Reformation. But in the post-reformation we got such an overweening desire to be respectable intellectually.

We have such a fear of superstition and allegory that we squeezed all the imaginative stuff out of Scripture so we could be sure that it was just precise and accurate. If it's the infallible Word, well then you've got to have the exact meaning and nothing else, so all ambiguity goes. Well, all good language is ambiguous. It's poetic. It has levels of meaning, so which one of those levels of meaning is infallible? We've got to squeeze all of that out and get one level so we have the exact truth. It's not just the evangelical or conservative church that did that, that was liberal scholarship, too. They had a different theological reason for it, but it worked out to the same thing.

TSF: And with that has come this overburdening emphasis upon doctrinal and theological formulations at the expense of spiritual formation.

Peterson: I have nothing against the emphasis on doctrinal and theological formation; in fact, I insist on it. But that's part of a family and we've killed off the kids, eliminated all the imaginative stuff which people like William Faulkner or Walker Percy bring back. You cannot read a good artist just with your analytical mind. You've got to use your imagination. And Scripture is no different, but we insist on reading Scripture in a sub-literary way, and thereby lose much of its genius.

TSF: In speaking and writing, you talk about "wholeness." What do you mean by that term?

Peterson: I mean something Christian. I mean the whole Christian thing where we're in a conscious and growing relationship with God and an insistence that our life as described in Scripture and as experienced in grace be developed on those terms. I don't mean "wholeness" in terms of psychological subjectivism, what makes me feel good. And I don't mean "wholeness" in terms of meeting cultural expectations of what it means to be a well-rounded person, so there's tension in the way I use the word. I insist on the validity of the word for the Christian, being in touch with all reality. But I am also conscious that it is easy to be misunderstood, because a lot of people when they talk about "wholeness" mean just "I have it all together the way I want it to be."

TSF: How would you suggest a seminary student pursue "wholeness"? It's one thing to talk to seminary students about the fact that they need to read more, it's another thing when seminary students have jobs, a spouse, and perhaps children, and seldom enough money. In the midst of all that, we want them to come out of seminary at least pursuing the direction of wholeness.

Peterson: I think the one thing that's realistic in terms of suggesting "wholeness" to the seminary student is to get a vision of it and an appetite for it. "Wholeness" is a quest and we have to know what we're questing. It's not reasonable to say, "Okay, now get a well balanced life and get it all put together." It is possible to get a taste for it and to see what's possible. It's important to read the best writers. It's important to know the people who had some "wholeness." We need to know something about Gregory and Bernard, Thomas, Calvin, and Luther, to go to the best instead of fooling with the secondary literature. The mystics, I think, were often the whole people in our past. If we can develop a taste for them, so at least we know what it sounds like, what it looks like, then we might be dissatisfied with any substitute thrown our way as we go along.

TSF: You've somewhat touched on this, but maybe you could follow this through again: what qualities would you like to see in today's seminary graduates? If you were to hire someone freshly out of seminary to be an assistant pastor, what kind of person would you be looking for?

Peterson: I'd want somebody who had a basic conviction that the heart of pastoral work or leadership in the church has to do with developing a lifelong relationship with Christ which involves all of life. In other words, I would want somebody committed to the task of spiritual formation. I would also want somebody who had some intellectual discipline and curiosity about how to understand and imagine the different ways in which life is experienced. Without that intellectual curiosity, the early experiences become clichés and are not reapplied in fresh ways in new situations. What starts out as a vital experience deteriorates into platitude. And so spiritual formation and intellectual curiosity are reciprocal because they keep each other growing and alive and fresh. That's what I'd look for. I said earlier that the twin pillars of ministry are learning and prayer, and I'd look for a desire for that.

TSF: You have talked about the temptation in ministry to lie about God. Do we lie about God out of a lust for power or out of a fear concerning an inability to answer questions?

Peterson: Both. I would think both of those things, but I think they're subtle. I think they would probably be unrecognizable if we were accused that way. We would say, "No, I don't want power, I'm not afraid." But I think part of that, Bill, comes because most people who go into ministry want to help people. We really are programmed to help people and that's good. When people ask us to do things, we want to do what they want to do. If they want answers, we give them answers because that's what they requested. So a lot of what I call lying about God, answers about God that obscure or distort certain ambiguities of life or a certain wholeness in the doctrine of God, is very well-intentioned. I think we do it out of the best of motives which makes it very difficult to detect in yourself, because if your motives are right then you think what's coming out is going to be okay, too, especially if it's orthodox.

TSF: What part does doubt play in your own spiritual development?

Peterson: Doubt pushes me deeper. Doubt pushes me past the intellectualizing, past the superficial, and makes me deal with issues on a life basis where I can't understand and control everything. I have to plunge in anyway. Doubt has never functioned in my life as a way to get out of things. It has always pulled me in further. I know it makes spectators out of some people, but somehow it has never worked that way for me. It's caused me to be involved in dimensions of faith that I wasn't aware of before.

TSF: You spoke recently about the balance between striving for excellence and humility. How does that work? You say, "I really want to be an excellent people-helper," but you are always forced into the position of marketing yourself and your ability to help other people.

Peterson: That question, Bill, can't be dealt with very adequately in this setting, but it's one of the key questions for ministry because there's no area of the spiritual life that's more subject to pride, to ambition, to self-assertion, to non-humility than leadership positions in ministry. Yet there's no area in which the pursuit of excellence is more important either. Learning how to discriminate between excellence and ambition is a very difficult task. It requires lifelong scrutiny and a sense of discernment. I certainly think it's possible to learn how to do our best, discipline our lives in such a way that we get the best out of them (or the Lord gets the best out of them), and at the same time shut the door to self-assertion, to self-aggrandizement, to self-promotion. The problem is that most of the models for excellence that our culture provides feed ambition, so we don't have any models to work on. That's why we really need to saturate our imaginations with people like Teresa of Avila and John of the Cross, Francis of Assisi, Gregory of Nyssa; these people who really did pursue lives of excellence in incredible humility and a complete indifference in terms of what people thought about them or whether they had any standing in life at all. It's too bad you have to go back five hundred years for your models, but that's better than nothing. Some helpful models are still around but we have to be very alert to spot them.

Of Passion, Prayer, and Poetry

By Kathy Bubel

It could have been just one more studied attempt to make the Bible easier to read, but the task was awarded to none other than a passionate pastor, professor, and poet, Eugene Peterson. The result — aptly titled The Message *— is a remarkable, poignant rendering of the New Testament that is perhaps the most eloquent and understandable translation around.*

At first I wanted to know what all the fuss was about. Flipping, through a press kit on *The Message,* I encountered a long list of authors, musicians, and spiritual leaders practically tripping over themselves to endorse this book. I had always thought of Bible translation as a rather boring process stolidly carried out by aging scholars in dusty libraries.

After meeting Eugene Peterson and reading *The Message* myself, I get it now.

We scheduled to meet outside the bookstore at Regent College in Vancouver, British Columbia, where Eugene serves as professor of spiritual theology. Regent is probably one of the brightest and airiest college buildings in existence, and though Eugene is over 60, the man who approaches looks like he could be hiking the mountains

"Of Passion, Prayer, and Poetry" was originally published in *Release ink Magazine* 1, no. 2 (December 1994/January 1995): 14-17. Reprinted by permission of Kathy Bubel.

or sailing in the bay just beyond the campus. Decidedly, *not* an aging scholar in a dusty library.

He invites me into his office, a small but uncramped space with one wall of window, one wall of books. Pictures of his family line the windowsill in front of his desk. Eugene seats himself comfortably in the rocking chair. He has just returned from an annual pilgrimage to the family home in Montana. He seems relaxed and well rested. All but his voice. It is almost a whisper, obviously well-worn by thirty-five years of hearty pastoring and teaching.

The interview begins with him asking me about myself. That's a first, and I'm caught a bit off-guard. Never at a loss for words, however, I launch in. For some reason, I'm drawn into confession. I tell him of my current disillusionment with "North American evangelical Christianity" — the place I come from and where I stay: albeit on the sidelines. I refer to countless friends and acquaintances who share my quandary, and then suddenly I realize that I could be alienating my host — not always the best way to begin an interview. Luckily for me, he understands.

Welcome to the First Church of Misfits

Luckily for all of us. It's us that Eugene had in mind when he undertook the translation of the New Testament from Greek to current English. The disenfranchised Christian and the "modern pagan." The people he pastored for thirty years.

His church in Bel Air, Maryland — a place he describes as "classic American suburbia" — included "misfits, odd people that didn't fit, the spiritually lost. There were a lot of people in 12-step programs, a lot of recovering alcoholics and drug addicts." He responds to my comments on the state of church by telling me about such a woman who wrote him about her church experience.

The woman, an artist, told him that she grew up in a culturally sophisticated home but without religion. She knew nothing about the church. She was invited to church by friends, became intrigued, and stayed. Eventually she embraced the faith.

But later her pastor left and when the new pastor came, she found herself in difficulty. The new pastor kind of promoted too much, talked too much, and hustled too much. "I got a letter from

258

her not too long ago saying 'I flunked church-going.' You see, when the church no longer functions out of a center, it just . . ." he trails off sadly. "I guess I feel that it's really hard to go to church. I think it's important to go to church — I wouldn't think of not going — but you've got to be mature. It's not for beginners."

When I question whether church has always been thus, he shakes his head like a concerned physician. "No, I think we're in a unique time in this North American culture. We're in a bad time, and the church is not healthy, it's not mature. It's not easy, it's not easy."

As the professor of spiritual theology at Regent College, Eugene is smack-dab in the middle of North American evangelical Christianity. But there's something different here. It has to do with that mystical "center" he referred to. An explanation of the term "spiritual theology" reveals just what that center is.

"Spiritual theology traditionally has been prayer, spiritual formation, development of Christian character, reading the Bible formationally, not just intellectually. And so this is the center of Regent. This is a place of prayer in which you study theology, ethics, and history. In all my courses, people write reflective and integrated papers on the conditions in which they deal with their spirituality, the ways that they learn to pray.

"It takes me half a semester to get my students with me. They want to take notes, they want to find materials they can use. And I'm kind of dodging them all the time, coming at them from all directions, trying to get them to take their lives seriously as a text studied by the Holy Spirit."

What Eugene is doing for his students at Regent, he does over and over again for the people he "pastors" and teaches through the many books he has authored. Prayer is a common theme. Prayer is the center.

From Pulpit to Paper

It was for this "congregation at large" that he decided to retire from the little church in Maryland in 1991 and devote full energies to writing. Though the parting was difficult, the transition was not. As he says in *Reality and the Vision*, "Being a writer and being a pastor

259

are virtually the same thing for me: an entrance into chaos, the mess of things, and then the slow, mysterious work of making something out of it, something good, something blessed — poem, prayer, conversation, sermon, a sighting of grace, a recognition of love, a shaping of virtue."

Within a month of that choice, NavPress called Eugene to ask if he would translate the entire New Testament in the same way he had done Galatians in his book *Travelling Light*. He agreed, and that was his first assignment as a full-time writer.

A fairly significant first assignment, I'd say. One that must have been accompanied by some fear and trembling.

"Often while I was doing it," he says, "I had the feeling of 'Oh, I've always been doing this — but now it's harvest time. This is the fruit of everything I've been doing already.' So it was a wonderful experience that way. But it was very pedestrian for me. All the time that I was [translating], I had the feeling that I was doing second-rate stuff. I was never as good as John, Mark, Paul. Sometimes as a writer you'll write a sentence and think, Ah, nobody's ever done it that well before, and that you've got it. I never had 'it' — and when it was finished, I told my wife, I'm glad that's done — I'm so tired of coming in second.'"

As he told *Publishers Weekly*, "I look at it and I'm pleased, but the work wasn't really mine. I felt as if I was a servant to the text for two years, and I was compelled to obey. Now I'm free to follow my own creativity again."

Unintentionally, that is Eugene's best defense against those critics who say *The Message* is a personal interpretation rather than a faithful translation.

A Voice Speaking

He seems unaffected by the criticism. "I think the controversy stems from a genuine concern that this is the Word of God, the authority of Scripture. So anytime someone does something like this, it deserves to be critiqued because people's lives are at stake here — the way they believe, the way they think, the way they live. Anytime someone does this [Bible translation], it's dangerous work, it's risky work.

"The other part of it, though, is that a lot of people don't understand how translation works and that all translations interpret. Every time you move from one language to another you interpret because we don't speak in words, we speak in sentences and paragraphs. When you graph dialogue, you don't see any separation between individual words — it's all continuous speech.

"So if you think of translation as something by which you scientifically, grammatically take a word from this language and put it into that language, then if I use three words to translate one Greek word, you'll say I'm interpreting and adding stuff. But I'm not — it's all there, but you need three words in English. I marvelled as I did this, that God the Holy Spirit used language as a revelation, because language is inherently ambiguous."

And I marvel, as I sit in this office, at the unique combination of teacher, pastor, and poet that is Eugene Peterson. That is why reading *The Message* is such a unique experience. Each book is given an introduction to put things into context for the reader, his student. Each word is carefully chosen to communicate in clear, straightforward language to us, his congregation.

As for the poet part, singer Michael Card said it best when he described *The Message* as "a translation of tone. I read not only the words, but I hear a voice behind them speaking — as, in fact, all these documents were originally experienced. Peterson's translation transforms the eye into an ear, opening the door of the New Testament wider than perhaps it has ever been opened."

Eugene explains, "I wanted to write this so people who have never heard of God, never heard of Jesus, would get it the first time. That's what a preacher does. So my main qualification for doing this is not that I know Greek or Hebrew — a lot of people do — but that I am a preacher and a pastor, and mostly to these North American pagans who don't know anything about the faith. My working assumption with *The Message* was that the people that first read the text of the New Testament got it the first time."

And people *are* getting it. People from assorted backgrounds and ages are reading the New Testament for the first time — or *as if* it were the first time. NavPress saw the light and realized it was more effective than any tract or video or evangelical crusade. On the initiation of The Parable Group, an affiliation of independent bookstores throughout the U.S., excerpts were taken from *The Message* and put into an unassuming evangelical booklet called *The Message of Hope.* Its nonthreatening title and cover lend to the ease with which it can be given away. That, and knowing what's inside. I even found myself passing on my publisher's sample to my nanny the other day.

This is what Eugene delights in. "I get a ton of letters," he says with a sparkle in his eyes. "The other day I got one from a 74-year-old woman who described herself as a KJV person who had been a Christian all her life. She said, 'I got *The Message* for my nieces and nephews, but then I started reading it for myself, and I'd say, 'That's what the KJV says! That's what it says!'

"Then there was the little girl, about 12 years old, who met me in the bookstore the other day. I love this, he grins. "She said, 'We're using *The Message* in our family devotions.' Then, lowering her voice, 'But I've been reading ahead.' Now I'd much rather have a commendation like that than [one] from any of my critics!"

What the critics have missed is that *The Message* is not about Eugene Peterson. No one is more aware of that than Eugene himself, who so rarely grants an interview. He closes our time together by recounting a memory that well conveys the way he sees himself — as interpreter, as messenger.

"My wife and I went to hear Paul Tournier speak. Driving home we were discussing how wonderful it had been, and my wife said something that made me stop. She said, 'And wasn't the interpreter good?' Suddenly I realized that Tournier had been speaking in his native tongue, which is French, and I hadn't even noticed." As the New Testament speaks to us in its native tongue — earthly Greek, heavenly Divine — Eugene hopes we won't notice him there, just to the side, translating.

Pray with Simplicity — Matthew 6

"And when you come before God, don't turn that into a theatrical production either. All those people making a regular show out of their prayers, hoping for stardom! Do you think God sits in a box seat?

"Here's what I want you to do: Find a quiet, secluded place so you won't be tempted to role play before God. Just be there as simply and honestly as you can manage. The focus will shift from you to God, and you will begin to sense his grace. . . . This is your

262

Father you are dealing with, and he knows better than you what you need. With a God like this loving you, you can pray very simply. Like this:

> 'Our Father in heaven,
> Reveal who you are.
> Set the world right:
> Do what's best — as above, so below.
> Keep us alive with three square meals.
> Keep us forgiven with you and forgiving others.
> Keep us safe from ourselves and the Devil.
> You're in charge!
> You can do anything you want!
> You're ablaze in beauty! Yes. Yes. Yes.'"